D1325422

Catholic Education: the Unobtrusive Partner

Catholic Education:
the Unobtrusive Partner

Sociological Studies of the
Catholic School System in England and Wales

MICHAEL P. HORNSBY-SMITH

Sheed and Ward
London

This book is dedicated
with love and thanks
to
LENNIE
for her love, support and encouragement
and to
MY PARENTS
who started it all

Contents

Tables

Preface

This book has grown out of a developing interest in Catholic education in England and Wales. The conflict in Northern Ireland led a number of people in the early 1970s to assert that Catholic schools were divisive. I did not believe this was true at all in England and Wales and the attempt to articulate a case for separate Catholic schools from a sociological perspective was published in *The Month* in October 1972. This article is reprinted substantially unchanged in chapter 3 of this volume.

Over the next three years, three students of mine at the University of Surrey—Ann Thomas, Margaret Petit and Johanna Fitzpatrick—carried out a number of small scale studies of the religious attitudes of senior pupils in a variety of Catholic schools. Several articles arising out of these studies were published in *The Journal of Moral Education*, *The Tablet* and *Catholic Education Today* and form the bulk of the material comprising chapters 4, 5 and 6 in this volume.

In 1974 I was invited to address the Annual Study Conference of the Catholic Teachers' Federation on the theme 'Education—A Continuing Process: The Catholic Contribution', and the paper was published later that year in *Catholic Education Today*. The following year I was invited to talk to a group of university and polytechnic chaplains on the theme 'Catholic Students in Higher Education' and the paper was later published in *The Month*. Revised versions of these papers appear in this book in chapters 9 and 7 respectively.

Since early 1974 I have been carrying out research into social change in the Roman Catholic community in England on two projects which have been funded by the Social Science Research Council. As part of this research Penny Mansfield and I interviewed lay members of some of the Bishops' Commissions in 1974. This led to the attempt to construct a typology of advisory bodies and to apply the analysis to the particular case of those bodies dealing with Catholic Education policy in an article in *The Tablet* in 1975. A revised and extended version of this article is given in chapter 10.

It is strange, and possibly a sad reflection of the continuing defensiveness of Catholics in this country, that the system of education which has been built up over the past century has been the subject of so much neglect by academics. It is in the hope of reducing this neglect and of stimulating a more systematic analysis of its growth and characteristics that this book is offered. In doing so I am aware of the limitations of some of the studies reported. Clearly it would be desirable to be able to report surveys of national samples of schools and pupils, comparisons with control groups of schools and pupils in the local authority sector and more intensive case studies involving a multiplicity of research strategies. The fact is that there have been no resources available for more intensive studies and those reported here are among the very few which have been published. It is hoped that they will stimulate others to go further in the investigation of the religious climates and outcomes of Catholic schools, their place in the British form of pluralist society, and other aspects of the Sociology of Catholic Education.

It is now commonly agreed that complete 'value-freedom' in sociology is not possible. In order that the reader might make allowance for my values and potential biases, I will attempt to make my own position explicit. I am a believing and practising Roman Catholic with four children in Catholic schools and a wife who teaches in a local authority school. Since 1970 I have been a diocesan representative on the Catholic Education Council. I believe that, all other things being equal, a Catholic school is likely to be more supportive of the religious beliefs and values of our family than a local authority school. However, I also believe that the extent to which this is or is not the case is an empirical matter and that variations of religious climates from school to school may be considerable. In my view the understanding of the processes of religious socialisation and the extent to which different outcomes in terms of beliefs, values, behaviour and commitment are structured are also essentially amenable to empirical investigation. This is because they are essential empirical issues and not ideological issues and on empirical issues, in the last analysis, the appeal must be to the evidence.

This book, then, is offered to two different audiences. In the first place it is hoped that it will be of interest to students of the Sociology of Education as an introduction to a major, but neglected, education sub-system. Secondly, it is offered to those Catholics with an interest in the Catholic education system: parents, teachers, priests, bishops and administrators, in the hope that it might inform or enlighten their consideration of the issues involved as the century-long period of expansion comes to an end and there is a period of contraction, consolidation, but also, hopefully, the vision to meet the demands of the changing world of tomorrow and the determination to improve the qualitative contribution which the Catholic community can make to the educational needs of this country.

I would like to thank the editors of *The Journal of Moral Education*, *Catholic Education Today*, *The Month* and *The Tablet* for permission to reproduce material previously published by them. I am grateful to them for the opportunities they provided to test and develop many of the ideas appearing in this book. I would also like to express my sincere thanks to Ann Thomas, Margaret Petit and Johanna Fitzpatrick with whom I published several articles on the religious attitudes of senior pupils, for their permission to use material here which was previously published jointly. I am particularly pleased to acknowledge the kind co-operation of the headteachers of the eight research schools mentioned in this book, the tolerance and integrity of the 766 senior pupils who either answered self-completion questionnaires or were interviewed in the course of the three small scale investigations reported, and to Mgr E. Mahony for arranging the administration of the Southwark schools survey and making available the data for analysis. Bishop Daniel Mullins, Philip Blake, Richard Cunningham, Raymond Lee, Martin Redfern and Marten Shipman made helpful comments on individual chapters and I am grateful to them for their help. Any errors which remain are, of course, entirely my own responsibility. Finally, to Jenny Scott, who coped marvellously with frequently appalling scribble, a very special thanks is due.

Michael Hornsby-Smith

PART I

1

Introduction

In the mid-1970s one child in eleven in England and Wales attends a Roman Catholic school.[1] In all there are over 900,000 children in nearly 3100 Catholic schools, staffed by over 44,000 teachers.[2] Given the size of the Catholic sector of the 'dual system' it is surprising that there have been no major sociological studies of its characteristics or its functions in the British version of the pluralist society. This volume attempts to commence this task by identifying some quantitative and qualitative features of the system.

Apart from the dearth of sociological studies of contemporary Catholic education there is also an absence of studies of the social history of Catholic education since the Butler Education Act of 1944. A number of significant contributions have been made to an understanding of the development of Catholic education in earlier periods[3] but there has been no systematic study of the various political negotiations since the 1944 Act, which have resulted in a series of increases in the rate of capital grant for school building from 50 to 85 per cent. These changes have occurred as a result of a developing political consensus based on a substantial acceptance of the permanence of the 1944 settlement, a reduction of divisive religious rivalries and antagonisms, and an acceptance of the pleas of the leaders of the Catholic community that the financial burden of a separate Catholic school system was becoming insupportable. Not surprisingly, Murphy has referred to 'the end of "passionate intensity" ' in the post-war years[4] after decades of sometimes bitter political battles over the place of church schools in our society.[5]

It may well be that the strategy of Catholic decision-makers in these political processes can accurately be characterised as 'playing the system', keeping a low profile, avoiding overt conflict and the antagonism of other interests and sections of the community and pursuing a policy of secret rather than open diplomacy. Although they were not alone in employing these strategies, it is perhaps worth noting that they were used in particular by the Catholic aristocracy in the long years before emancipation, for coping with the strong latent, and frequently manifest, hostilities of a population deeply suspicious of the extra-national links of Roman Catholicism. In the dark years of persecution and discrimination such a strategy was necessary for the survival of the small Catholic recusant community prior to the nineteenth century growth occasioned by famine-induced Irish immigration. These defensive responses linger on, however, and are to be seen in the disproportionately small involvement of Catholics in politics in England. In educational politics, following the aggressive mobilisation of Catholic public opinion and the public demonstrations in support of Catholic claims for a fairer deal in education in the early 1950s,[6] the policy of 'playing it cool' by the Catholic negotiators appears to have been enormously successful in facilitating a massive school building programme for a quarter of a century after the second world war. This resulted in an increase in the proportion of the school population in Catholic schools from 7 to 9 per cent.[7] Social changes in British society generally, notably post-war affluence enjoyed by all sections of the community and the decline in the salience of denominational religious antagonisms, contributed to the success of the Catholic strategy.

What have the consequences of this strategy been? In the first place Catholic schools in England and Wales have clearly not been a significant cause or focal point of social conflict, at least at the national level. Quite obviously they have not been divisive. It is perhaps worth asking whether this is because they are indistinguishable from other schools, no worse than other schools, but also no better or innovative or pioneering compared to other schools. The successful consolidation of the Catholic schools system might possibly have been bought at the cost of any distinctive character or educational contribution.

There are relatively few documented cases where it would seem that Catholic schools are significantly different from other schools. An early study of social class and educational opportunities showed that in Middlesbrough Catholic children from large families gained a disproportionately large number of grammar school places.[8] Wiseman reported some rather contradictory results about attainment in Roman Catholic schools on the basis of his investigations in the Manchester conurbation in the 1950s and of Kemp's study in London.[9]

Mays has published a number of studies of inner-city Liverpool where the proportion of Roman Catholics ranges from one-third to one-half of the total population. He reports that in the 1930s there was evidence that a not inconsiderable proportion of Catholic six-year-olds did not attend school, class sizes were large and there was much overcrowding in the Catholic schools. Many of these problems had been overcome by the late 1950s as a result of praiseworthy Catholic school building programmes.[10] The parish priests were a dominant influence in these schools and they generally considered PTAS were unnecessary on the grounds that the Roman Catholic school was so intimately linked with the parish.[11] In the main the school seemed

> to place emphasis on indoctrination and an attempt to secure conformity to authority and dogma rather than on wide cultural interests and the attainment of a balanced, liberal view of human life.[12]

The links between the school and the parish were strengthened by the fact that many working class teachers were born and bred in the same area. Although most of the Catholic children claimed to attend mass weekly,

> the Catholics were no less delinquent than the non-Catholics which suggests that there is not an immediate transference of values learned in church into the sphere of everyday conduct.[13]

More recently Grace has reported an instance of role conflict in the particular context of religious teaching in a Catholic school.[14] In his controversial study of teaching styles, Bennett observes that teaching methods in Roman Catholic schools tended to be more formal.[15] This accords with the common conception of Catholic schools as generally placing greater stress on authority relationships and discipline. This is particularly the case where the traditional involvement of the local parish priests has continued to be an important feature of the social control mechanisms exercised by the local community. Some evidence that this might be the case was obtained in a study of two neighbourhood comprehensive schools in Glasgow, one Catholic and one Protestant, in the mid-1960s. It was found that both teachers and parents gave higher priority to 'good behaviour' in the Catholic school and that the priests had a close relationship with their parishioners and provided additional supportive supervision, an important link between the school and parish, and continuity with the feeder primary schools. One result was a significantly lower delinquency rate in the Catholic school and a higher level of scholastic attainment in the case of the Protestant school.[16]

The stress on general welfare functions in the Catholic school is echoed in Benn and Simon's report on the early stages of comprehensive re-organisation. On progress in the denominational (mainly Roman Catholic) comprehensive schools they observe that they 'were much impressed by the quality of their care for the whole education of their pupils'.[17]

Further evidence that there might be significant differences between Catholic schools and local authority schools was provided by a literacy survey of nearly 16,000 eight-year-olds in all the ILEA (Inner London) junior and junior-infant schools in October 1968. It was reported that the mean reading scores were 99·2 in the Roman Catholic schools compared to 96·9 in Church of England schools and 94·3 in county schools.[18] What is the explanation for these figures and what do they mean? In the absence of more thorough analysis one can do little more than hypothesise. For example, it may be that Catholic primary schools use more formal teaching methods, as Bennett suggested, and that in a narrowly defined area of goal attainment, for example reading, these are more effective. It would be interesting to see whether the advantage persists in the secondary schools where there are wider curricular demands and different teaching methods. Of course, this is speculative, but it does illustrate the point that if differences in the processes taking place in Catholic schools were investigated more systematically, it would increase our understanding of the complex social processes of learning in schools generally. In particular the close inter-relationship between Catholic home and parents, Catholic school and teachers, and Catholic parish and priests, potentially offers enormous educational advantages in terms of a supportive community and the absence of 'culture conflict'. With the current vogue for community schools,[19] it is surprising that more note has not been taken of the interlocking web of Catholic institutions in many of the deprived inner-city areas.

These few studies provide little more than hints for the generation of hypotheses which might be tested further in more systematic research. Generally the religious complexion of a school has not been considered to be an important independent variable even in major national surveys.[20] It would be a fascinating exercise to explore the political sociology of this neglect. One might hazard the guess that neither the local authorities nor the Catholic diocesan administrators wanted to 'rock the boat'. On the Catholic side there has always been a deep suspicion of the social sciences,[21] quite apart from the defensiveness of a minority group with a history of hostility and persecution. In Catholic ideology the Catholic school was seen as intrinsically desirable and a political right[22] and therefore research findings were often considered to be irrelevant. On the local authority side, provided that minimum standards of competence were maintained, there was probably no desire to awaken the latent political resources of one of the largest interest groups in British society. At the same time in this post-war period, sociologists of education were overwhelmingly concerned with social class and later ethnic group inequalities in the distribution of educational opportunities and, given the ameliorative orientation of British sociology, religious inequalities paled into insignificance beside the deep and persistent class differentials which seemed impervious to change and unaffected by post-war expansion of educational opportunities.[23]

Given the strength of the ideology of the Catholic school, it is nevertheless important to note that the views of religious leaders are couched far less in dogmatic and assertive terms now than half a century ago. In his encyclical letter *Divini Illius Magistri*, written in 1929, Pope Pius XI repudiated 'neutral' or 'secular' schools from which religion is entirely banned as 'subversive of the whole foundation of Christian education'. He endorsed and confirmed

the prescriptions of canon law which forbid Catholic children on any pretext whatsoever to attend . . . schools open indiscriminately to Catholics and non-Catholic alike.

Furthermore, he taught

nor can the church tolerate the type of mixed school . . . in which Catholics, although receiving religious instruction apart, are taught other subjects in common with non-Catholics by non-Catholic teachers.

In order to satisfy the rights of the church and family and render a school fit to be attended by Catholic pupils

the whole of the training and teaching, the whole organisation of the school—teachers, curriculum, school-books on all subjects —must be so impregnated with the christian spirit under the guidance and motherly vigilance of the church, that religion comes to provide the foundation and the culminating perfection of the whole training.[24]

In the more ecumenical climate of the Vatican Council the teaching was far less inflexible. There was a recognition of the pluralist character of modern society and of varying forms of Catholic schools according to different local circumstances and needs. The church's involvement in education was thought to be 'demonstrated especially by the Catholic school' and the Council reminded Catholic parents of

their duty to entrust their children to Catholic schools, when and where this is possible, to support such schools to the extent of their ability, and to work along with them for the welfare of their children.[25]

The recent Vatican document on *The Catholic School* takes this process a little further.[26] The basic assertion of the educational value of the Catholic school is still made. It is considered to be a privileged means of promoting education with reference to a specifically 'christian concept of life centred on Jesus Christ' (33). However, no longer is the duty of supporting Catholic schools simply asserted. In this document an attempt is made to refute various objections to the Catholic school: that there ought not to be separate Catholic institutions, that there is a danger of proselytism, that they have no place in a modern society where the civil authorities have assumed responsibility for educational provision, that they contribute to social and economic discrimination in education and that they are ineffective (17–23). There is a strong defence of the Catholic school in a society marked by cultural pluralism and suggestions for improving the Catholic school system. No longer are parents instructed without question to send their children to Catholic schools. Rather, an ideal model of a Catholic school is presented, which is a community of those united in the faith, stimulated and fed by 'constant reference to the gospel and a frequent encounter with Christ' (55). The document rejects the view that the work of the schools can

be assessed by the same rationalistic criteria which apply to other professions. (75)[27]

and therefore, in the last analysis, admits that

to commit oneself to working in accordance with the aims of a Catholic school is to make a great act of faith in the necessity and influence of this apostolate (83).

It is interesting to note a similar shift of orientation from the assertive to the critical among Catholics in England over the same period. Writing during the second world war of the significance of the Catholic schools in England, Evennett claimed that:

The hierarchy of values taught by Catholicism is one which runs directly counter to much modern social and moral ideology . . . Death and original sin are the constants in the light of which the Catholic Church surveys humanity. Life is a preparatory stage and its values are secondary . . . If education is what remains after we have forgotten all we learnt at school, the quintessential left by a Catholic education is a lasting consciousness of the fact and the meaning of death . . . The child is . . . progressively indoctrinated with the principle that worldly success and happiness are not the final values, that they are not necessarily the concomitants of virtue . . . Genuinely to apply these principles to life involves the development of a sense of proportion and realism, of a permanent quality of discretion and self-control that should, if properly cultivated, ultimately inform all the actions and thoughts of the adult individual.[28]

It is one of the purposes of this book to suggest that such essentially empirical assertions about the goals of Catholic schools are amenable to empirical testing. Are Catholics more aware of death than anyone else? Are they less concerned with worldly success? Are Catholics socialised to noticeably different sets of values and beliefs? What is the evidence?

In the political battles concerning Catholic schools in the early post-war years, Bishop Beck quoted Evennett with approval and in his turn asserted

> We Catholics are the only body in the country *consistently* concerned with the content of education; we are the only body who have clear ideas on what education is for, and how its whole purpose is to be achieved.[29]

Furthermore, in a commentary on the Ministry of Education pamphlet *Citizens Growing Up at Home, in School and After*, he claimed that

> We Catholics are the one community in this country who, in this field of education are trying consistently, even at the cost of great sacrifice, to live up to these high ideals; and in doing so we are rendering an immense service to the country.[30]

A third example illustrates the sense of isolation and defensiveness which Catholics in England felt after the 1944 Education Act. Reviewing 'The Struggle for the Schools' on the centenary of the restoration of the hierarchy, Beales wrote

> Mr Gladstone, by supplementing the Dual System, advanced it. Mr Butler has halted it, and outflanked it. Over half the Anglican schools were expected to opt for 'control'. Few, except the Catholics, see any longer anything vital to revelation that an Agreed Syllabus cannot give; for few, except the Catholics, subscribe any longer to the bedrock educational truth, that the Christian formation of the child can be secured only by a dedicated partnership of the home, the church and the school, through the trinity of parent-priest-teacher. In England and Wales today the Catholic schools are more than ever, then, missionary schools. In measurable time they may be the only ones left. Were they to be lost to the country, as God's Church sees it *all* would be lost.[31]

Such were the interpretations and assertions made by officially recognised Catholic apologists up to the early 1950s. From that time onwards all efforts appear to have been focused on the task of expanding the Catholic school system in line with population increase and movement. In spite of the assertions or assumptions about the *quality* of Catholic schools in all the above quotations, in fact the prime concern, at least until the peak of the post-war growth in the early 1970s, appears to have been with the *quantity* of school building, the Catholic share of school building programmes, and so on.

It was not until the early 1960s that the first significant piece of empirical research on Catholic schools was undertaken. Joan Brothers' study[32] was a pioneering attempt to explore the implications of post-war social change in the affluent society on the Catholic community. In a study of the impact of grammar schooling and the consequential upward social mobility of Catholics in Liverpool, she drew attention to the decline of devotion and loyalty to the traditional parochial structures on the part of these young Catholics. Social change in the wider society was significantly changing the social structure of Roman Catholicism in England.

Around this time the questioning spirit unleashed by the Vatican Council led a number of Catholic critics to challenge publicly previous assumptions about Catholic schools.[33] It is interesting to note that the shift of concern about the effectiveness of Catholic schools in terms of their qualitative outcomes is paralleled by increasing comment about the financial implications of the secondary school system. Several dioceses were thought to be near bankruptcy and the financial obligations of the continuing school building programme in the 1960s and early 1970s threatened to get out of control in the mid-1970s during a period of unprecedented inflation and high interest rates.[34] All the same, Catholic parents continue to send their children to Catholic schools and an overwhelming majority support the continuation of separate Catholic schools and the financial obligations implied.[35]

In sum, the Catholic education system since the war has changed significantly in response to post-war affluence and urban and social change generally, on the one hand, and to the shifts in the climate of opinion within the church given focus and direction by the second Vatican Council, on the other. The political power of Roman Catholicism in England has been sufficient to maintain and even slightly increase its share of the school population and building provision, even during a period of unprecedented expansion. The ideological justifications for the separate Catholic school system have also become muted over the past two decades, partly as a result of the decline of religious intolerance and possibly also of the salience of religious values generally, and partly in response to the less authoritarian, more self-critical and more ecumenically-minded approaches of Roman Catholicism to the wider society since the Vatican Council. The post-war period, then, can be characterised as one of growth, consolidation and adaptation for Catholic education in England and Wales.

This, then, is the background to this book, which attempts to address four main issues. In part II there is a consideration of the Catholic system of education in England and Wales. Its size and growth and changing characteristics since the second world war will be outlined in chapter 2. In chapter 3 the existence of the separate Catholic schools system, at least for England and Wales, will be defended. It will be shown that there is no research evidence to suggest that Catholic schools are not reasonably efficient in terms of both religious and academic goals and argued that they have a legitimate role to play in our sort of pluralist society.

It seems that the dominant concern of the administrators of the Catholic system since the second world war has been the size and expansion of the school system. In part III it will be argued that there is a need to shift the emphasis more towards the qualitative outcomes of a Catholic education and the consideration of its effectiveness in terms of both academic and religious goals. A number of research studies of Catholic secondary school pupils and students will be reported. In chapter 4 there will be a tentative consideration of Catholic education and social justice and the question of the distinctiveness of the atmosphere or climate of a Catholic school will be raised. Chapter 5 will outline some findings from questionnaire surveys of senior pupils in Catholic comprehensive schools. The results provide some evidence that the religious outcomes of Catholic schools are different from those of local authority schools in some respects, even though there is a wide variety of responses from Catholic pupils and a considerable amount of deviation from official religious beliefs and moral norms. In chapter 6 the process of religious disaffection of a large proportion of Catholic adolescents is examined further on the basis of three different research studies, including the interviewing of fourth formers in Catholic comprehensive schools. One of the conclusions is that much leakage appears to be due more to drift and laziness than to choice and conviction, and is a process which often begins as early as twelve years old when some parents remove sanctions for non-attendance at Sunday mass. There is a consideration of the case of Catholic students in higher education in the following chapter from Marxian, Weberian and Durkheimian perspectives. The con-

cluding chapter in this section examines more closely the two
research studies of Catholic education in the United States by
Greeley[36] and that by Flynn of Catholic schools in Australia.[37] Each
of these studies has relevance for the consideration of the relative
effectiveness of Catholic education in this country.

Part IV of this book consists of two chapters which look at some
policy implications for the Catholic community. In the first place
it can be argued that the religious education of Catholics in the
fifty or so years following the end of their secondary schooling has
frequently been neglected in this country. Some implications of
considering education as a continuing process throughout the life
cycle of the individual are examined in chapter 9. In the following
chapter it is argued that the size and coverage of the Catholic
education system in England and Wales is such that it presents
considerable organisational problems of control, goal specification,
task achievement, co-ordination and management styles. In particular it is argued that present structures of advice need to be
overhauled if the co-ordination of the different parts of the Catholic
education system is to be more satisfactorily achieved in the more
difficult years ahead when there is likely to be some contraction
in the school system, a scarcity of resources and the re-allocation
of them in the light of newly defined missionary goals of the
Catholic community in England and Wales.[38]

Part V attempts to draw some of these themes together and interpret the developments in the post-war years as responses to social
changes in the wider society. It has been said that 'the party is over'
and the long period of post-war expansion in a period of population growth and continuous economic prosperity is at an end. New
problems and a new situation face the Catholic community today
as it consolidates its school system and reappraises it in the light of
the perceived needs of tomorrow. In this process of re-evaluation,
faith in the Catholic school and dogmatic assertions about it are
likely to be replaced by a more pragmatic assessment based on
empirical evidence. In this process, systematic research is likely to
play an increasingly important part.

PART II

The Catholic System of Education

2

Catholic Education in the Post-War Years

In this chapter the growth and development of the Catholic system of education in England and Wales in the post-war years will be traced and an attempt made to interpret the major changes which have taken place. In the hundred years since the 1870 Forster Education Act the number of Catholic schools increased from 666 to 3060 and the number of pupils on the registers from 75,127 to 882,709. The number of fully qualified teachers increased from 799 to 36,850 and public expenditure on Catholic schools from £41,527 to an estimated £150 million. Correspondingly, the financial contributions made by Catholics increased from £25,640 to around £3 million.[1]

The period up to the outbreak of the second world war can perhaps be divided simply into two by the 1902 Balfour Act. In the thirty-two years between the two Education Acts the Catholic community undertook a massive school building programme which quadrupled the number of Catholic school places and ensured that large numbers of poor working class children were educated in a Catholic atmosphere rather than in the Board schools. This expansion was all the more impressive because Catholics at that time were heavily concentrated in the poorer sections of the community. The Balfour Act required the new Local Education Authorities to assist church schools from the rates. This, together with the 1936 Education Act which provided for grants of 50 to 75 per cent for new senior schools, enabled the Catholic community to consolidate its school system and by the outbreak of the second world war over one-third of a million children, or nearly 7 per cent of the elementary school population, were being educated in 1266 Catholic assisted schools.[2]

After the Butler Education Act of 1944 and the introduction of 'secondary education for all' there followed another quarter of a century of continuous growth. By the early 1950s there were 400,000 children in Catholic maintained schools and this figure reached half a million by 1960 and exceeded threequarters of a million in the early 1970s.[3] Apart from these children in schools partly supported by public funds there were probably around 70,000 children at Catholic independent schools in the late 1940s.[4] By 1975 nearly 9 per cent of the children in the maintained sector in England and Wales and more than two-fifths of the children in voluntary schools were in Catholic schools.[5]

The identification of the key trends in the provision of Catholic schools in recent years has been facilitated by the publication of summary statistics by the Catholic Education Council.[6] In table 2.1 it can be seen that the number of maintained Catholic schools increased to 2061 in 1960 and 2678 in 1977 and the total number of Catholic schools (including independent, special and approved schools and those in the Channel Isles and Isle of Man) to 2748 in 1960 and 3071 in 1977. Within this pattern of overall growth, several important trends can be discerned. First of all it can be seen that it took nearly a quarter of a century after the 1944 Act to complete the re-organisation of Catholic 'all age' schools, mainly because of the shortage of building resources after the war, government controls on school building programmes, and the introduction of specific building programmes only in the late 1950s and early 1960s. Secondly, the growth of a system of maintained secondary schools along tripartite lines continued steadily until the middle 1960s when a major programme of comprehensivisation got under way, so that by 1977 over two-thirds of the pupils in maintained Catholic secondary schools were in secondary middle or comprehensive schools or sixth form colleges (table 2.2). As a result of amalgamations the total number of maintained secondary schools declined after 1970 although the number of pupils in them continued to increase.

Thirdly, the number of independent schools has almost halved since 1960. Whereas at that time one Catholic school in five was independent, reflecting the major provision for the Catholic upper and middle classes which has historically been made by the religious orders,[7] the proportion now is one in ten. Several factors are likely to have contributed to this decline. Some have participated in schemes for secondary reorganisation along comprehensive lines while many are likely to have closed for financial reasons, especially following the Houghton pay award to teachers in the state sector in 1974.[8] The viability of the schools has, no doubt, become more problematic where there has also been a decline in the number of vocations to the various religious orders and an ageing of the existing membership. It is difficult to say how important public criticisms of what are seen by many as the inequitable social functions of the independent schools on behalf of the socially privileged have been.[9] Finally, the general reappraisal of their service functions in a changed society by the religious orders in the light of the exhortations for 'renewal' since the second Vatican Council, may also have contributed significantly to decisions to re-define their purposes and shift to other types of ministry, although this has been discouraged in the recent Vatican statement on the Catholic School.[10] From table 2.1 it might also be noted that the proportion of independent schools recognised as efficient has increased over this period from under three-fifths to over three-quarters.

The post-war trends are also indicated by the numbers of pupils in the schools (table 2.3). These figures indicate more clearly that the major increases in Catholic school provision since 1960 have been in the maintained secondary schools, where the rise in the school population, the raising of the school leaving age to 16, and the long term trend to stay on at school after the statutory leaving age have all contributed to a maintained secondary school population two and a half times that of 1960. By contrast the expansion in the primary sector has been more modest and there has been a decline of over one-quarter in the number of pupils in the Catholic independent schools.

Another significant change which is currently taking place is the phasing out of direct-grant status. Here the Catholic schools have responded differently from the other direct grant schools. Whereas 48 of 51 Catholic direct grant schools intended to seek aided status as comprehensive schools or part of a comprehensive scheme,[11] 116 of 119 other direct grant schools originally opted for independent status.[12] In some cases the Catholic schools have provided the only available Catholic grammar school provision and it is therefore not surprising that they have largely opted for aided status. On the other hand, it also suggests that the Catholic independent sector might be too large to be viable, given the distribution, density and economic resources of the Catholic population in comparison with the rest of the population. However, in spite of these recent changes, one pupil in eight in Catholic schools still attends a direct grant or independent school, a proportion more than twice that in the school population as a whole.[13]

The implications of the rapid decline in the birth rate since 1964[14] can be clearly seen from the age distribution of pupils in table 2.4. The figures for 1974 have been included because it was in this year that the period of expansion, which had lasted for over a century, ended. The total population in Catholic schools declined by 26,000 in the three years to January 1977. The table illustrates clearly that the major expansion up to 1974 was in the secondary schools. The effect of raising the school leaving age to 16 in 1972–3 is clearly seen in the doubling of the size of the top age group in the decade 1964–74. There was also a significant increase in nursery provision from a small base and the youngest age group continued to grow in the three years from 1974. However, from this time there has been a decline of 39,000 children in the primary schools and, no doubt, this partly explains the increase in the size of the youngest age group which includes over 7500 children under four. Apart from this it can be seen that the big reduction in primary school numbers is likely to have repercussions for the smaller secondary schools by the early 1980s. Since there is a considerable amount of population movement between regions and because many of the smaller secondary schools are in regions of population growth, these repercussions may not be as serious as might otherwise have been feared.

Table 2.5 shows that the proportion of non-Catholic children has tended to decline overall over the past two decades. Over 2 per cent of the children in the maintained schools are non-Catholics, a proportion which has trebled since the late 1960s. Since 1960 the proportion of non-Catholic boys in the direct grant schools more than doubled to just under 5 per cent but the proportion of non-Catholic girls in direct grant schools fell by one-half in the 1960s and in the mid-1970s remains under 8 per cent. The proportion of non-Catholic pupils in the Catholic independent schools has always been much greater than in the maintained schools so that by the mid-1970s one-quarter of the boys and nearly half of the girls were non-Catholics. This fact is probably an important consideration for the religious orders as they reappraise their priorities and pastoral contributions in the light of the theological reorientations legitimated by the second Vatican Council. It is also interesting to note the recent rapid rise in the proportion of non-Catholic pupils in Catholic special and approved schools although the total numbers involved are quite small. Taking all schools together, the proportion of non-Catholic pupils declined from one in fourteen in 1960 to one in seventeen in 1977.

Apart from the rapid growth in the number of schools and pupils in the years since the second world war there has been a corresponding increase in the size of the teaching force in these schools. In the decade after 1964 the number of teachers increased by nearly one-half to over 44,000. At the same time there have been significant changes in the composition of the teaching force (table 2.6). In the first place it is not unexpected that at a time when there has been a decline in the number of vocations to the priesthood and the religious life and a reconsideration by the religious orders of the value of teaching the relatively privileged children of the middle classes, there was a reduction in the number of secular clergy and men and women religious of one-third or over 2000 over the last twelve years. It is of some interest to the contemporary discussions about pastoral strategies and the efficient deployment of the church's specialised manpower[15] that in 1976 more than two-fifths of the secular clergy and religious teachers in Catholic schools were still teaching the one-eighth of the pupils in the direct grant and independent schools.

An increase of over 8000 in the number of Catholic lay teachers over the same period was not however sufficient for the needs of the schools in a period of rapid expansion and there was in addition a massive increase of over 7000 non-Catholic teachers which more than doubled the proportion to nearly one-quarter overall. Further analysis indicates that proportionate increases had occurred in every sector but that these were particularly striking in the secondary and independent sectors where one-third of the teachers are not Catholic. Even in the primary schools one teacher in twelve is not a Catholic but the number has declined from a peak of 1846 in 1974 to 1559 in 1977. These trends, which resulted inevitably from the rapidity of expansion at a time of teacher shortage, are clearly relevant to the question of the 'Catholic atmosphere' of a school which is formally Catholic. Finally it may be noted that in each sector there was a steady increase in the proportion of graduate teachers, even at this time of rapid expansion.

At the time of the centenary of the restoration of the hierarchy for England and Wales in 1950 it was reported that there were significant differences in the provision of Catholic school places in rural and urban areas. Four categories of area were distinguished and the distribution of schools and pupils in them reported by Beales for 1949.[16] In table 2.7 the distribution of Catholic maintained schools in 1976 has been given for the same groups of dioceses. While Beales' descriptive categories can be challenged,[17] they enable a crude measure of changes in the distribution of schools and pupils and the broad patterns of mobility of the Catholic population in England and Wales since the war to be made. Two conclusions can be drawn from the figures. In the first place there is now a greater balance between the distribution of schools and pupils. The industrial dioceses of the north in 1949 contained over half the pupils in only one-third of the schools while the rural dioceses had 15 per cent of the schools for only 7 per cent of the pupils. Secondly, there has been a significant shift of the school population from the older, industrial cities of

the north to London and the South-East in particular, but also to
the more rural dioceses in the South of England. Whereas well
over half the children in the Catholic maintained schools in 1949
were in the four northern dioceses of Liverpool, Salford, Leeds and
Hexham and Newcastle, by 1976 their share had fallen to two-
fifths. Taking groups A and D together (table 2.7) it can be seen
that whereas at the end of the war just over one-fifth of the pupils
in Catholic schools were south of the line between the Humber and
the Bristol Channel, by the mid-1970s the proportion had risen to
well over one-third. These changes reflect the major post-war
changes in the social structure of English Catholicism and are
indicative of a substantial amount of social and geographical
mobility in the post-war years in response to the social, economic
and urban changes in the wider society.[18]

Apart from the provision of Catholic schools for Catholic children, a key aspect of Catholic education policy has been the training
of Catholic teachers to staff these schools in Catholic colleges of
education.[19] At the beginning of the 1960s there were two male
and ten female colleges with about 2800 students.[20] In preparation
for the anticipated increase in the school population in the 1960s,
one additional female and three new mixed colleges were built and
the teacher training capacity of the Catholic colleges more than
trebled in the decade. In the peak year of 1971 there were 10,782
students, of whom just under one-quarter were men, in the fifteen
colleges, all but four of which were now mixed.[21] With the dramatic fall in the birth rate since 1964 the student population declined
by 28 per cent in the next five years.[22] Successive drastic cut-backs
in planning proposals have resulted in the closure of several of the
colleges and a number of amalgamations, those in Liverpool and
Roehampton involving federal arrangements with non-Catholic
colleges, in the battle for the survival of this major institutional
presence of the Catholic community in the provision of higher
education in this country. It now looks as if the Catholic colleges
will provide only two-fifths of the number of teacher training places
in 1981 that they had done a decade earlier. On the other hand, it
could be argued that the trauma of the past decade will have
resulted in two lasting improvements: the ending of single sex
educational institutions for young Catholic adults and the potential
opportunities for making contributions to the higher education of
students for a range of occupations in addition to teaching.

To summarise, therefore, it can be seen that the Catholic system
of education in England and Wales experienced a century of continuous growth up to the early 1970s in the numbers of schools,
pupils, teachers, financial commitments, colleges of education and

student teachers. Something like 60 per cent of Catholic children are now being educated in Catholic schools,[23] a figure which might well represent near the practical limit because of the operation of factors such as the availability of Catholic schools in areas of low Catholic population density.[24]

In the past few years the situation has changed dramatically as a result of the sharp drop in the birth rate since 1964. It takes some time for the changes to effect gross school numbers but teacher training places in the colleges of education have already been affected. After a decade of very rapid growth they are now experiencing a decade of equally rapid contraction. Primary school numbers have started to fall and the decline would have been more rapid if there had not been an increase in their numbers of under-fours and non-Catholic pupils. By the early 1980s pupil numbers in the secondary schools will also fall, in spite of the tendency for a greater proportion of pupils to stay on at school after the statutory school leaving age. It may be though that in the search for a more adult environment senior pupils will increasingly prefer to attend local authority sixth form colleges or colleges of further education. Such a tendency, if realised, would clearly put considerable strains upon the smaller Catholic secondary schools and it is interesting to note that there are already several Catholic sixth form colleges.

Before concluding this review of the changing size and characteristics of the Catholic system of education in England and Wales in the post-war years, it is important to emphasise the constraints on its development. In particular, the Catholic maintained school system is an integral part of the state system of education in this country and its pattern and development are therefore inevitably affected by the changes in the educational priorities of successive governments. Hence if in future there was a massive shift of emphasis towards nursery schools, community schools or in standards of educational achievement in schools, then these priorities would, in all probability, be reflected in the Catholic schools system. At the moment it seems that a century of continuous expansion is likely to be followed not so much by one of contraction as one of consolidation. The problems of financing new buildings to cope with the expansion and mobility of the increasingly affluent Catholic population and the stress upon the *quantity* of provision, which has characterised the period of expansion, have increasingly been replaced in the past few years with problems of *quality*. This has been indicated, for example, by the recent appointments by the Catholic Education Council of former headteachers as national advisers in primary and secondary education and also by the

B

appointment of an experienced College of Education lecturer to the post of national adviser on religous education. In the short term, therefore, one might predict a period of retrenchment as the Catholic community attempts to consolidate the provision built up over the past century, and also a shift of emphasis from the provision of places to the consideration of the processes occurring within the Catholic schools and colleges. It is these issues which will chiefly be addressed in part III of this book. Before that, however, the case for a separate Catholic school system in our type of pluralist society will be outlined in the following chapter.

3

A Sociological Case for Catholic Schools

In recent years[1] the traditional Catholic insistence that Catholic children from Catholic homes should be taught by Catholic teachers in Catholic schools[2] has increasingly come under attack from Catholics themselves. It has been claimed that Catholic schools in this country are too costly, that they are socially divisive and anti-ecumenical, that they are intellectually inferior, authoritarian, over-protective and singularly ineffective in their aims of producing practising, knowledgeable and committed Catholics. Furthermore, the strategy is only coping with some two-thirds of Catholic children.[3] The most articulate criticism of the school-centred strategy was published in 1971 by the Catholic Renewal Movement[4] and a number of attempts have also been made recently to re-appraise the educational needs of Catholics in England and Wales at the present time.[5] A number of the critics have referred to some recent findings in the social sciences in their support. In particular in the absence of substantial British research, reference has frequently been made to the massive Greeley-Rossi study of Catholic schools in the United States.[6]

The purpose of this chapter is threefold. First of all it aims to show that in the light of much of the educational research of the 1960s and on theoretical grounds a good case can in fact be made for the continued existence of a separate Catholic school system in this country. Secondly, it aims to show that what limited research there has been on Catholic schools by no means indicates their ineffectiveness. The research findings are best interpreted as indicating the relative unimportance of the school as compared to the home, family and environmental variables in the determination of the various outcomes of formal educational provision. Thirdly, it is argued that since it is not possible at the present time to evaluate adequately the relative effectiveness of Catholic schools in achieving whatever goals they set themselves, a programme of systematic research should be initiated in order to appraise the existing educational strategy and to provide a sound basis for future policy decisions.

Before undertaking a review of this sort it must be recognised that 'ideological predispositions and inclinations' intrude into the selection of areas of social research and in an attempt to take these into account it has become the common practice among professional sociologists to make these as explicit as possible in order the better to appraise the value of their work.[7] The assumption underlying this present chapter is that the effectiveness of Catholic schools is an empirical matter of fact rather than an article of faith. From this perspective the Catholic Renewal Movement are right to identify areas of uncertainty about the effectiveness of Catholic schools. However, their evaluation of what evidence there is does not, in my view, do justice to the Catholic schools. The traditional aim of a Catholic school with Catholic teachers for Catholic children seems to make educational sense to this sociologist and it is one aim of this chapter to suggest that this belief is well founded on the evidence of social science research.[8] As a parent it has also seemed to make sense that my young children have attended a Catholic primary school while they have been prepared for the sacraments of confession and communion. At the same time my personal experience would lead me to value attendance at a Catholic school during the adolescent years.

The limits of the argument presented here should also be noted. There is no claim that the existing strategy and distribution of resources, both of manpower and finance, is the best of all possible arrangements. The relative distribution of effort between primary and secondary schools, university and college chaplaincies, catechetical centres and provision for adults, the youth service, chaplaincies in local authority schools, and so on, is a matter for empirical investigation. Secondly, there is no claim that Catholic schools can by themselves produce high rates of religious commitment. Indeed it will be suggested later that the indications are that the school is not the crucial variable. Thirdly, there is no claim that the argument can be generalised to all societies at all times. This leaves open the question of the most appropriate formal education provision for Catholics later this century. Furthermore, it is not claimed that the argument is relevant to either Scotland or Ulster. Many critics have indeed argued that separate denominational schools in both these areas are socially divisive and likely to contribute to the perpetuation of religious prejudice and bigotry. On this point my own judgment is that where a main function of denominational education is the socialisation of successive generations into sectarian myths and hatreds and where this process is underpinned by the persistence of rigid socio-economic inequalities, as is probably the case in Ulster and possibly the case in Scotland, the existence of Catholic schools may in fact contribute to the perpetuation of prejudice and discrimination. Even in Ulster, however, Rose has shown that attendance at mixed (Catholic and Protestant) schools is only marginally associated with the reduction of extreme views.[9] There is no evidence to show that Catholic schools in England and Wales in the 1970s, with which this book is concerned, are socially divisive.[10]

The Catholic Sub-culture

There is now general agreement among sociologists that a model of society which presumes a high measure of shared norms, values and beliefs is inadequate to account for the reality of pervasive conflict between different groups and interests. A model of society which recognises a plurality of groups with not only different interests but also distinctive norms, values and beliefs seems to accord better with reality. A pluralistic model is better able to explain the facts of industrial conflict, race relations, political and religious differences and a host of other aspects of complex industrial societies. In line with this there is a realisation that it is more meaningful to refer to the sub-cultures of recognisable groups in society rather than to assume the existence of a single pervasive culture. From this perspective it is meaningful to identify a distinctive Catholic sub-culture with its own norms of religious, social and moral behaviour (for example Sunday mass attendance, sexual continence, life-long marriage), its own values (for example those relating to the dignity of the unborn child) and beliefs (in particular religious beliefs about the Trinity, Christ's redemption of mankind, the mass and so on).

The evaluation of Catholic schools is concerned with their effectiveness not only as institutions for the learning of skills and dispositions required by the wider society but also with their effectiveness as agencies of socialisation to the distinctive features of the Catholic sub-culture. In other words this evaluation relates not only to the success of Catholic schools in terms of academic or vocational achievement but also to their effectiveness in producing young Catholics knowledgeable about their faith, affectively attached to it, and committed to the christian transformation of the world.

In the achievement of the goals of the Catholic community there would appear to be two major arguments in favour of Catholic schools. The first argument emphasises the desirability of identity of purpose in the various institutions concerned in the process of the socialisation of the child, especially family, church and school. Pius XI wrote prescriptively about this in his encyclical over forty years ago.[11] More important from the perspective of this book, however, is the empirical support given to the importance of close home-school relationships by educational research in the 1960s. Two British studies are particularly relevant. In the follow-up study of a representative sample of over five thousand children born in 1946, Douglas reported for primary school children that 'the influence of the level of the parents' interest on test performance is greater (as judged by the level of the statistical significance of its effect) than that of any of the other three factors—size of family, standard of home, and academic record of the school—which are included in this analysis, and it becomes increasingly important as the children grow older'.[12] Secondly, the Plowden Report on *Children and Their Primary Schools* stated on the basis of a survey of a national sample of over three thousand parents of primary school children that 'the variation in parental attitudes can account for more of the variation in children's school achievement than either the variation in home circumstances or the variation in schools'.[13] Both these researches were concerned with academic performance but there seems to be no reason to suppose that the findings cannot be extended to the learning of prevailing norms, values and beliefs. There is certainly strong evidence of the importance of parental influence in the determination of both religious[14] and political beliefs.[15] Yet the child socialised in terms of values which do not closely accord with those dominant in the school is exposed to the stresses and strains of adapting to an alien culture. Thus the early leaving of the working class grammar school boy or his failure to realise to the full his potential ability have frequently been attributed to this form of 'culture conflict'.[16] In order to minimise the destructive aspects of such culture conflict between the religious values and beliefs of the home and the school for Catholic children it is clearly desirable that there should be that measure of community of interest which is to be found in a Catholic school staffed by Catholic teachers.

The second argument for Catholic schools derives from the work of political sociologists concerned with the analysis of pluralist industrial societies. Kornhauser,[17] for example, has argued convincingly that liberal democracy is best promoted by a plurality of independent and limited-function intermediate groups which represent diverse and frequently conflicting interests. In the absence of strong intermediate relations between elites and non-elites they are directly exposed to each other and vulnerable to widespread mass behaviour. Socially heterogeneous religious organisations are particularly important in contributing to 'extensive cross-cutting solidarities (which) favor a high level of freedom and consensus . . . (and) help prevent one line of social cleavage from becoming dominant . . .'[18] In England and Wales at the present moment the social composition of the Catholic maintained schools approximates to that of the corresponding local authority schools. The Catholic community has shared in the general educational, social and economic advancement of the country as a whole in the post-war years and, unlike the position in Ulster, there is no reason to suppose that there is a potentially divisive superimposition of class differences along the lines of religious cleavage.[19]

It can therefore with confidence be contended that the existence of a strong, healthy Catholic community, with its distinctive subculture and schools, contributes to the maintenance of a healthy democratic society in this country. Indeed, there are clear signs that spokesmen for other religious communities, fearful of a pervasive secular materialism in our society and the limitations of nonsectarian christian formation in local authority schools, are more sympathetic to the traditional Catholic defence of denominational schools.[20] There seem to be sound theoretical reasons, therefore, both in terms of the socialisation process and in terms of the needs of a pluralist industrial society,[21] for the continued existence and development of a Catholic schools system in England and Wales.

Some Empirical Evidence
In the previous chapter the scale of the involvement of the Catholic community in its own schools was indicated. In the mid-1970s there are over 3000 Catholic schools serving over 900,000 pupils in this country. These include nearly 2700 Catholic maintained primary, middle and secondary schools with over three-quarters of a million pupils staffed by over 38,000 teachers. Only 2 per cent of the pupils and 21 per cent of the teachers in these schools are not Catholics. In the past decade many independent schools have become aided, frequently as part of programmes for the reorganisation of secondary education. There can be no denying the massive commitment these figures represent. A system which involves one child in eleven is not seriously likely to disappear, at least in the foreseeable future. It is a hard political fact and it could be argued that the really serious questions relate to the quality of the contribution which the Catholic schools of this country can make to the health of our society.[22]

A number of critics have pointed to the massive financial burden which the Catholic community has borne since the 1944 Education Act.[23] An emphasis on this additional burden has been a major part of the political strategy of Catholic representatives in their negotiations with successive governments for increases in the grant for post-war school building programmes.[24] The Secretary of the Catholic Education Council has estimated gross expenditure on Catholic school buildings since the war to be approximately £150 million, net Catholic liabilities after grant to be approximately £50 million, financed in large part by some £30 million total borrowings. Annual interest and loan repayments are estimated to be about £6 million.[25] This averages about thirty to thirty-five pence weekly for a family of five mass attenders. This is not to deny that the burden is significantly greater than this in some areas. For example, the Development Fund payments required in the Diocese of Arundel and Brighton are approximately double the average figure but this is a prosperous area.[26] What these figures indicate is that the financing of the Catholic maintained schools cannot seriously be considered to be a crippling burden for the Catholic community.[27]

A social scientist faced with the problem of evaluating a programme for the achievement of specified goals would wish first of all to define the goals of the programme as explicitly and as fully as possible, secondly to devise appropriate indicators for the measurement of the extent to which these goals were being achieved, and thirdly to carry out the necessary data collection using these indicators for subsequent analysis and interpretation. It can safely be claimed that the first of these requirements, the defining of the goals of Catholic schools in England and Wales, has scarcely been attempted, although the basis exists in the prescriptions of papal encyclicals and the teachings of the Vatican Council. Virtually nothing has been done in this country on the second and third requirements though the Greeley-Rossi study in the United States offers a model for comparison.[28]

Several Catholic apologists have emphasised that the distinctive aim of a Catholic education is to prepare for man's last end.[29] Thus Archbishop Beck, in his introduction to *The Case for Catholic Schools*[30] quoted with approval the statement by Evennett[31] that 'if education is what remains after we have forgotten all we learnt at school, the quintessential left by a Catholic education is a lasting consciousness of the fact and the meaning of death'. More recently in the *Declaration on Christian Education* the Vatican Council suggested that, apart from pursuing the same cultural aims as all other schools, the Catholic school in addition had a number of distinctive purposes: the creation of an atmosphere of freedom and charity, the development of the adolescent personality in the light of faith, the effective promotion of secular welfare and the advancement of the reign of God.[32] Earlier the principal aims of a christian education are said to be consciousness of the gift of faith, adoration of God and morality of personal conduct. Finally, three behavioural indicators of the achievement of these goals are suggested: maturity, witness and the promotion of the 'christian transformation of the world'.[33] Spencer has summarised these threefold aims as the transmission of the main elements in christian culture, the internalisation of christian values and the socialisation of the child for adult membership of the church.[34] He has also argued that potential conflict exists between some of the norms relating to christian education, particularly those relating to the role of parents.[35] The only criterion used by Spencer in his evaluation of the effectiveness of Catholic schools was that of mass attendance.[36]

Monica Lawlor in a study of young Catholics used more sophisticated measures of social and religious values[37] and in the United States, Greeley and Rossi used a wide variety of measures of religious knowledge and belief, attitudes and practice.[38] They not only used Sunday mass attendance as a criterion but also constructed sacramental, church-as-teacher, religious knowledge, doctrinal orthodoxy, ethical orthodoxy and sexual mores indices from their interview and questionnaire data. Other criteria often suggested include leakage, Catholic marriage, and vocation rates. The effectiveness of the secular aims of Catholic schools might be judged in terms of GCE 'O' and 'A' level pass rates, university places obtained, and various indicators of occupational success, for example, average salaries, occupational status and so on. In addition indicators of social involvement or commitment might include activity rates in political and other voluntary organisations, and the election as members of parliament and local councillors of former pupils. Many Catholics claim that there is a distinctive atmosphere in a Catholic school but this assertion has yet to be adequately tested in this country. Much work in recent years has been done in the United States to measure high school climates mainly in terms of academic-orientation[39] but the systematic measurement of the religious climates of schools remains in its infancy.[40]

The paucity of research findings relating to the achievements of Catholic schools has been noted above but there are a number of reasons to question Spencer's conclusion 'that the empirical basis of the strategy of providing a place in a Catholic school for all Catholic children is extremely doubtful'.[41] Thus he appears to discount[42] the findings of a Catholic Education Council enquiry which indicated that a higher proportion of school leavers in 1963–64 from Catholic schools compared to non-Catholic schools entered full-time higher or further education. While a lower pro-

portion of Catholic boys proceeded to universities, higher proportions of both boys and girls proceeded to teacher training or
full-time further education.[43] Similarly in the United States Greeley
and Rossi reported a generally weak but persistent and positive
association between Catholic education and academic and occupational achievement.[44] In the absence of any hard evidence of a
significantly lower academic or intellectual orientation in Catholic
schools compared to local authority schools or of any significantly
poorer educational outcomes it cannot seriously be claimed that
the secular results of Catholic schools will inevitably be poorer.
Indeed, the results of research in the United States would lead us
to anticipate no major differences in the academic outcomes of
Catholic schools.

This is not to claim that there will be no distinctive outcomes. In
her study of Catholic schoolchildren and students in the early 1960s,
Monica Lawlor referred to the evidence of an impressive, real and
deep religious commitment.[45] At the same time she commented on
the other-worldly nature of their religion which resulted in their
contracting out of this world and the human community, and the
comparative lack of concern shown by her respondents for each
other. Her pioneering study draws attention, not only to the successes of the process of religious socialisation in Catholic schools
but also to some of the potential weaknesses and imbalances of it.
When one considers Spencer's own studies of mass attendance it
appears that whereas one-quarter of Catholics who never experienced Catholic schools did so, nearly two-fifths of those who had
always experienced Catholic schools did so. This association between mass attendance and Catholic schooling in thirteen parishes
held when controlling for age, sex, social class and terminal education age, although it was not very strong for those who entered
higher education.[46]

The Greeley-Rossi study reported that

there is a moderate but statistically significant relationship between Catholic education and adult religious behaviour

in terms of

Sunday Mass, monthly Communion, Confession several times a
year, Catholic education of children, financial contribution to
the Church, acceptance of the Church as an authoritative
teacher, acknowledgement of papal and hierarchical authority,
informality with the clergy, strict sexual morality, more detailed
knowledge about one's religion.

The authors conclude that

there does not seem to be much doubt that the schools have made a substantial, thought not overwhelming, contribution to the achievement of these goals . . . One could say that the Catholic experiment in value-oriented education has been a moderate . . . success, and that therefore there is some reason to think that value-oriented education can affect human behaviour and attitudes in matters that are invested with heavy symbolic importance.[47]

Furthermore, in a replication of the earlier study carried out in 1974, Greeley and his colleagues reported 'so not only absolutely but also relative to other factors, the importance of Catholic education has *increased* since 1963.[48]

It may be safely concluded, therefore, that there is no evidence which suggests that Catholic schools are detrimental to the achievement of either academic or religious goals. In all the researches quoted there has been a positive, if slight, association between Catholic schools and the achievement of religious goals.

Further Considerations
The main purpose of this chapter has been to show that on both theoretical and empirical grounds there is a strong case to be made for the continued existence of a distinctive system of Catholic maintained schools. This is not to claim that Catholic schools are the major causal factor in the achievement of academic or religious goals. Indeed, it is necessary at this point to insert a note of caution about the power of schools to produce approved social, educational or religious goals. Although Bronfenbrenner[49] has recently reported major differences in the socialisation processes in American and Russian schools with corresponding differences in the educational and social outcomes, the findings of educational research in the late 1960s both in this country and in the United States have increasingly suggested that school variables within any one society are of relatively minor importance in the determination of educational, religious or social outcomes. Reference has already been made to the fact that both the Douglas study and the Plowden research showed that parental and environmental variables were more important than school variables in the determination of educational achievement.[50] In the United States the Coleman Report on Equality of Educational Opportunity showed that school variables affected achievement much less than the family and peer group variables.[51] Thus the report concludes that

Schools bring little influence to bear on a child's achievement that is independent of his background and general social context . . . For equality of opportunity through the schools must imply a strong effect of the schools that is independent of the child's immediate social environment, and that strong independent effect is not present in American schools.[52]

A more recent study of educational climates in American high schools similarly reported

school quality . . . can have only modest effects on the achievements of students. Thus the large discrepancies in achievement are primarily attributable to differences in factors such as native ability, child-rearing practices, and peer-group membership.[53]

These findings are in line with the general failure of programmes of compensatory education.[54] Thus the main conclusion of much recent educational research is the relative unimportance of the school in producing desired social or academic outcomes.

The reported research on the influence of Catholic schooling on religious attitudes or behaviour by Spencer in this country[55] and Greeley and Rossi in the United States[56] give added support to this conclusion. These latter authors also note that 'the association (between Catholic education and adult religious behaviour) is strongest among those who come from very religious family backgrounds'.[57] Their analysis of the relative influence of the home and the school shows that the Catholic school does not simply duplicate the efforts of the family but that

the religiousness of the family reinforces the impact of the school and that it is only among those from highly religious families that one can expect the school to have much influence . . . We can go so far as to say that, for all practical purposes, the religious impact of Catholic education is limited to those who come from highly religious families . . . the impact of Catholic education on the religious behaviour of adults coming from families who were not highly religious is limited to their religious knowledge . . . It appears that a school cannot be expected to carry out effectively a religious socialisation process for which there is little sympathy at home . . .[58]

This is a very important qualification with obvious policy implications. However, given a school-centred strategy it is important to ask at what level or for what age group the Catholic school is most effective. Given that one-third of Catholic children do not attend Catholic schools, should there be priority for primary or secondary schooling? There is no serious claim that in this country attempts should be made to provide a separate Catholic system of higher education. It is true that there are a number of Catholic colleges of education but these exist in order to service the Catholic schools and it may be that they will become increasingly anachronistic in any major restructuring of the higher education system which substantially broadens the functions of the colleges in the next decade or so. Within the schools Berridge has offered a convincing case from the perspective of developmental psychology for Catholic schools at the pre-adolescent stage.[59] However, her view contrasts with the finding of the Greeley-Rossi study that although the association between religious behaviour and social attitudes was greater for Catholic colleges than for primary and secondary schools, this was so only among those who had already gone to Catholic primary and secondary schools. The authors of the American study interpreted their data as indicating a 'multiplier effect', the most desirable effects of religious education being produced principally in those who have had a comprehensive religious education extending over a prolonged period.[60] This is an area where systematic research in this country might be particularly relevant at the present time, when local authority sixth form or further education colleges may be offering serious competition to relatively small Catholic comprehensive schools.

Finally, the foregoing review of what relevant research findings there are both in this country and in the United States suggests that the important question at the present time is not 'are Catholic schools effective?' but 'how can Catholic schools be made more effective and what is their *relative* effectiveness in terms of measurable social, educational and religious achievements given their inputs of manpower and finance, compared to actual or potential alternative methods of religious socialisation?' The contribution which research can make to the answering of these questions will be addressed in chapter 11 but first, in part III of this book, a number of studies of the religious outcomes of Catholic schools in England will be reviewed.

PART III

Qualitative Outcomes of Catholic Schools

4

The Quality of Catholic Schools

It has already been suggested that the exigencies of the post-war expansion of the system of Catholic schools in England and Wales resulted in a relatively strong concern with the *quantity* of school building and the size of the school and pupil populations and with a relatively weak concern with the *quality* of Catholic schools. There is some evidence that with the commencement of the contraction of the school population in the early 1970s and possibly in response to some of the critics of Catholic schools since the late 1960s[1] there has been an increasing concern to explore the facts about the quality of Catholic schools.

There are a number of examples of this growing concern. In the first place a Catholic Schools Humanities Project to parallel that of the Schools' Council Humanities Curriculum Project was undertaken under the direction of a member of staff at St Mary's College, Strawberry Hill.[2] Secondly, the Catholic Education Council appointed two headteachers as national advisers on secondary and primary education.[3] Much of their work seems to have involved the dissemination of examples of 'good practice' on the part of school or teacher exemplars and the holding of seminars and the publication of reports on such issues as 'The Catholic Secondary School and Its Community', 'The Joint Church Secondary School', 'Problems of the Inner City Schools', 'The Role of the Head of the Religious Education Department' and 'The Christ We Present to Children'.[4] In this way it is hoped that communications between schools and teachers have been improved and standards in schools have been raised. It is perhaps important to distinguish this work of public relations from research, at least as far as it is understood by academic social scientists, and involving the generation and testing of specific hypotheses within some sort of body of theory of social interaction.[5] Thirdly, a national adviser for religious education has also been appointed.[6] One of the outcomes of his work has been a consideration of the relationship between christian revelation and educational theory in the light of theological developments since Vatican II.[7] At the same time the Bishops' Commission has initiated a study into the theology of education and, in the light of the theological conclusions, intends to make a full enquiry into the present educational needs of the Catholic church in England and Wales.[8]

The five chapters which comprise part III of this book aim to make a contribution to the knowledge and understanding of the qualitative outcomes of Catholic schooling from the perspectives of empirical sociology. A number of relatively small-scale studies will be reported which it is suggested have been cumulative in the knowledge they have generated. But first of all it is proposed to raise questions about some of the latent functions[9] of Catholic education. In particular it is suggested that there is a need to be aware of actual and potential areas of injustice in Catholic education.

Justice in Education[10]

The consideration of matters of social justice has come to play an increasingly important part in the life of the church in recent years. This has been reflected in papal encyclicals[11] and was a major concern of the 1971 Synod of Bishops.[12] This re-thinking of the gospel message in terms of the imperatives of justice and the pre-requisites of peace has been largely promoted in terms of the global concerns with war and peace, population and food, world development and trade, urbanisation, racialism, pollution and the environment and so on.[13] The bishops saw endeavours to transform the world according to the demands of justice as an essential part of the preaching of the gospel and urged that the church must be particularly concerned with education for justice.

While it is true that the bishops recognised that much of the world's contemporary education 'is individualistic and geared towards the accumulation of possessions', the overriding impression given is that we should educate in our schools for the external injustices in the world outside and mainly abroad. The argument put here, however, is that this perspective may inhibit a critical appraisal of injustices in our own institutions, including Catholic schools. At least five areas of enquiry seem to be relevant.

First of all a number of critics have argued that the very existence of separate Catholic schools is divisive. My own judgment would be that where a main function of denominational education is the socialisation of successive generations into sectarian myths and hatreds and where this process is underpinned by the persistence of rigid socio-economic inequalities, as is probably the case in Ulster and possibly the case in Scotland, the existence of Catholic schools may in fact contribute to the perpetuation of prejudice and discrimination. Even in Ulster, however, Rose's study[14] showed that attendance at mixed schools was only marginally associated with a reduction of extreme views and there is no evidence to show that Catholic schools in England and Wales are socially divisive. Current explorations of the possibilities of combined Anglican-Catholic schools may in fact indicate that inter-denominational suspicions are declining in the face of common fears of a pervasive secular materialism. The existence of separate Catholic schools may in fact be a valuable contribution to a healthy pluralism in our society.

Secondly, there is the continuance of a strong independent sector. One of the main moral criticisms of the powerful independent sector is that its advantages can be purchased by an elite to perpetuate existing socio-economic privileges through favoured entry to prestigious and powerful occupations. This is held to be a structural injustice in a society which proclaims an ideology of equality of opportunity. This is a particularly relevant challenge for the Catholic community which still has a higher than average proportion of independent schools and places in spite of the fact that in recent years many independent schools have become aided, frequently as part of schemes for the reorganisation of secondary education.[15]

The third area of injustice relates to the persistence of social class inequalities of educational opportunity even on a weak definition in terms of measured intelligence. All the evidence shows that a massive increase in the provision of university places has done nothing to alter the proportion of undergraduates from working-class homes, and in the schools a series of sponsorship hurdles, including streaming in the primary school, selection for secondary school, and entry into the sixth form serve to remove working-class children disproportionately from the system at all stages. Recent research has indicated that the independent influence of the school may be less than was once supposed and that the roots of social class inequalities are firmly established in differences in pre-school socialisation patterns. Even so it may be wondered if Catholic schools are doing all they might to reduce existing structural inequalities. Indeed, it may be that because of its strong grammar school traditions, resistance to the changes necessary if there is to be any reduction in social class inequalities is greater in the Catholic than the local authority schools.

While studies of structural rigidities in the educational system have concentrated almost exclusively on class differences, it seems particularly important that Catholics appraise their educational policies with respect to sex differences. It seems to me that Catholics with their special devotion to our Lady, their celibate religious, and their interpretation of the biblical predominance of man in prescriptive rather than culture-bound terms, are particularly prone to the ideology of the permanent maternal vocation. This ideology serves to legitimate the socialisation of women into permanently subordinate familial and work roles. The roots of this process are found not only within the family but also in the system of 'progressively contracting opportunity' in the schools. Catholic schools are particularly prone to distinguishing girls' subjects from boys' subjects and it might be expected that this subtle form of sexual discrimination is gradually eroded in mixed Catholic comprehensives.

One unintended consequence of a policy of Catholic schools for Catholic children may very well be that they are failing to participate in society's attempts to assimilate large numbers of coloured immigrants and their children.[16] Early reports suggest that the schools are not being very successful in their endeavours to ensure equal opportunities even for second generation children. It is surely a matter of justice and an essential part of the church's mission to the poor and deprived to be fully committed to making a contribution to the education of these children whatever their religious adherence.

Fourthly, it has sometimes been said that because of the strongly hierarchical nature of the church, Catholics are particularly likely to perpetuate inappropriate authority structures within the school system which are either simply traditional or which are not legitimated in terms of some relevant criteria such as merit, representativeness and so on. Such structures are likely to be destructive in promoting either alienation, apathy or docility and are to be found, for example, wherever a parish priest has an automatic or dominant control of school managers; where a head teacher treats his school as an extension of his private property or treats his staff as subordinates to be controlled rather than as professional colleagues to be consulted; where, in spite of the ideology of parental responsibility, parents are not involved in the education of their children and where their wishes with respect to their children are of no account; where teachers treat children as inferiors to be directed rather than as clients to be encouraged towards independence and responsibility; and where students in colleges of education are not treated with the dignity their adult status demands. In all these cases there are deficiencies of justice. Catholics can be particularly prone to authoritarianism.[17]

Social justice in Catholic schools implies a recognition of the fact that children too have rights.[18] They have a right to be respected as human beings and not as subordinates to be directed or receptacles to be moulded. They have rights to a proper care and attention to their needs. As far as their religious education is concerned they have a right in justice to honesty, to clear if unpalatable guidelines to moral behaviour where these can be identified, and to the candid admission of uncertainty where doubt exists. They have a right to a reasonably structured syllabus with regard to the main tenets of the christian beliefs and also an experience of a living christian commitment on the part of their teachers and an indication of its relevance to them not only in their current dilemmas, for example those concerning sexual relationships, but also those relevant for their future lives, marriage, work and the adult world generally. In sum, children have a right to be treated seriously.

The fifth area of injustice is the most difficult to elucidate and yet in many ways it is the most important. Very broadly, parents and pupils can reasonably demand that Catholic schools provide a satisfactory introduction to the common cultural heritage of the land, a preparation necessary for future employment in a complex industrial society and for rapid social change, a deep grounding in the faith, a commitment to the christian transformation of the world, and an awareness of and preparation for death. A deficiency in any of these areas may be viewed as an injustice to the pupils concerned.

In her study of Catholic school children and students in the 1960s, Monica Lawlor referred to the evidence of an impressive, real and deep religious commitment.[19] At the same time she commented on the other-worldly nature of their religion which resulted in their contracting out of this world and the human community, and the comparative lack of concern shown by her respondents for each other. Her pioneering study drew attention, not only to the successes of the process of religious socialisation in Catholic schools, but also to some of the potential weaknesses of it. Clearly a Catholic schooling which is 'out of this world' may be an inadequate education for social justice. More fundamentally, attention might be drawn to 'the unchristian effects of competitiveness and of intellectual segregation'. In these respects there may be little which is specifically distinctive or just about Catholic schools.

These five areas of injustice may plausibly be found in Catholic schools. It is an empirical issue to determine whether or not they actually do appear disproportionately, and a policy issue to determine to transform these schools and strive to inculcate a greater sensitivity in matters of social justice in education.

Three Exploratory Studies

In the remainder of this chapter and in the following two chapters some findings from three small exploratory studies carried out at the University of Surrey in the mid-1970s will be reported. In the first study, Ann Thomas aimed to compare two independent girls' schools with the boys' public schools surveyed by Lambert.[20] Since one of the schools was a Catholic convent and the other an Anglican school it was incidentally possible to explore the distinctive features of the Catholic school. Data were obtained in the summer of 1972 from questionnaires, based on Lambert's research instruments, which were completed by 139 senior girls in the two schools. In addition, a number of extended interviews were carried out with selected girls. The convent school had been founded by a religious congregation nearly half a century ago and was currently attended by some 600 girls. Most of the teachers were part-timers and only a few sisters taught in the school. Two-thirds of the girls were aged 14 or 15 and one-third 16 or 17 when surveyed. Two-thirds had entered the school before the age of twelve and so had experienced the socialising influences of the school for a significant period of time. Half the sample were boarders. With only one exception all the girls had fathers in professional or managerial occupations and two-fifths were either foreign or normally resident abroad. Only one in six of the English girls were Catholics, compared to two-thirds of the other girls.[21] In the Anglican school all the girls were in the sixth form, two-thirds were boarders and more than four-fifths were aged 16 or 17.[22]

In the autumn of 1973 the religious attitudes of 578 fifth formers in three Roman Catholic maintained mixed comprehensive schools and one mixed county secondary school in the south of England were surveyed by Hornsby-Smith and Margaret Petit, again using self-completion questionnaires. All three comprehensive schools had recently been created by the amalgamation of single-sex grammar or independent schools and in all three cases there were transitional problems resulting from the change of status. For example, School 1, which was run by a religious order and had a religious head teacher and deputy head, comprised separate boys' and girls' sections nearly a mile apart. Consequently, at the fifth form level with which this study was concerned, the classes were in fact single-sex classes though there was a measure of staff interchange between the two sites. In this school pupils were streamed by ability in three broad bands. The amalgamation of schools to create School 2 a few years previously had aroused fierce local controversy and considerable resentment on the part of many of those pupils now in the fifth form. While there were clear signs that this resentment was becoming muted, it was a factor which was reflected in some of the responses in this school where pupils were also streamed by ability. School 3 had recently been created by the amalgamation of two single-sex independent schools and again there had been a considerable amount of friction when it was first established. Fifth form pupils were divided alphabetically so that there was no direct streaming in this school, though a process of 'guided choice' operated. Both Schools 2 and 3 had recently appointed lay head teachers. The fourth school was a county secondary school where the pupils were streamed by ability into three major bands. A summary of the main characteristics of these four schools and the two schools of the previous study has been given in table 4.1.[23]

In the third study Johanna Fitzpatrick obtained focused interviews[24] during school hours in the autumn of 1974 with 48 fourth-formers in two London Catholic mixed comprehensives. These interviews, which were tape recorded, on average lasted half an hour. The 25 boys and 23 girls in the sample were selected randomly from the fourth formers in the two schools. All were aged 14 or 15 and had at least one Roman Catholic parent. Nearly all had attended a Catholic primary school and reported that most of their friends were Catholics. Only six of the 40 pupils for whom data were available had fathers in non-manual occupations. In 'St Peter's, Newtown' the socio-economic status of the parents was slightly higher, but both parents were Catholics in a rather lower proportion of cases compared to 'St Paul's, Oldtown'. A survey of mass attendance in all the Catholic secondary schools in the Southwark diocese in 1975[25] had suggested that there was a significant decline of Sunday mass attendance before the fifth form. By interviewing fourth formers it was hoped to explore the early stages of any process of religious disaffection.[26]

School Differences: A Case Study
As has already been mentioned the first of these studies arose out of the attempt to compare girls' independent schools with the boys' public schools studied by Lambert. The girls' perception of the school goals, their adaptation to the school regime and their general religious, social and moral attitudes will be reported in the following chapter. Some of the findings of this study are, however, relevant to the question of the distinctiveness of the atmosphere of a Catholic school and because they resulted in hypotheses which were tested in the subsequent investigations.

In his study, Lambert was concerned to explore the relative weight put on instrumental and expressive aims by boys in public and state schools. One question asked them if they could be one of an outstanding scholar, head of school, sportsman or artist, which they would prefer to be. The girls in this study were asked the same question and their responses have been compared to those of Lambert's two samples of boy boarders in table 4.2.[27] It can be seen that by comparison with the boys, the girls were much more likely to select the more expressive and artistic alternatives and to be much less concerned with sporting achievement. The girls in the Catholic school were much more likely than those in the Anglican school to aspire to outstanding scholarship or sporting achievement. Although the largest group of girls aspired to artistic achievement, the proportion in the Catholic school was much lower than in the Anglican school. This appeared to be related to the fact that the girls in the Catholic school were much more pre-occupied with the state of family life in this country, a concern which was closely related to their more critical views on television and modern art and drama.

The general religious, moral, social and political attitudes of the girls were surveyed by means of a question devised by Lambert.[28] Girls were presented with a list of twenty-five controversial statements and asked to indicate the extent of their agreement or disagreement with each on four point scales. On the basis of twenty of these items Lambert constructed a scale of acceptance of traditional values.[29] Lambert's results for boy boarders have been compared to those of the girls in the two research schools of this study in table 4.3. The results suggest that traditional values have been strongly rejected by the pupils in the Anglican school, whereas those for both Catholic and non-Catholic girls in the convent school are intermediate between Lambert's boys' public school and state or integrated school boarders. There are, however, a number of reasons for suspecting the validity of Lambert's scale on the basis of the findings of this study. First of all he gives no indication of how he treated the case of non-response on any item. Secondly, several items on Lambert's scale were found to be *negatively* correlated with each other. Thirdly, the scale is too crude to detect the nuances of religious, moral, cultural, social and political traditionalism which may not operate in identical ways.

Further analysis of the correlation matrix of the scores on the twenty-five attitude scales led to the construction of six separate scales. Average values for each of these scales were computed for each school and also separately for the Catholic and non-Catholic girls in the convent school. The results of this analysis have been summarised in table 4.4. It can be seen that there were significant differences between the schools in terms of three of the six values:

the salience of christian morality, anti-intellectualism and acceptance of the woman's traditional sex role.

However, none of the differences between the Catholic and non-Catholic girls from the convent school reached the level of statistical significance, and could therefore have arisen by chance. This was also true of the scores on the twenty-five individual items, for most of which the proportions of Catholics and non-Catholics agreeing or disagreeing were practically identical. This continued to be true after controlling for residence in England or abroad. There were again no significant differences in the responses of those girls with English parents resident in this country or those normally resident abroad. These are extremely interesting findings because they mean that in this study, between-school differences are far more important than those within the convent school in terms of religious affiliation, nationality or normal residence (ie England or abroad). It also suggests that irrespective of differences in the entrants, the convent school is a far more powerful institution for the religious and moral socialisation of adolescent girls than much recent educational research would have led one to expect.[30]

Two suggestions might be made about these researches. Most of them have been concerned with effectiveness in achieving the instrumental goals of schools in terms of academic outcomes. In terms of Etzioni's analysis of complex organisations[31] it might be that in these cases coercive or remunerative (in terms of long-term occupational prospects) types of power predominated and that the corresponding involvement of the pupils was either alienative or at best only calculative. The relative ineffectiveness of the school under these conditions, therefore, is not unexpected, given the coercive nature of much secondary education[32] and the pervasiveness and rigidity of the structural inequalities in the wider society.[33] When considering questions of religious socialisation in the schools, however, the power employed by teachers is more likely to be normative and pupils are consequently more likely to show what Etzioni calls moral involvement and to express high levels of support for the social, moral and religious attitudes and values promoted by the school.

In those researches concerned with the outcomes of Catholic schooling, on the other hand, it is important to recognise that effectiveness has generally been measured in terms of long-term adult behaviour well after the supportive influence of the school has been left behind. Again it can be argued that in the absence of an adult environment favourable to the maintenance of earlier school influences, the relatively weak long-term outcomes of Catholic schools are not unexpected. What is erroneous is the inference drawn from this that Catholic schools are ineffective.

In the light of these considerations it is possible to resolve the apparent contradiction between, on the one hand, the findings of educational researches in recent years which have demonstrated a relatively weak independent influence of the school, and, on the other hand, those findings reported here of significant between-school differences and significant similarities in the attitudes and values of Catholic and non-Catholic pupils within a convent school. Firstly, weaker school influences are likely to be found in those areas concerned with the predominantly instrumental, academic goals of schools, associated as they frequently are with the coercive nature of secondary school attendance. Secondly, the ineffectiveness of Catholic schools in terms of long-term adult religious practice in the absence of family and other supportive influences is not to be confused with the short-term effectiveness in inculcating distinctive social, religious and moral attitudes while in the school. The conclusion is not that Catholic schools are ineffective but that their influence wears off in a hostile or non-supportive adult environment. This is only to be expected since the school is only one of a number of major formative influences in the process of religious socialisation.

Important policy implications derive from these conclusions. Firstly, further research is necessary to identify those pastoral strategies which are most effective in maintaining the influence of the Catholic school even where the family environment is not supportive. Secondly, more attention should be paid to the development of new or more effective institutions for school leavers and adults for the continuation of the process of religious socialisation commenced in the Catholic school. The exploitation of family or friendship or occupational groups may well be a more effective strategy than the almost exclusive concern with traditional parochial structures for this purpose.[34]

In this chapter it has been argued that the quality of Catholic schooling has become a matter of greater importance to the Catholic community as the decline in the birth rate has taken the pressure off the need to build more schools in order to approach the goal of a Catholic school for every Catholic child who wishes it. It has also been urged that this shift of emphasis should be promoted. A number of potential weaknesses in the Catholic system have been identified but it has been stressed that empirical research would be necessary to indicate the extent to which these weaknesses are in fact realised. To this end a number of empirical studies of the religious outcomes of Catholic schools have been initiated. In the first of these, a study of a convent school, there appears to be evidence of a successful process of religious socialisation of both Catholic and non-Catholic pupils. In the next chapter this will be taken further with an analysis of the religious attitudes of senior pupils in a number of different secondary schools in the south of England.

5

The Catholic Adolescent and Religion

In the previous chapter details were given of the studies carried out by Ann Thomas in 1972 and Margaret Petit in 1973. In this chapter there will be a consideration of the major findings from these studies. Firstly, pupil understanding of school goals and their evaluation of the success or not of the school in achieving these goals will be summarised. Secondly, there will be an appraisal of pupil adaptation to their school regimes. Thirdly, the responses to a battery of religious, social and moral attitude questions will be outlined and social correlates of the variations in these attitudes will be reported.

Data were obtained from pre-coded questionnaires completed anonymously during school hours by a total of 717 pupils in six schools.[1] In the Anglican girls' school and the three Catholic mixed comprehensive schools the questionnaire was administered by the researchers and no teacher saw the completed forms. In the event, permission to carry out a comparative study in two local authority comprehensive schools in the same area as one of the Catholic comprehensives was not given and we are indebted to a teacher in a local authority secondary school in this area for making arrangements to administer the same questionnaire to her own pupils. In our judgement she was unlikely to have influenced the responses in any way. In the Roman Catholic convent the questionnaires were administered by the headmistress and it is likely that some of the girls might have been intimidated by this fact. In addition, they were wrongly advised by her to select one option for each of the questions on school goals so that the results from this school are not directly comparable to those from the other schools. However, the results are reported for completeness and are certainly suggestive, if not conclusive. Furthermore, in this school 22 girls were interviewed in private and this enabled a number of clarifications to be made. Seven girls from the Anglican girls' school were also interviewed.

School Goals

For the purposes of this study pupils in the four mixed schools were given a list of eight possible school goals. These were based on those devised by Lambert.[2] Pupils were asked to indicate which of the eight items they considered their school was (*a*) *trying* to do, (*b*) *should* try to do, and (*c*) was *succeeding* in doing. Comparable data were available for the two girls' independent schools for four of these goals. Details of the proportions of students in each school checking each of the three questions for each of the eight given goals have been given in table 5.1. Although there are minor differences of emphasis between the three Catholic comprehensives it can be seen that in at least two respects they differ markedly from the local authority school. Whilst the Catholic schools are considered by their pupils to put more emphasis on the teaching of christian doctrine, the practice of christian values and moral education in terms of recognition of right and wrong, and are generally seen to be more successful than the local authority school in pursuing these goals, by contrast they are held to be relatively less successful in the development of the pupils' individual interests and talents. For the reasons stated above a simple comparison of these responses with those of the girls in the convent school is not possible but it is of interest that the girls in the Anglican independent school considered their school to put a higher emphasis both on examination success and on christian and general moral education in comparison with the four mixed schools but to be relatively unconcerned about career preparation. It is also of note that pupils not only in the local authority school but also in the three Catholic comprehensive schools considered that the two goals of teaching christian doctrine and putting into practice christian values *should* be given less emphasis than any of the other six goals. This finding parallels that found by Lindsay[3] in a comparison between a Catholic comprehensive school and a Protestant comprehensive school in the same area on the outskirts of Glasgow.

These differences between the Catholic and the local authority pupils and also those between the sexes in the four mixed schools can be seen more clearly when the eight goals are ranked for each of the three questions in table 5.2. The rankings demonstrate clearly that there are surprisingly few significant differences between the Catholic and local authority schools in spite of not only the religious factor, but also the relatively lower educational status of the secondary school. The differences are confined to the higher emphasis placed on christian values in the Catholic schools and their correspondingly higher level of success, according to the assessment of the fifth formers, not only on this goal but also in the teaching of christian doctrine and the moral education goal of enabling students to distinguish right from wrong. Against this the Catholic schools were seen to be relatively much less successful in pursuing the three personal growth goals of developing the students' individual interests and talents, encouraging students to challenge traditional ideas and opinions, and preparing students for adult life. On the other hand, there was general agreement that all the schools had most success in pursuing the instrumental goals of career preparation and examination success and that they should put far more emphasis than they did on developing individual interests and talents and promoting independent thinking by encouraging students to challenge ideas and opinions which were simply traditional.

The religious orientation of the convent school was apparent in the interviews with senior girls. One summed up the efforts of this school in these terms:

> The school is trying to educate girls, to bring them up with a sense of true values . . . Because it's a convent it's quite based on religion but it's not forced on you at all; you make up your own mind. It's really to bring up the girl to be useful in society more than exam results . . .

The assessment of the strength of the goal of 'putting into practice christian values' in this school was also indicated in some critical observations in the interviews which hinted at the alienating potential of an imposed emphasis on religious practice:

> We're too strict in some things, especially religion . . . You have to go to Mass . . . They say you can say your own views, so you say them and then you get picked out for it.

> We shouldn't go to church so much—twice a week we have to go. I think it's OK Catholics can go that much. It's a bit rotten on Protestants and Hindus here.

Thus the prominence of the religious orientation of this school is explicitly recognised, not always with approval, by the senior girls of this school. In the second study of the four mixed schools there were few differences between the sexes in their assessments of school goals as can be seen from table 5.2. When the ratings of the male and female pupils in these schools were compared the only difference of any note was that the boys considered their schools should put relatively more emphasis on the challenge goal than the girls.

Pupil Adaptations

In his classical study of the way in which the frequency of deviant behaviour varied within the different social structures, Merton[4] identified five types of individual adaptation in terms of the 'dissociation between culturally prescribed aspirations and socially structured avenues for realising these aspirations'. Lambert devised measures of the pupils' adaptations to six parts of the school's structure or values. In each part or situation five possible reactions were offered and pupils were required to select in each instance the reaction they would actually have.[5] For the purposes of this present study one situation was chosen for comparison between the schools. As Lambert's measures had been devised for boys it was necessary to make a number of minor modifications in the wording but otherwise the test used was identical. Pupils were asked to indicate which of five specified reactions they would have if they were in a responsible position in the fifth form. (A slightly different wording had to be employed in the girls' schools where some of the sample were in the sixth forms.) The responses to this question have been given in a simplified form in table 5.3. It can be seen that there was very little evidence of significant patterns of either rebellion or retreatism in any of these six schools. The dominant mode was that of conformity selected by between two-fifths and three-fifths of the pupils in all the schools. The innovation mode, which represented an acceptance of the school goals but also a pursuit of them by channels which were not formally approved, was selected by between one-quarter and two-fifths of the pupils in all six schools. But the widest variations between schools were recorded for the ritualism mode, that is the rejection of the goals promoted by the schools whilst going through the motions of adhering to the means of pursuing these goals. This represents 'playing along with the system' and many have suspected that authoritarian methods of socialisation in Catholic schools were particularly likely to result in this mode of adaptation by young Catholics who went through the motions of religious adherence (eg by regular Sunday mass attendance) without particularly internalising the religious values or becoming committed to them in any serious way.

The data provide only partial support for this view. Two of the three Catholic comprehensive schools have the same proportion of selections of the ritualism mode as the local authority school whilst the third had double this proportion. However, one-third (or four times the proportion in the local authority school) of the girls in the convent school selected this mode. It seems, therefore, as if ritualism is not so much a feature of Catholic schools, per se, as of certain types of school. Half the pupils in the convent school, which had a headteacher who was a nun, were boarders and the regime appeared to be particularly favourable for the development of this mode. It is also noticeable that the second highest selection of this mode was in the Anglican school, also an independent girls' school and having two-thirds of the sample boarding. The differences between the girls in the two independent schools and those in the four mixed schools were statistically highly significant.

Finally, it may be noted that there are highly significant differences between the sexes in the four mixed schools of this study. Three-fifths of the girls selected the conformity mode compared to two-fifths of the boys whilst over one-third of the boys chose the innovation mode compared to one-quarter of the girls. Males were also nearly twice as likely to select one of the minor options—retreatism, ritualism or rebellion.

Adolescent Attitudes[6]

This section of the chapter will report the findings on five questions which explored the social, moral and religious attitudes, beliefs and values of the 578 fifth formers in the three Catholic comprehensive schools and the local authority secondary school. Where possible, comparison will also be made with the results obtained in the earlier study of two girls' independent boarding/day schools. In each case the research instrument used was a self-completion questionnaire which was completed anonymously during school hours.

The first question invited the pupils to indicate their level of agreement or disagreement on four point scales with each of sixteen controversial statements. Eight of these statements had been on the questionnaire used in the previous study and were derived from Lambert's original instruments. The level of agreement with each of the sixteen statements for each of the four schools of the second study and for the two schools of the first study has been given in table 5.4.

The strong socialisation to the traditional role of the woman in the home does not appear to be a characteristic of Catholic schools, per se, but simply a characteristic of the education in a convent school. Similarly, a distrust of intellectuals is not confined to the Catholic schools although the high proportion agreeing with this item in the local authority school largely reflects the significantly lower social class background of the pupils attending, compared to all the other schools. Social class factors also seem largely to explain the rather different attitudes of the pupils in the local authority school to statements 9, 10, 11 and 14. Apart from the responses to some questions relating to religion (statements 1 and

13) it is remarkable how few differences there are between the schools, even though the secondary school has a lower status than the three comprehensive schools.

The second question on belief in God and the third on belief in Jesus were both taken from the studies of contemporary American religion by Glock and Stark.[7] Variations of belief in God have been summarised in table 5.5. Only one-fifth of the pupils in the three Catholic schools selected the first statement, the traditionally orthodox view, and a further two-fifths the less certain statement. These proportions were twice those selected by the pupils in the local authority secondary school. By contrast these pupils were seven times more likely to select the agnostic position compared to those in the Catholic schools. All these differences were statistically highly significant. The figures reveal a much wider range of conceptions of God and level of conviction, even in the Catholic schools where the processes of religious socialisation might have been expected to have been particularly powerful, than had ever been imagined.

The third question explored beliefs in the divinity of Jesus, the central figure of christianity. Details are given in table 5.6. Again it can be seen that the proportions accepting the orthodox conception of Jesus are twice as high in the Catholic schools as in the local authority school and the agnostic view is selected four times as frequently in the local authority school as in the Catholic schools.

In an attempt to simplify these data and isolate significant clusters of attitudes and values, the data were subjected to factor analysis using the SPSS program. The assumption was made that the selections of beliefs in God and Jesus could be treated as interval scales (neglecting the final option in both cases) though Labovitz's work[8] would indicate that correlation procedures are sufficiently robust for this assumption not to be crucial. On average 554 pupils scored each of the 18 items on the relevant scales (neglecting don't knows, no responses, statement 7 in table 5.5 and statement 6 in table 5.6). Principal factoring with a maximum of 25 iterations was used, five factors with an eigen-value greater than 1·0 being extracted. The default rotational method was Varimax. Pairwise deletion of missing data was selected for the computation of correlation coefficients.

Details of the factor loadings on the five factors which together accounted for 35 per cent of the variance have been given in table 5.7. A consideration of these loadings and of the multiple correlation matrix for the 18 variables suggested that the data could be best simplified by the construction of six scales from those items indicated (*, **). The six scales constructed from the raw data, the

c

average inter-item correlations measuring the internal consistency of the scales, and McKennell's Alpha coefficients measuring the reliability of the scales[9] were therefore:

I   Salience of Christian Religious Morality, CHRELM
     (Items 1, 7, 13, 17 and 18)
     $n = 5$, $\bar{r} = 0.40$, Alpha $= 0.77$

IIa   Deference to Parents and Teachers, DEFPTS
     (Items 4 and 5)
     $n = 2$, $\bar{r} = 0.45$, Alpha $= 0.62$

IIb   Sexual Morality, SEXMOR
     (Items 6 and 12)
     $n = 2$, $\bar{r} = 0.33$, Alpha $= 0.48$

III   Anti-Intellectualism, ANTINT
     (Items 3 and 9)
     $n = 2$, $\bar{r} = 0.29$, Alpha $= 0.45$

IV   Independence within a Framework, INDFRM
     (Items 15 and 16)
     $n = 2$, $\bar{r} = 0.21$, Alpha $= 0.34$

V   Rejection of Contraceptive Morality, CONMOR
     (Items 8 and 12)
     $n = 2$, $\bar{r} = -0.16$, Alpha $= 0.28$
     This scale was computed after reversing the direction of FAMLIM (Item 8).

It can be seen that it was decided to split the items with high loadings on factor II into two separate scales after a consideration of the inter-correlation matrix and the meanings of the various items. Values for each of these six scales were computed for all cases where there were no missing data and subsequent analysis consisted in the cross-tabulation of each of the six scales by school, sex, social class (in terms of father's occupation), maternal employment, pupil religion and parental religion, in an attempt to identify factors significantly related to variations in pupil attitudes. The results of this analysis have been summarised in table 5.8. Note that high proportions of low scores represents high levels of agreement with statements 1–16 and orthodox christian beliefs about God and Jesus.

There was a wide variation between the four schools in the scores on the Salience of Christian Religious Morality scale. It is noteworthy that a higher proportion of pupils in the local authority secondary school expressed high levels of agreement on this scale compared to those in school 2 where the proportion of low scorers was only one-half that of school 1. Otherwise there were no statistically significant differences between any of the groups although as might have been predicted, a higher proportion of girls, children of non-manual fathers, Roman Catholics and those with Roman Catholic parents scored less than the average.

The second scale measured deference to parental and teacher authority figures. Again there were no statistically significant differences when scores were simply dichotomised into high and low, as indicated in table 5.8. It is, however, of interest that girls, pupils with white collar fathers, working mothers, and those from Roman Catholic homes scored higher measures of agreement than the average.

The third scale measured the strength of the belief that premarital sexual relations and contraceptive intercourse were wrong. As can be seen from table 5.4, only one-fifth of the fifth formers in the four schools agreed with the condemnation of premarital sexual relations compared to the two-fifths in the two girls' schools of the previous study. When the two separate items were scaled there were again no significant differences between the four schools. The only statistically significant difference occurred between pupils both of whose parents were Roman Catholic compared to those pupils both of whose parents had other religious allegiances. As for the previous two scales, girls, pupils with non-manual fathers, and Roman Catholics expressed higher levels of agreement than the average.

The earlier study of the two girls' schools had suggested that a significant measure of anti-intellectualism might be a feature of Catholic schools. This present study provides no support for this notion. The highest proportion of low scores on this scale were obtained in the local authority secondary school but this result clearly needs to be interpreted cautiously. This school has a lower status than that of the comprehensive schools (all of which had grammar or independent school origins) and also a much larger proportion of pupils from working class homes. On this scale, social class differences were highly significant and ideally should be controlled for in any future comparative study. In addition, a significantly higher proportion of boys than girls had low scores. Finally, the possibility that there might be a deep-seated anti-intellectualism component in the Catholic sub-culture was given no support by our data. Roman Catholic pupils and those from Catholic homes had lower scores on this scale than pupils with other religious affiliations. Thus it would seem that anti-intellectualism is not necessarily a characteristic of Catholic schools per se, though it did appear to be a feature peculiar to the convent school of the first study.

The fifth scale was made up of the only two items with high loadings on factor IV, items 15 and 16 on table 5.4. Virtually all the respondents in all four schools agreed with both the statements but it was possible to dichotomise the scores by distinguishing those scoring only 2 or 3 from the rest. At first sight one might have anticipated a negative relationship between these two items, one stressing the need for rules and regulations and the other the importance of individual decision making. In the absence at this stage of interview material which might have explored these views in greater depth, it would appear that this scale measures the strength of the desire for individual independence but within a framework with clear guidelines and recognisable boundaries. It seems to represent a dual rejection of both personal alienation and structural anomie. One might speculate that a rejection of both powerlessness and meaninglessness is particularly emphasised.[10] With the selected cut-off point there were three very highly significant differences in the scores on this scale. First of all the proportion of pupils with low scores in the Catholic schools was about one-third higher than that in the local authority school. Similarly, the proportion of pupils with low scores was about one-third higher where one or both parents was a Catholic compared to those both of whose parents had other religious allegiances. A balanced interpretation of these findings requires further in-depth study but there would appear to be at least two possibilities. On the one hand the high levels of agreement by young Catholics with item 16 could reflect a measure of resistance to the pervasiveness of a specifically Catholic viewpoint and a desire to be allowed more personal freedom in decision-making on a wide range of controversial social, moral and religious issues. On the other hand the high levels of agreement with item 15 could reflect an acceptance of a traditional Catholic viewpoint that clear guidelines are essential and that it is a function of an authoritative church to provide such guidelines. It must be emphasised that these observations are largely speculative. The two items comprising this scale are not very discriminating and therefore can serve at this stage only to generate hypotheses for further research. Finally it may be noted that a much higher proportion of boys than girls had low scores on this scale.

Four items from table 5.4 did not load sufficiently highly on any one of the factors to be included in any of the scales. In the previous study two-fifths of the convent girls agreed with the statement that 'women are best kept in the home', a proportion fourteen times greater than that recorded by the girls in the Anglican school. In this study, however, there were no significant differences between the four schools, just under one-fifth of all respondents agreeing with the statement. Boys and pupils with mothers who were not working were far more likely than girls and pupils with working mothers to agree with this traditional view of the woman's role. Two-fifths of the fifth formers in the four schools thought that school uniform ought to be abolished altogether. However, fewer students in school 3 agreed with this, possibly because they had been intimately involved in the decision-making process regarding a new uniform. Males and pupils in the local authority school and those with fathers in manual occupations were much more likely to favour the abolition of the school uniform requirement. This, no doubt, reflects variations in the strength of the youth sub-culture by sex and social class, working class boys being particularly susceptible to its influence. Agreement with the view that 'politics should be left to the leaders' implies a certain deference which seems to be particularly strong in the secondary school and to be influenced by social class. The final statement that 'nationalisation is better than free enterprise' was answered by fewer pupils than any other and was perhaps the nearest approximation to a question on political preferences. The results showed the expected social class differences but also, unexpectedly, a stronger agreement on the part of the girls compared to the boys.

There were two open-ended questions on the questionnaire which invited the fifth formers to write briefly on what they thought religion was and how important they considered it to be both to themselves and to other people. The response rates to these questions were lower than to the precoded sections of the questionnaire. The majority of the interpretations of religion were found to fall into five broad categories.

1 *Religion as a belief in God*
   A high proportion of pupils in all four schools described religion in these terms, all centred around God (eg the understanding or acceptance of, teaching about or getting into contact with God), seen as a single personal being.

2 *Religion as a belief in some other being or power*
   In this category God is not specifically mentioned (eg 'the idea of believing in one or more gods and conforming to their beliefs and teachings'). In this category the belief in some form of external power is far more diffuse.

3 *Religion as a way of life*
   The second highest proportion of pupil definitions fell into this category, which considered religion to be a comfort in time of need, a help and a type of security or a form of moral code (eg

the understanding and loving of other people; a moral code; a guide or rule book).

4 *Religion as a belief in eternal life*
A small proportion of respondents in all four schools expressed religion in these terms (eg the striving of all men to the goal of eternal happiness; the fulfilment of life after death).

5 *Religion as a social institution*
A small proportion of pupils viewed religion simply in terms of its institutional forms or practices (eg going to church).

Most of the respondents in the Catholic schools considered that religion was important to them whereas a high proportion of those in the local authority school thought it unimportant. Those for whom religion was important referred to the need for belief, security, an explanation of the finite nature of this life, and a moral code. The ideas of worship and adoration were rarely mentioned but the ideas of dependence and powerlessness were prominent.

It is important to me because you have to have something or someone to believe in.

Very important because it acts as a guide and a basic hope that this world is a beginning not an end.

Religion is a major factor of the way I lead my life, not in worship necessarily but leading a life which will benefit my sense of achievement and the lives of others.

Religion gives me . . . a guideline to follow in everyday life.

To me religion is important most of the time but not all. While I am safe and secure I do not think of it but as soon as I feel lost it gives me something to fall back on.

Among those who considered religion to be unimportant in their lives several distinguished clearly between beliefs in God and (institutional) religion:

I don't think religion is very important to me as I don't go to Church but I believe in God.

I don't think religion is really worth it but I do believe in God.

Religion means nothing to me and as soon as I leave my parents I will stop going to church or practising my religion.

Others distinguished clearly between its importance to them now and its likely importance in the future:

At the moment religion is not very important to me and I hope it will become so as I grow older.

Not very important at the moment but might be later on.

Others viewed religion in instrumental terms and judged it to serve no purpose in their present lives:

It is not important; I don't need a faith.

Religion isn't important to me; I'm happy.

It doesn't seem very important to me as it doesn't help me in any way.

I do not think religion is important because you have got to enjoy life while you can.

From this brief review it is apparent that many pupils even in the Catholic schools considered that religion had no relevance to their lives or to the forming of their moral and social values and beliefs. Nevertheless the results reported earlier do indicate that there are significant differences in the attitudes, values and beliefs of the fifth formers in the three Catholic schools when compared with those from the local authority school. This would suggest that the Catholic school is a powerful enough agency of socialisation to generate some distinct clusters of social, moral and religious attitudes on the part of its senior pupils. At the same time, this study has indicated that large differences do occur within Catholic schools themselves. In particular it has been shown that the anti-intellectualism and the effective internalisation of the traditional 'house-bound' model of the role of the woman, both of which were very prominent in the convent school of the earlier study, were not a significant feature in the three Catholic comprehensive schools.

Apart from the school and religious variables, the results of this study have also demonstrated the importance of the sex of the pupil, social class in terms of paternal occupation and maternal employment. Social class differences were most significant when measuring anti-intellectualism. Finally, it is particularly interesting, especially given the strong Catholic sub-cultural support for the home-based mother, that maternal employment was not significantly related to differences on any one of the six scales identified by means of the factor analysis in the present work.

Having briefly reviewed the findings it is important to recognise two limitations in particular of this small study which has perhaps raised more questions than it has answered. In the first place the survey included only one local authority school and that of a lower status and different social class intake compared to the three Catholic comprehensive schools. Secondly, no comparison was made between Catholic pupils in Catholic and in local authority schools. Nevertheless, given the complete absence of research data in this area, this study has hopefully clarified a number of issues, indicated the need for more broadly based research, and opened up a number of new lines of enquiry for the future.

Catholic Adolescents and Catholicism[11]
The final section of this chapter reports the responses to two questions addressed to Roman Catholic pupils on the questionnaire administered only to fifth formers in the three Catholic comprehensive schools in the south of England in the autumn of 1973; 419 of the 479 respondents were Roman Catholics.

The first question invited the respondent to indicate on a four-point scale how important he/she considered each of ten distinguishing characteristics of a Catholic to be. Since there were no significant differences in the replies between the three schools, they have been aggregated in table 5.9 On average 385 pupils, an estimated 92 per cent of the Catholics in the sample, judged the importance of the ten statements on the scales. According to these adolescent Catholics, the most important characteristic of a Catholic is that he 'makes a firm effort to try again after personal sin and failure'. Only one respondent in ten did not rate this important. The second most important characteristic was thought to be that the Catholic 'has a personal relationship with God'. It is perhaps a disturbing reflection of Catholic values that as many as three Catholic adolescents in ten in these Catholic secondary schools thought this to be unimportant, a proportion not much lower than that for 'goes to mass weekly' and 'obeys the laws of the church'. Well over half the pupils rated 'models his life on the example given by Christ in the new testament' as not important and only one-half thought 'prays regularly and frequently' important.

The second question asked the pupils to indicate the level of their agreement with each of ten controversial issues within the church on four point scales. The answers have again been aggregated in table 5.10. On average 358 pupils, an estimated 85 per cent of the Catholics in the sample from the three schools, indicated the level of their agreement with each of these statements. Particularly noticeable is the fact that nine young Catholics in ten considered that 'you should act according to your conscience and not just blindly follow the laws of the church' and correspondingly disagreed with the statement 'Catholics ought to obey the laws of the church without question'. A refined interpretation of these views requires further research involving in-depth interviewing rather than questionnaire methods, and some work in this area by Johanna Fitzpatrick will be reported in the following chapter. Other statements which received overwhelming support included one recognising that 'the unity of the christian churches is very important' and rejecting the view that 'mixed marriages are wrong'. This last finding must, however, be treated with some caution since a number of pupils in the lowest streams in one of the schools indicated that they thought the question related to racially mixed marriages rather than to marriages where only one partner was a Catholic.

In order to analyse these data more fully and in an attempt to identify significant clusters of attitudes and values, the data were subjected to factor analysis using the statistical package for the social sciences (SPSS) program FACTOR. Principal factoring with a maximum of 25 iterations was used, five factors with an eigenvalue greater than 1·0 being extracted. The default rotational method was Varimax. Pairwise deletion of missing data was selected for the computation of correlation coefficients.[12]

Details of the factor loadings on the five factors which together accounted for 38 per cent of the variance are given in table 5.11. A consideration of these loadings and of the multiple correlation matrix for the 20 variables suggested that the data could best be simplified by the construction of four scales from those items indicated (*). Factor 3 was omitted because it did not appear to isolate a meaningful cluster of variables. The four scales constructed from the raw data, the average inter-item correlations measuring the internal consistency of the scales, and McKennell's Alpha coefficients measuring the reliability of the scales,[13] were therefore:

I Personal Religious Orientation, RELORN
   (Items 1, 2, 7 and 8)
   $n = 4$, $\bar{r} = 0.37$, Alpha $= 0.70$

II Democratic Orientation to Use of Power in Church, DEMPWR
    (Items 12, 14, 16, 17 and 19)
    $n = 5$, $\bar{r} = 0.34$, Alpha $= 0.72$

III Emphasis on Conformity to Church Laws, CONFOR
     (Items 3, 9 and 13)
     $n = 3$, $\bar{r} = 0.46$, Alpha $= 0.72$

IV Emphasis on Voluntary Additional Religious Practices, VOLUNT
    (Items 4, 5, 6 and 10)
    $n = 4$, $\bar{r} = 0.28$, Alpha $= 0.61$

Values for each of these scales were computed for all cases where there were no missing data. Four variables (items 11, 15, 18 and 20 in table 5.10) were not employed in the construction of the four scales. Subsequent analysis of the data consisted, therefore, in the cross-tabulation of each of the four scales and the four remaining variables by school, sex, social class (in terms of father's occupation), maternal employment and parental religion, in an attempt to identify factors significantly related to variations in pupil attitudes. The results of this analysis have been summarised in table 5.12.

An emphasis on a personal religious orientation (RELORN) was highest in school 1, the only school run by a religious order and with an estimated 6 per cent non-Catholic pupils in the sample compared to an estimated average of 18 per cent in the other two schools. In addition, both parents were Catholics in 63 per cent of the cases in school 1, compared to 53 per cent in the other two schools. Most of the other variables appeared to have no significant influence on the strength of this orientation with the exception of social class where nearly one-half of the children of non-manual fathers scored highly compared to under one-third of the children of manual fathers. This finding lends support to the view that the working classes in England are becoming relatively more alienated from the contemporary church. One might speculate that this is a dysfunction of an 'embourgeoisement' process in the church in this country.[14] Girls scored more highly than boys on the personal religious orientation scale, as did pupils from homes where both parents were Catholics compared to homes where only one parent was a Catholic, though the differences were not statistically significant.

The second scale (DEMPWR) measured the strength of a broadly democratic orientation to decision-making and the use of power within the church. As can be seen from the component items of this scale in table 5.10, this orientation seems to be highly critical of existing decisions and decision-making procedures in the church. It is noticeable that pupils from mixed marriages scored significantly higher on this scale than those from homes where both parents were Catholics. Males and those with manual fathers and working mothers also scored more highly than the average.

The third scale (CONFOR) measured an emphasis on conformity to church laws. Although there were no significant differences in the scores between the various groups, it is perhaps unexpected to find that boys scored more highly than girls. Pupils with non-manual fathers and working mothers also scored more than average while those where only the father was a Catholic scored less than average.

The final scale (VOLUNT) gives a measure of the importance

placed on voluntary, additional religious practices such as going to mass occasionally when not of obligation. No group gave much emphasis to this scale and there were no significant differences between them.

On the remaining four items there were no significant differences in the responses between the various groups except that a significantly higher proportion of boys compared to girls considered that 'the church and politics should not be mixed'. Three-quarters of these fifth formers agreed with this view which appears to indicate the continuation of the 'other worldly' view of religion criticised by Lawlor over a decade ago.[15] What is perhaps disturbing is that this view of religion did not receive any encouragement from the second Vatican Council with its strong missionary and pastoral emphases on 'making all things new'. On the other hand the data indicate a healthy acceptance of ecumenism and the importance of the individual conscience. One policy implication for those responsible would seem to be the need to ensure in programmes of religious education that ecumenism is interpreted in a positive and constructive manner and not simply as a rejection of the distinctive claims of the Roman Catholic church, and that the individual conscience is properly formed by the teaching of the church. As has been mentioned above, a fuller interpretation of the meanings which these Catholic adolescents attached to these views on personal conscience and christian unity requires more in-depth study by interview methods. A start on this work has been made by Johanna Fitzpatrick in the research reported in the following chapter. Such research would seem to be essential if religious educators are to be fully aware of the climate of opinion among contemporary secondary school children in Catholic schools and adapt their approaches accordingly.

Finally, it is necessary to comment briefly on the importance of the five independent variables used in the above analysis (table 5.12). It is interesting to note that the differences between the three Catholic schools in this study are relatively small, though pupils from school 2 did not emphasise a personal religious orientation, conformity to church laws, and voluntary additional religious practices, as much as those from schools 1 and 3. Again, while this might be indicative of real differences between the schools, it would be necessary to undertake far more in-depth studies of the actual working of the schools to place any significance on these results. The problems of these schools in a period of transition must be recognised. Even so, there are statistically significant differences between the three Catholic schools and the local authority school on the religious variables, as has already been indicated above.

Sex differences do not appear to be very important although it may be noted that girls scored higher on the personal religious orientation scale than boys, who believed much more strongly that 'church and politics should not be mixed'.

It is of interest to record here that girls also scored significantly higher on a separate scale of christian unity (ECUMEN) constructed from the four items comprising the scale RELORN, the score for UNITY and a score on a question relating to belief in the divinity of Jesus (n = 6, $\bar{r}$ = 0·33, Alpha = 0·75).

A number of interesting differences appeared between the social classes in the analysis. Adolescents with fathers in non-manual occupations were much more likely than those with fathers in manual occupations to score highly on the personal religious orientation, conformity to church laws and voluntary additional religious practices scales. On the other hand, children with fathers in manual occupations were far more likely to emphasise a democratic orientation to the use of power in the church and to urge the separation of the church from politics. Again, it is clear that the bald statement 'church and politics should not be mixed' is subject to some ambiguity. On the one hand it could mean that the church should not concern itself with social, economic and political matters, including questions of social justice. Such a view would oppose the critical appraisal of the existing social order by the church authorities. On the other hand, support for the statement could simply indicate a rejection of an established relationship between church and state which was thought to prevent the church from critically commenting on social issues. One view would favour a critical church while the other would not. Clearly further research would be necessary to clarify the matter but it is apparent that the belief systems of adolescents from different social backgrounds are very different and this needs to be taken into account in any programme of religious education.

In Catholic mythology, the non-working mother has a special place. The results of the present survey do not lend support to the notion that the child inevitably suffers where his mother is in full-time or part-time employment. Indeed, pupils whose mothers were employed scored more highly on the personal religious orientation, conformity to church laws and voluntary additional religious practices scales.

On the other hand, there was evidence of the importance of the religious background of the homes of our respondents. Two conclusions can be drawn from the data. First of all, where both parents are Catholics, scores are higher on the personal religious orientation and voluntary additional religious practices scales.

Secondly, where only the mother is a Catholic, the scores on these scales are only a little less, and are higher on the conformity to church laws scales. All three scores are lowest where only the father is a Catholic. These findings are important in demonstrating the socialising influence of the home and of the mother in particular, and in drawing attention to the different pastoral needs of those mixed marriages where the father is a Catholic from those where the mother is a Catholic. Too often the assumption is probably made that the pastoral needs of all mixed marriages are the same.

Conclusion
There is increasing concern about the effectiveness of the religious socialisation process in Catholic schools. This chapter has provided some quantitative data relevant to the debate. It is suggested that such data are a necessary prerequisite for the proper appraisal of the outcomes of Catholic schooling and provide a basis for the modification and adaptation of the programmes of religious education in the schools to meet the different needs of children from different social and religious backgrounds. Further research, with particular emphasis on the exploration of the meanings attached to their religion by Catholic adolescents, is necessary to clarify areas of ambiguity. In the meantime, it might be suggested that the results of the studies reported in this chapter demonstrate a general absence of a deep religious commitment, an acceptance of a measure of conformity to church laws and ritual observances, an absence of a christocentric religion, and a highly critical valuation of the institutional church on the part of a large majority of these Catholic adolescents from Catholic schools in the south of England. These findings, which clearly need to be explored in more depth, are nevertheless important for all those concerned with devising more effective approaches to the religious education of young Catholics.

6

The Religious Disaffection of Catholic Adolescents

Since only about one-third of Catholics attend mass on Sunday[1] and two-thirds attend Catholic schools[2] it follows that at the very least, one-half of the children attending Catholic schools subsequently cease to practice, at least in terms of the crude indicator of mass attendance. Many priests and teachers believe that a process of disaffection with the church and/or with religion in general, sets in well before the end of secondary education. There are plenty of speculations about this process; some consider it a temporary adolescent fling against all forms of authority and coercion, a rebellion against the constraints imposed by parent, teacher or priest. Some believe it reflects a reaction against an institutional church or against its perceived imperfections only, and that a more privatised or latent religious adherence and belief continues. There are plenty of explanations in circulation but very little or nothing in the way of scientific certainty or even probability. The fact is that we just do not know the nature or the reasons for this process and in the absence of a serious systematic attempt to find out by painstaking research it would appear that we just don't care.[3]

In the previous chapter some findings which indicated that for many Catholic adolescents, even in Catholic secondary schools, there was an absence of any deep religious commitment and a large measure of heterodoxy of belief and deviance as regards moral values were reported. This chapter aims to explore the process of religious disaffection among Catholic adolescents. In the first place the findings from the Southwark Diocese Mass Attendance Survey which confirmed that there is a decline in the observance of this institutional norm from the early secondary school years will be outlined. Secondly, a comparison will be made between 'disaffected' Catholics and other Catholic adolescents from the study of fifth formers in three Catholic comprehensive schools in the south of England which was reported in the last chapter. Thirdly, the attempt made by Johanna Fitzpatrick to explore more fully the meaning and process of this disaffection among fourth formers by means of in-depth interviews will be described.

Southwark Survey[4]

In the summer of 1975 a survey which was sponsored by the Diocesan and Youth Commissions, following a resolution from the Senate of Priests, was carried out in all the 45 aided secondary schools and two middle schools in the Southwark diocese. At the time, estimates of lapsation of adolescents from the church ranged from 20 per cent to 70 per cent and the survey aimed to obtain more reliable information and to determine the extent to which it was more pronounced among the older age groups.

All Catholic pupils in these schools were asked to answer the single question, 'How often do you usually attend mass outside the school?' in one of four ways: (1) more than once a week (ie not just on Sundays and holidays of obligation) (2) on Sundays and holidays of obligation only (3) occasionally and only when I feel in the mood, or (4) never really. Pupils answered this question anonymously during school hours and added their sex, age and form number. The staff in each of the schools aggregated the responses separately for each age and sex group. Overall replies from the 11 to 18 age groups were received from every school (with the exception of examination classes in one school) and from a total of 10,921 boys and 11,032 girls from 20 ILEA schools, 20 schools in the Greater London Boroughs and seven Kent schools. The proportion of children on the school roll answering the question was only given for three schools and ranged from 82 per cent to 97 per cent. The suggestion was made by one headteacher that truancy probably accounted for a higher proportion of older children but in general there is little reason to suspect that non-response has introduced any significant bias in the results.

The proportions of boys and girls giving each of the four alternative responses have been given separately for each age group in table 6.1. It can be seen that there is a steady reduction in the proportions attending mass at least weekly. Eighty-three per cent of the 11-year-old boys attend to this extent compared to 56 per cent of the 15-year-old boys. The decline for the girls is less rapid; 87 per cent of the 11-year-olds attend at least weekly compared to 63 per cent of the 15-year-olds. Conversely, the proportions reporting that they never attend mass outside school increased from 4 per cent of the 11-year-old boys to 19 per cent of the 15-year-old boys and from 3 per cent of the 11-year-old girls to 15 per cent of the 15-year-old girls. It must be remembered that these figures relate only to children in Catholic secondary schools in an area where there is a shortage of Catholic school places and where the Catholic practice of parents is a factor usually taken into account when selecting pupils. Given the importance of peer group norms the probability is, therefore, that these figures represent higher practice rates than for the total Catholic adolescent population in this area.

The results show a jump in reported mass attendance for the 16- to 18-year-olds in these schools. This jump needs to be explored further but it is unlikely to indicate a return to practice of those whose mass attendance had previously been less regular. It is much more likely to reflect a disproportionate tendency for those who have played 'good pupil' roles in the schools to stay on beyond the statutory leaving age. Thus one headteacher comments 'that admission into our VIth (form) was based on "application and hard work" (*not* on ability) so we tend to select conscientious pupils'. It is also possible that pupils from more stable homes or homes where both parents are practising Catholics are more likely to stay on although it should be stressed that no data exist from this present survey which would enable these hypotheses to be tested.

While the general pattern of decreasing mass attendance with age holds for both boys and girls, the girls record higher mass attendance rates (responses 1 and 2 together) in each age group from 11 to 17. It seems that whereas the biggest decline in mass attendance occurs among the 13–14-year-old boys, the crucial age for girls is one year earlier. There also appear to be big sex differences in the responses of the 18-year-olds where over one-fifth of the girls reported never attending mass. The numbers in this age group are, however, very small and replication of this finding in further studies would be necessary before it could reasonably be inferred that this reversal in the distribution of responses by sex was significant. Thus it may be noted that all the girls in this age group reporting that they never attended mass outside school came from two of the four schools in this survey with 18-year-old girls. While school-specific factors might explain the responses it should be noted that the 15-year-old girls in these two schools reported slightly *higher* mass attendance rates than 15-year-old girls at all schools in the same area.

Detailed tabulations from two schools enabled an estimate to be made of the effect of measured ability on reported mass attendance. The results, summarised in table 6.2, suggest that there was a decrease of mass attendance among the less able children. In one school this was a factor in all age groups while in the second school it only manifested itself in the third form. These results suggest that the degree of conformity to or deviance from the school's religious norms may be determined partly by the type of school organisation, streaming, banding or labelling employed, in the same way that academic achievement is related to organisational features in the school.

There are some significant differences in the reported mass attendance rates in the different local authority areas. Table 6.3 shows that a much higher proportion of both boys and girls attend mass at least weekly in the 40 London schools than in the seven Kent schools. At first sight this is surprising in that a greater measure of alienation might have been predicted in the inner-urban areas. An important consideration is likely to be the relative shortage of places in London so that the schools are likely to be selective in terms of known religious behaviour. Another factor could be the greater distances which children might have to travel to mass in the more rural area of Kent.

There does not seem to be any one variable which is clearly related to mass attendance rates. This can be seen from table 6.4 which summarises the findings from the 44 schools which had data for 15-year-old pupils. Twenty-three schools had weekly mass attendance rates of 60 per cent or over for this age group and 21 schools had lower rates. The distribution of these schools by sex, size, type, control and area shows no differences which are statistically significant using the Chi-Square test. The table also gives the school mean attendance rates together with the range of school rates for each category. The latter figures indicate clearly the considerable variability which exists between schools. It seems that there are strong school factors operating to generate these different rates, quite apart from the five test variables.

An attempt was made to extend the analysis further. Thus there were five schools with the favourable characteristics according to the data in the table—large, single-sex, comprehensive or grammar schools, run by a religious order in London. These schools had an average mass attendance rate for fifth formers of 65 per cent but it is interesting to note that the school with the highest reported rate of 84 per cent (school 18) was a 3-form entry girls' secondary modern school run by a religious order. The schools with the lowest reported rates in both Kent (25 per cent) and London (28 per cent) were 3-form entry mixed secondary modern schools. The number of schools in the sample was too small to control for several variables at the same time. Thus there were no mixed, grammar or comprehensive schools run by a religious order in London. However, some comparisons were possible when considering the seven boys' grammar or comprehensive schools in London. Four were run by a religious order and three were not. Even so, a wide range of mass attendance rates existed. Of the two 3-form entry boys' grammar schools run by a religious order one had a reported weekly rate for 15-year-olds of 40 per cent (school 51) while the other reported 73 per cent (school 53).

The analysis cannot be taken any further at this stage. However, it does seem clear that there are determining factors within the schools themselves, which are crucial in the processes of religious socialisation, in general, and to the norms of weekly mass attendance in particular. These factors appear to be more important than the sex, size, type, control and even the area of the school. Further research might therefore attempt to isolate, by means of intensive case studies of selected schools, those key processes within the schools which favour the development of a continuing religious commitment on the part of young Catholics. Studies such as the present one might provide a useful starting point by identifying schools which deviate markedly from the norm.

However, in any future replication of this present study it is recommended that consideration be given to improving the design in a number of ways. First of all, there appeared to be ambiguity in the administration of the questionnaire at two points in particular: the classification by age or form, and the inclusion by at least some schools of voluntary mass attendance within the school. Secondly, it would be desirable to attempt to collect data relating to the two key variables of social class and parental religious identification and practice. There is evidence that both variables are important in the determination of the outcomes of school programmes of religious education and it would be desirable to attempt to devise appropriate measures of them for each pupil.

Disaffected Catholics[5]
The study of the religious attitudes of 479 fifth formers in three Catholic mixed comprehensive schools in the south of England in 1973, which was reported in the last chapter, provided the opportunity for an exploratory analysis of factors related to adolescent religious disaffection. Data were obtained from questionnaires completed anonymously by the students during school hours. Pupils were asked to indicate their own religion (if any) and their parents' religion. From these three questions and for the purposes of this present study, disaffected Catholics were defined as those explicitly indicating that they were *either* non-practising or non-believing Catholics *or* those who did not give their religion as Roman Catholic although they identified one or both parents as Catholics. Using these criteria a total of 45 disaffected Catholics were identified and compared with 374 self-defined Roman Catholics and 60 non-Catholics. Validation for the criteria used in identifying disaffected

Catholics was obtained in the responses to two questions about belief in God and in the divinity of Jesus which were taken from the study of contemporary American religion by Glock and Stark.[6] The responses to these questions have been summarised in a simplified form in tables 6.5 and 6.6. It can be seen that there are highly significant differences in the responses of the disaffected Catholics when compared to the self-identified Catholics in the same schools. Considering the first two statements together in each table, it can be seen that only one-quarter of the disaffected group compared to three-quarters of the control group recorded orthodox beliefs. This has been taken to confirm the fact that the disaffected Catholics comprise a distinct group within the Catholic schools.

The first question on the questionnaire completed by the pupils invited them to indicate separately for each of eight possible goals of their school whether they thought it *tried* to attain the goal, whether it *should* do so and whether it in fact *succeeded* in achieving it. These items were modifications of some of those originally used by Lambert in his study of the goals of boys' public schools.[7] When considering what goals their schools tried to pursue, the disaffected group scored lowest on every item except one; a higher proportion of them than either of the other two groups considered their schools tried to 'put into practice christian values'. When next considering what goals their schools should pursue, the disaffected group scored highest on two items. They thought the schools should 'develop students' individual interests and talents' and 'encourage students to challenge traditional ideas and opinions' more strongly than either of the other two groups. On all the remaining six items they scored lower than the other groups. Finally, a lower proportion of the disaffected Catholics compared to the other two groups considered their school succeeded in achieving seven of the eight goals.

In order to extend the analysis two efficiency indices were calculated for each goal. An *Achieved Efficiency* was calculated from the ratio of the proportion considering their school succeeded in achieving the goal to the proportion considering it tried to do so. Secondly an *Ideal Efficiency* was calculated from the ratio of the proportion considering their school succeeded in achieving the goal to the proportion who considered it should try to do so. A comparison of these two indices between the three groups indicated that in most respects the group of non-Catholic pupils was very similar to that of the self-identified Roman Catholic pupils except that the Ideal Efficiency score of the non-Catholic group on the goal to 'prepare students for adult life' was only half that of the Roman Catholic group. In other words the non-Catholic students thought these Catholic schools particularly inefficient in this respect. Finally, to simplify the analysis further, the ratios of the Ideal Efficiencies scored by the disaffected Catholics and the self-identified Catholics were calculated. These have been called *Indices of Disaffection* and have been summarised in table 6.7. From these final figures it can be seen that the disaffected group thought the schools gave far more emphasis to 'teach Christian doctrine' than they considered desirable. On the other hand, on the two goals related to adult careers, this group was very critical of what it judged to be school inadequacies. It also considered the schools failed to 'encourage students to challenge traditional ideas and opinions' as much as they should. It is also interesting to note that the disaffected Catholics were very critical at what they saw as their school's inability to 'enable students to recognise what is right from wrong'. This last finding needs careful interpretation but it would seem to indicate a clear separation on their part between moral education and religious instruction in terms of christian doctrine.

In his study of boys' public schools, Lambert devised measures of student adaptations to six parts of the school's structure or values.[8] One of these was selected for the present study. Pupils were invited to select the reaction they would have if they were in a responsible position in the fifth form. The five alternatives offered are given in table 6.8 together with Lambert's labels in terms of Merton's classic typology.[9] The results show again, that there are no significant differences between the self-identified Roman Catholic pupils and the non-Catholics. In both groups one-half selected the conformity mode and one-third the innovation mode. By contrast only between one-quarter and one-third of the disaffected group selected the conformity mode and half selected the innovation mode. This is interesting because it appears to confirm earlier comments regarding their concern with education to enable students to recognise right from wrong, that in large measure they accepted the school goals but rejected their means of pursuing them. These differences in the modes of adaptation between the disaffected Catholics and the other two groups are statistically highly significant.[10]

Pupils were next given a list of sixteen controversial statements on various social, moral and religious issues and asked to rate their agreement on four-point scales. The proportions of each of the three groups of pupils agreeing with each of these statements have been given together with Indices of Agreement, measured by the ratio of the proportions of disaffected and self-identified Catholics agreeing with each statement, in table 6.9. There are no significant differences in the responses of the three groups to the last three statements. For half of the remaining statements there are no significant differences between the Roman Catholic and non-Catholic pupils, a fact which appears to be related to the higher levels of conformity selected by these groups. By contrast the disaffected Catholics more frequently express independence from authority figures (items 4, 5 and 11). Other differences between the disaffected Catholics and the Roman Catholic controls include the much lower support for christian religious morality (items 1, 7 and 13) of the former group and their stronger rejection of the traditional Catholic sexual morality (items 2, 6, 8 and 12). Finally it can be seen that the two items where there is strongest similarity between the disaffected Catholics and the controls (items 3 and 9) are those constituting the anti-intellectualism scale discussed above in chapter 5.

The final two questions were asked of Roman Catholic pupils only. In the first they were asked to indicate, on a four-point scale, which of ten statements they considered to be important in characterising a Catholic. The results given in table 6.10 indicate that on three items, having a personal relationship with God, the importance of prayer, and on the personal commitment to try again after sin, there were no significant differences between the two groups. On all the remaining items, however, the disaffected scored much lower levels of importance. In particular, a christocentric religion was considered important by only one-fifth of the disaffected group compared to nearly one-half of the controls. Other responses (especially items 3 and 9) suggest a rejection of the constraints to the exercise of a personal, privatised religion imposed by the institutional church or even of its non-obligatory recommendations (items 4, 5, 6 and 10).

The last question invited the fifth formers to indicate the level of their agreement on four-point scales with each of ten issues of controversy within the contemporary church. Significant differences on items 13 and 14 confirm the rejection of or resistance to the claims to authority by the church as a major factor in the religious disaffection expressed by this sample of adolescent Catholics in three Catholic comprehensive schools.

Further insight into their disaffection is provided by the analysis of their replies to open-ended questions which invited them to write a paragraph on what they thought religion is and how important they thought it was, firstly to themselves and secondly to other people. Only five pupils did not make any comment. One-fifth of the disaffected Catholics explicitly referred to belief in God and another fifth to belief in some supreme being or higher power as essential elements in any definition of religion. Another one in seven pupils referred in one way or another to various ontological beliefs while another one in seven considered religion to be mythical or unscientific, functioning especially for the old, the dying and the needy. One-fifth of the pupils considered religion to provide a basis of morality, for a philosophy of life and an ingredient in the upbringing of children. However, one in ten emphasised the view that true religion was a personal or individual matter and one in five rejected various constraints imposed by institutional religion.

These interpretations of religion were elaborated in their comments on the importance of religion to themselves.[11]

Half the sample of disaffected Catholics asserted that religion was unimportant to them. For some it was simply irrelevant to their lives:

To myself religion is of no importance whatsoever. I am just out to enjoy my one and only lifetime and achieve satisfaction.

Religion is not very important to me because it will not necessarily help me to get a good job.

I have a scientific nature which needs facts to satisfy myself. I don't think that we have enough data to have a belief in God. Thus in my life religion is not very important.

Some considered that an acceptable social morality did not require organised religion:

To myself religion is not important. What is important is loving mankind and treating them accordingly. To be taught to love everyone is all that is needed.

(Religion is) not very important although I believe in the basis of Christian Doctrine (helping those in need etc.).

Others implied criticisms of the contemporary church:

I think it is not very important. I don't go to Mass although I believe that there is a God and devil. I think the Church only wants money off people.

Religion does not play any part in my life: it does not 'grab me'. I think this is due to Mass which is in dire need of modernisation.

On the other hand at least one-quarter of the sample admitted that it was more frequently very important to them for personal comfort, in times of trouble or as a basis for morality:

Religion keeps me from doing what I think to be bad.

I don't believe in Religion on the whole but I believe in God. To me when I am in trouble or someone near me is in trouble, God is a comfort; He is something to turn to.

Religion is something I know I need although some of the time I like to think I don't!! I only seem to realise I have a God when I am in trouble or need something badly.

This was sometimes qualified by the claim that this did not necessarily mean they thought church-going was essential and they reacted against the element of coercion. Others qualified their remarks by saying they thought the institutional church was corrupt:

I believe in God but I can't be bothered to go to Church every week. I think the only time I could go to Church through my own free will would be if I really wanted to without someone pushing me.

Religion is fairly important to me but I don't feel myself obligated to keep it.

Religion is a major factor of the way I lead my life, not in worship necessarily, but leading a life which will benefit my sense of achievement and the lives of others.

My religion is important but I do not feel I have to go to Church regularly to keep it up.

It forms for me a basis for morality though on the whole I do not agree with the runnings of the present day Church and its teachings since they are to my mind corrupt.

Thus for a sizeable minority of disaffected Catholics there was no disaffection with religion per se, but only with its institutional forms and with the elements of coercion which were resented as extraneous.

Several pupils implied that there had been a process of disaffection in their lives and that the process might conceivably be reversed in the future. On the other hand, some implied that they would cease to practise as soon as the constraints of school and home were removed:

Personally, religion does not have any effect on my life now but when I was younger, it was important.

Not at the moment; maybe later it will seem more so.

It is not very important although I always go to Mass and other functions etc.

This is important as it seems to confirm that there is a *process* of disaffection which starts before the end of secondary schooling. It is my view that progress in understanding this process will best be made now by research which includes a significant component of interviewing with adolescent Catholics, preferably with a longitudinal element to facilitate the study of the process of change with a panel of students over several years.

Finally, having outlined the ways in which the beliefs and values of the disaffected Catholics differed from self-identified Catholics and non-Catholic pupils in three Catholic schools, it remains to indicate how they differed from the other groups in terms of their social and religious backgrounds. Overall one in eight of the male Catholic pupils compared to one in fifteen of the female Catholic pupils were classified as disaffected according to the criteria employed in the present study.

However, there were wide differences between the three schools which appeared to reflect the different problems of the transitional period in the recent change of status of all three schools.[12] Thus, as many as one in five of the boys in one school and one in five of the girls in another school were disaffected. On average one pupil in nine in the three schools were so classified but the proportion ranged from one in fourteen in the school run by a religious order to one in five at one of the other schools. It is relevant to note that the proportion of non-Catholic pupils was under 6 per cent in the former school and 20 per cent in the latter school. This is probably reflected in the peer group values, the influence of which will almost certainly be crucial. Parental religion also appears to be significantly related to the chances of disaffection. Overall 8 per cent of the children of marriages where both parents were Catholics, were disaffected, compared to 14 per cent where the mother only was a Catholic and 24 per cent where the father only was. These figures confirm the importance of home background and particularly maternal influence and point to increasing problems as there is a softening of religious group identity and boundary maintenance with the relaxation of regulations and social pressures to inhibit mixed marriages in an ecumenical era.[13] Finally, the disaffected Catholics in these schools appeared to come disproportionately from middle class homes. In terms of father's occupation, 84 per cent of the disaffected had non-manual fathers compared to 63 per cent among the self-identified Catholic control group.[14] This probably indicates that a cohesive group identity remains strongest amongst the working classes where possibly the proportion of mixed marriages remains lowest. On the other hand, there were no significant differences in the proportions of the three religious groups where the mother was working. It cannot then be argued that this is a significant factor in any process of disaffection.

This section has reported on an exploratory study of a group of disaffected Catholics in three Catholic comprehensive schools in the south of England which arose out of a survey of the religious attitudes of 479 fifth formers in three schools. It has been shown that compared to the control group of self identified Catholics, they expressed orthodox beliefs in God and Jesus only one-third as frequently. They considered their schools over-emphasised christian doctrine and under-stressed the preparation of students for independence in adult life far more frequently. They were twice as likely to select the innovation mode of adaptation and only half as likely to select the conformity mode. In a number of ways they expressed their resistance to authority figures and to religious and social forms of coercion. However, they shared with the control group a propensity to anti-intellectualism when compared with non-Catholic pupils in the same schools. Their religion was personal and privatised and was not christocentric, though it appeared to be related to a form of morality which was humanistic. For many of them, religion was irrelevant to their lives though a large minority distinguished between personal belief in God and the submission to the rules of the institutional church. The strong impression was given that the process of disaffection had taken place over some time and this lent support to the view that longitudinal studies of panels of young Catholics, involving in-depth interviewing methods, might be the best way of extending our understanding of this process and hence the likelihood of our developing appropriate pastoral responses. The disaffected Catholics were disproportionately male, middle class and children of mixed marriages, but the data indicated wide variations between the three schools which appeared to be related not only to the size of the non-Catholic student body but also to the particular circumstances of the recent amalgamations of schools to create the new comprehensive schools and the transitional problems which amalgamations and changes of status entailed.

Clearly this analysis is limited by the nature of the sample studied (only three schools, none of which was situated in a major conurbation) and the method employed (self-completion questionnaires with only two open-ended questions). Nevertheless, it has provided, possibly for the first time, some data as a basis for informed public discussion, analysis, interpretation and decision making.

Interviews with Young Catholics[15]

The limitations of questionnaire surveys have been acknowledged previously and it has been stressed that clarification of adolescent views requires further research involving in-depth interviewing, with an emphasis on the exploration of the meanings attached to their religion by Catholic adolescents.[16] In this section the findings arising from focused interviews with 48 fourth formers in two London Catholic mixed comprehensives will be summarised. The interviews, which were tape-recorded, on average lasted half-an-hour. The Southwark Survey discussed above had suggested that there was a significant decline of Sunday mass attendance from the age of twelve or thirteen. By interviewing fourth formers it was hoped to identify some of the relevant causal factors in the early stages of any process of religious disaffection.

Twenty-four fourth formers from each school were interviewed by Johanna Fitzpatrick during school hours in the autumn of 1974. The interviews opened with questions about the respondent's home and school background, whether or not he had been to a Catholic primary school and what he and his parents felt about Catholic schools, and to which ability group he belonged. By asking about the Religious Education lessons in the school and about the school's attitude to religion it was hoped indirectly to elicit some information about the respondent's own views on religion. Questions about his family aimed to encourage him to give a picture of the place of religion in the home. Questions about the sacraments and his local parish aimed to explore his feelings about the sacramental and institutional aspects of the church. After discussing the influence of his friends on his religious attitudes, the interviewer concluded by asking the respondent's opinion on several controversial issues in order to estimate the extent to which the church's official teaching affected his viewpoint, and with two questions on belief in God and the divinity of Jesus Christ.

Although it is a primary purpose of this section to report in their own words the attitudes towards religion of these fourth formers, and although the sample was small, a number of systematic variations in the reported religious outcomes can be noted. Seven outcomes were measured: the response to the school's RE lessons; belief in the divinity of Jesus; belief in God; frequency of mass attendance; voluntary prayer; regular reception of communion; and attendance at confession. In addition to these dependent variables, data were collected for nine independent variables: school, sex, ability (whether or not the respondent was taking any O-level courses), social class (in terms of father's occupation), ethnic origin (both parents British, one British and one Irish, both Irish, and a residual category including West Indians, Italians, Maltese, Swiss and Indian), family position, family mass attendance, parental religion, and parental practice. The detailed analyses have been summarised in table 6.12. For simplicity all variables were dichotomised. In the case of ethnic group it was found that for all seven religious outcomes the mixed Anglo-Irish children were sharply distinguished from the remaining three ethnic groups. In the case of family position, for six of the seven outcomes the youngest children were distinguished from the oldest and other categories. The first two of the six and seven Glock and Stark categories for belief in the divinity of Jesus and belief in God, respectively, have been grouped together.

These results go beyond those reported in previous studies in a number of respects. It appears that although the girls in this sample were less likely than boys to attend mass weekly, this was mainly because three times the proportion of them attended 'only when they felt like it'. Girls were less likely never to attend and they scored more highly on the sacramental and prayer outcomes. On five of the seven measures higher scores were reported by the higher ability groups, in line with a finding of the Southwark survey. Previous research had suggested that disaffected Catholic adolescents were disproportionately middle class. In this present study weekly mass attendance and voluntary prayer are less frequent among the higher social class but the continuance of a sacramental life was more frequently reported by them. On all seven measures lower religious outcomes were recorded by the children of Anglo-Irish marriages. Although numbers are small, this group had a higher than average proportion of mixed marriages which generally had a lower practice rate. This suggests that the key variable is parental practice rather than ethnicity per se. It is interesting to note that family position appears to be related systematically to religious outcomes. On six of the measures youngest children scored more highly than either oldest (or only) children or middle children. This suggests that the religious socialisation of the youngest child may be significantly different from that of other children.

Finally, it is instructive to note the relative importance of the school and home variables. It appears that for all seven outcomes the family or parental practice has a stronger effect than the school effect. Parental religion (both Catholic compared to mixed marriage) appears to be less important than parental practice. It is also interesting to note that full family practice (ie parents and siblings) reinforces the influence of parental practice taken by itself; the example of older brothers and sisters appears to operate independently.

It was a concern of this study not only to map these systematic variations but also to explore some possible explanations for them by discussing their attitudes to religion with these fourth formers at some length. Three themes in particular emerged from the interview transcripts. Firstly the process of religious socialisation during the secondary school years is strongly influenced by the structural position of adolescents in our society. The adolescent is experiencing a period of transition from the status of dependent child to independent adult. Authority is seen as relevant only to children and the adolescent rebels against perceived forms of coercion in order to assert his autonomy. This rejection of the authority of the home, school and church and assertion of the right of personal choice was apparent in many interviews:

> They want to push you this way, and you may want to go that way.

> I don't like some of the teachers; they treat you like little kids.

> No-one really wants it (RE), only the teachers and the priests.

> It's up to you what you do; it's not up to the Pope.

> It doesn't matter what the Church thinks; it's what I think . . . (on morality).

> I don't think they should tell you what to do; it's your life, not their's (the church).

A large number of our respondents insisted that they would give their children 'the choice' in the matter of mass attendance:

> I'd want them (my children) to be Catholics, but if I force it on them when they're young, they won't want to go when they're older.

Many of them quoted the age of sixteen as a time they looked forward to having 'the choice to do what I want'. Some, however, particularly from non-practising homes, commented that their mother had allowed them the choice from the age of twelve. If this is general in urban areas it helps to explain the decline of mass attendance from the early secondary school years, as noted in the Southwark Survey above.

The rejection of the norms of authority, however, results in a feeling of insecurity. While some adolescents reject the norms of the church, others find in them a support and guide:

> (Religion) kind of gives you faith, something to live for, like.

> (Religion) It's believing in God, having something or someone to believe in when you're feeling down. It's something to trust in . . . it's very important to me. I don't know what I'd do if I didn't have a religion.

> It's important, some of it; believing in God, Jesus and that . . . it helps you . . . it protects you from trouble.

It's having something to believe in and to trust in, instead of leading a life of nothing.

I'd feel lost if I didn't belong to some Church. I just couldn't go around not belonging to anything.

The adolescent frequently, however, finds support in his peer group in a commonly shared situation of uncertainty. As Matza has said: 'They conform to the norms of the group because not to do so would threaten their status'.[17] It was noticeable that when questioned about their friends' feelings on the subject of religion, a common reply was 'oh, they feel the same way as I do'. The importance of the peer group is illustrated by the following quotations:

I'd go if my friends would too (to a church youth club).

Sometimes I go (to mass) on Thursday. Me mate goes, so I go with him.

Everyone has sex before marriage now, don't they? It's up to them, isn't it?

There's nothing I don't like about it (mass) really. If my mates'd go, I'd go with them.

As well as looking to his peers for norms, the adolescent may see in the media an impersonal source of norms and values such as equality. A frequent assertion was that 'everyone is the same' and this was reflected in the following typical observations:

I think it would be better; get rid of the Pope and have one big unified Church, all worshipping the same (on ecumenism).

. . . they (priests) should get married; they're the same as ordinary men.

(A mixed marriage) wouldn't bother me at all. She's a human being; there's no difference really.

The pervasiveness of a scientific spirit demanding proof was also apparent in a number of comments:

I can't believe that Holy Communion is really the body and blood of Christ, or that it's really Him who forgives us in confession. Why doesn't He show Himself now?

I read a book about the shroud—the thing they wrapped Him in when He died. It was really good; it really made me believe in it . . . that's what really made me believe in Him.

I get fed up hearing the same old thing all the time, that God's all good. If there is a God, there's been no proof of it just recently—wars, Northern Ireland and everything. If there was a God, surely He wouldn't let that happen?

(I don't like) . . . the way they say that God does all these miracles, but you never have any proof.

Asked whether they thought 'it is best to act according to your conscience or to obey the laws of the church without question' thirty-five respondents stated they would act according to their conscience compared to five who said they would obey the laws. Thus, not many agreed with the church's teaching on sex before marriage because 'I can't see much wrong with it'. On the other hand the vast majority said that abortion was wrong because '. . . you can see that's murder'. Many could see no intrinsic point in going to mass and so did not go because '. . . you don't get anything out of it'.

However, in a situation of normlessness, without adequate support from their family or peers, much lapsing from mass attendance appeared to be due to laziness, certainly much more 'drift' than 'decision'.

It's very important . . . I like going to Mass, because I go every Sunday, except the last two 'cos we got up late . . . then we don't bother.

. . . there's nothing I don't like about it (the church). I just can't be bothered to go really. If my mates would go, I'd go with them.

I just gave up going out of laziness I suppose.

Sometimes there appears to be more than laziness, perhaps a fear of suspected restrictions on freedom that any commitment may hold. This seems to be implied in a quotation from one of the girls:

Sometimes I get really frightened by it. I think that if I get too involved with it, I'll get like the nuns so I won't be able to do anything else. I'd go mad I think.

A second theme which emerged from the interview material was the perception of the church as alienating inasmuch as the institutional church is incomprehensible to them:

The sermon takes quite a long time. You try to listen to what you can understand, but it gets a bit boring.

The ubiquitous word 'boring' appeared to be used to dismiss that which was seen as too difficult to understand. The fourth formers complained repeatedly about RE lessons, mass, teachers being 'boring':

I thought Mass was boring. I didn't understand it.

There was little evidence in the interviews of a sense of belonging to an institutional church. On the contrary, most of the respondents were at pains to point out that 'there isn't any difference' between Catholics and non-Catholics, or between Catholic and local authority schools and so on. This suggests a failure on the part of the institutional church, in spite of recent liturgical changes, to promote a sense of common membership of 'the People of God'. Few of our respondents thought their parish clergy ever visited their homes, or knew the priests well. Indeed, 'some people say he's only there to collect money' was a widely held view. Only one commented favourably:

> The parish priest is good; he organises lots of things. It's good; you feel as though you belong.

This is not to say that priests were generally unpopular, just that many of them seemed to be rather distant so that for many adolescents there appeared to be no place for them in the church which, as they saw it, was irrelevant to their lives and had nothing to offer them: 'you don't get anything out of it'. Although several said that they would feel lost without a religion, there appeared to be no feeling of dependency on the church. There was little evidence in the interview material that the mainly working class respondents saw the institutional church as alienating because middle class although teachers, school, priests and the church were seen to be apart from them and referred to as 'they'. Only one boy remarked on the grandeur of the church as something he disliked but several hinted at the turning to a more privatised religion:

> I'd say I'm a Christian, not a Catholic, because they believe in the Pope, and everything's attached to grandeur. I believe in worshipping God and nothing else . . . I just don't like the grandeur of the Church, and the way they say that God does all these miracles, but you never have any proof. All these bishops and things think that their religion is the only one; I don't like that.

> I believe in God and I believe in Jesus, but I don't see why you should have to go to Church to believe in God.

Thirdly and more tentatively and impressionistically, it is suggested that one reason why so many Catholic adolescents are becoming disenchanted with Catholicism and ceasing to practise is their own childish conceptualisation of God and religion. Religion is something for the simple-minded or childish because the adolescent's own ideas about religion are simple and childish:

> I take it for granted now. When I first made my Holy Communion I thought it was fantastic . . . I *think* it's the body and blood of Christ, but it's hard to believe . . .

> I got old enough to realise that everything in the Bible isn't true.

> I liked it (religion) as a kid, but I sort of grew out of it.

In struggling for adult status the adolescent rejects what is seen as childish. If this interpretation is correct it implies the need for more advanced conceptualisations of religion for adolescents. This is consistent with the finding that the more able children more frequently found their present RE lessons 'boring' and it was only among the respondents in the remedial forms that there was evidence of an unquestioning conformity whereas their more questioning peers were more likely to observe:

> You have to be stupid to believe in all that.

It seems that there is a vacuum of knowledge which the adolescent frantically wished to fill. Many said they wanted more 'religion' in the RE lessons, possibly because of a fear of facing the world as a Catholic who can only explain what he believes in childish terms:

> We don't do enough reading from our Bibles . . . we could have more of that . . .

> I wouldn't tell anyone I'm a Catholic, 'cos they might ask me questions on it and I wouldn't know nothing, and then they'd think I was a bad Catholic.

In this section an analysis of tape-recorded focused interviews with forty-eight fourth-formers from two London comprehensive schools has been attempted. Seven measures of the religiosity of these adolescents have been considered and shown to be related, particularly to the religious practice of the home. Further analysis of the interviews suggested the importance of three themes in the interpretation of the process of religious socialisation of the young Catholic. First of all the adolescent, in struggling for the personal autonomy of the adult, frequently rebels against the authorities of the school and the church. While some find support from religion in a situation of normlessness, most rely on their peer group. Where there is no support for regular practice from family or friends much lapsing appears to be due to laziness: 'more drift than decision'. Secondly, many saw the institutional church as incomprehensible, the RE lessons, mass and sermons as 'boring' or irrelevant while turning to a more privatised form of religion. Many appeared to be uninterested in rather than antagonistic towards the institutional church. Thirdly, it was suggested that part of the adolescent's rejection of Catholicism stems from his predominantly impoverished conceptualisation of God and religion and a fear of being identified with childish things while struggling for adult status and autonomy.

Research Methodology[18]

Three concluding methodological comments might be made. Firstly, all the studies reported above have been 'cross-sectional'—ie they have been based on surveys of one or more age groups at one moment in time. The findings from such surveys can only result in *plausible* hypotheses about the process of learning to be a knowledgeable and committed Catholic over a period of time, for example, the years from early adolescence to the early years of marriage. Ideally, the study of this process requires the follow-up of a panel of children over a period of several years in a longitudinal study. Only in this way would it be possible to determine whether the supposed adolescent rebellion against religion is temporary or permanent. Secondly, it has become apparent that while questionnaires can provide useful data, they are limited as a means of achieving insight and understanding into the meanings which young Catholics attach to religion and to the norms, values and beliefs of Roman Catholicism. Hence there is a need for more in-depth interviewing in any future research. Thirdly, it is clearly necessary that further research aimed at identifying more clearly the key processes within the schools which favour the development of a continuing religious commitment on the part of young Catholics should be undertaken.

D

Catholic Students in Higher Education

The number[1] of students in higher education has more than doubled in the decade since the Robbins Committee[2] reported in 1963. It is proper therefore that the implications of this expansion for the Roman Catholic community should now be reviewed. It has generally been assumed that the expansion of opportunities in secondary education since the 1944 Education Act would have revolutionary consequences for the Roman Catholic community with its traditionally strong Irish urban working class. Indeed, Joan Brothers first explored the implications for parish life of expanded grammar school opportunities in the early 1960s.[3] Catholic grammar school leavers were making their way into the universities in significant numbers around this time. The awareness of this was reflected in three issues of *The Dublin Review*. First of all, Bishop Beck saw the extent to which the loyalty of Catholics could 'stand up to the erosive influence of university life' as a key problem. His solution appeared to be expressed in terms of theological content and he asked at the Pax Romana Congress at Nottingham in 1955:

> Are our graduates being provided with the theological equipment which they need if they are to exercise effectively the apostolate of the Catholic intellectual or the educated Catholic layman?[4]

A. C. F. Beales, writing about a Conference on Higher Education at Strawberry Hill in 1958, reported Bishop Beck's stress on 'the *formation* of Catholic students in the universities, with a religious education commensurate with their secular, specialist education' and on the need 'that more of the money raised by Catholic self-sacrifice must go, from now on, into Catholic higher education'.[5] Two years later a conference of Catholic university teachers at Liverpool pondered on the question, 'What are universities for?' and Michael Fogarty reviewed the evidence from a Newman Demographic Survey which showed that in the early 1950s Catholics 'had about two-thirds as much chance . . . of reaching a university as members of the population in general'. However, the gap was narrowing rapidly and it was anticipated that by the 1970s 'Catholics will then have attained equality of opportunity at the university level'.[6]

It is interesting to note three aspects of this concern of nearly twenty years ago. First of all, the concern is exclusively with the universities as the elite sector of higher education. In this Catholics were, and still are, as guilty of elitism as any other section of the population. The whole area of non-university higher or further education might never have existed. Secondly, the worried responses to expanded opportunities for Catholics suggest that higher education was seen as a threat to the unquestioning loyalty and cohesion of the Catholic community. It might be suggested that this reflected a pre-conciliar model of the church and that we do not today see social change so much as a threat as a challenge. Thirdly, the tentative prescriptions proposed to meet this threat appeared to be largely cognitive, that is, the answer was seen to lie in more courses in theology, dogma and so on. Again, this is an area where there have been major shifts of orientation in the growing emphasis on the sociology of knowledge and the awareness that what counts as knowledge has been defined by powerful disciplinary interest groups.[7] This has been paralleled by a shift to discovery methods of learning and a concern with curriculum development and innovation. In the same way it might be argued that the formation of Catholic students has shown an increasing concern with group work, shared prayer, meaningful liturgies and commitment and, correspondingly, a reduced emphasis on didactic courses in theology and ritual forms of worship.

There is certainly some evidence that Catholics have in recent years been more upwardly socially mobile than the general population.[8] This 'new middle class' is likely to have increased in influence in the church in this country at the parish level and also on the various commissions at the diocesan and national levels. A study of the social origins of Catholic students in higher education, their socialisation to various professional roles, and the pastoral responses to new needs by the Catholic community seems particularly apt at this time as we reflect on the twin sources of change in the Catholic community: the expansion of educational opportunities and the changes in theological orientation legitimated a decade ago by the second Vatican Council. It seems fruitful to begin by asking how the three great founding fathers of sociology, Marx, Weber and Durkheim, would have set about such a study of Catholic students in higher education.

A Marxian Perspective

Marx would no doubt have got down to basics: social and economic basics. He would have wanted to know the facts about the social origins of Catholic students. Where were they located in the British class structure? Was there any evidence to suggest that because of their peculiar value system they more exactly reflected the socio-economic distribution of Catholics than students in higher education generally reflected the total population? He would of course have hypothesised that their prevailing values reflected those of the ruling class. For historical reasons Catholics in this country have been concerned first of all with elite provision and only secondly with its distribution downwards. This has been reflected in the dominance of the Catholic public (ie independent) schools and university chaplaincy provision. In table 7.1 an attempt has been made to estimate the size and distribution of the Catholic student body and the broad outline of the contemporary pastoral provision in terms of the resources of chaplains and chaplaincies. Wherever possible the estimates have been based on published figures. Where these are not available, estimates have been made on the basis of the best sources and information available. From the table it can be seen that broadly speaking any hypotheses deriving from a Marxian perspective would have strong support. The various social institutions of the Catholic community are no more capable of bridging the class barriers in this country than any other institutions.

It would seem that there are probably something like fifty to seventy thousand Catholic students in the higher education system in England and Wales at the present time. Although only about one-third of these students are in the universities, most of the specialised religious manpower, the chaplains, and virtually all the stock of buildings, the chaplaincies, are devoted to the pastoral care of university students. Over the past decade or so a reasonably comprehensive system of university chaplaincies has been set up. The days are not far gone when a university chaplain could refuse access to the chaplaincy facilities to those unfortunates who happened to be studying technological subjects or who attended non-university institutions. The scars of our recent past remain, however, and we are only just beginning to tackle the question of chaplaincy provision in the polytechnics. One fruitful approach appears to be the appointment of Catholic priests as full-time members of the academic staff at some polytechnics. In addition to the polytechnics there are several hundred institutions undertaking advanced level work, quite apart from the nearly seven thousand establishments of further education attended by about three million students taking lower level courses.

Of all the institutions in higher education the colleges of education are currently facing the biggest problems of adaptation to the changing economic and social conditions. The rapid decline of the birth rate in recent years has resulted not only in a reduction in the number of Catholic colleges and the size of their student intakes but also to some mergers to form ecumenical colleges. Serious consideration has also been given to the design of new courses. In the struggle for survival the Catholic institutions of higher education able to attract students for courses other than teacher training may well have the best chances. The ecumenical college or the diversified Catholic college, possibly with a large non-Catholic intake, will be a very different institution from the old monotechnic with its overwhelmingly Catholic intake. The pastoral problem will then become quite different and will clearly have implications for the role of the chaplain.

At the moment most of the Catholic colleges of education have a priest specifically appointed as chaplain. In addition, all the colleges have priests on their academic staff; in at least one college these priests are adamant that they too fulfil a chaplain's role with the students. Not all chaplains to students in higher education have full-time appointments and it seems that a substantial proportion have some sort of parish responsibilities. The number of religious sisters involved in chaplaincy work is also increasing at the present moment.

It appears that most chaplains now consider that they have a duty towards all students in higher education in their own area. Since, for historical reasons, a special building was first provided for university students, the university chaplaincy tends to be the focal point for the work of the chaplain. The financing of the university chaplaincies merits some consideration. The National Catholic Fund for Chaplaincies in Higher Education reported in 1974 on the present situation of chaplaincies and their immediate and long-term capital and income requirements. It is interesting to note that the report referred exclusively to university chaplaincies. It was stated that in 1973 'the financing of the 37 chaplaincies and 65 chaplains has cost £154,882. Some £100,000 of this was raised through the efforts of chaplains and their committees and the remaining £50,000 was financed from diocesan sources'. The report concluded that 'on the basis of the figures presented . . . we have estimated the future annual income requirement of the Chaplaincy service to be £209,000'.[9] It should be noted in passing that this figure exceeds by a considerable amount the annual income of the National Catholic Fund which finances the various commissions set up to advise the Bishops' Conference.[10] On the other hand it must be compared with the £6m estimated annual cost to the Catholic community of the school building programme.[11] The report of the National Catholic Fund for Chaplaincies in Higher Education concluded that a capital fund of £1¼m would be necessary for immediate capital requirements and to meet the annual income requirement. Again, it must be stressed that these figures related only to the existing university chaplaincies. To make similar arrangements for all polytechnics would almost certainly double or treble the figures given.

A Weberian Perspective

The insights of a Max Weber might lead us first to consider the bureaucratisation of chaplaincy provision.[12] There are clear signs that the office of the Department of Higher Education under Bishop Mullins is serving as an administrative centre for the co-ordination of chaplaincy work, printing and circulating newsletters between the chaplains and student leaders and informing chaplains of the names of school leavers from Catholic schools known to be entering their institution. In 1974, for example, information about 3852 school leavers was obtained from 253 of the 664 Catholic secondary schools surveyed. If the estimates in table 7.1 are accurate then this exercise succeeds in informing chaplains of one-fourth to one-fifth of their likely intake. By comparing the different ways of financing chaplaincies, a start has been made along the road to national provision and financing. The present structure developed in an ad hoc way and arguably a national system of higher education requires a national system of chaplaincy provision with national financing and some form of national, specialist, career structure which insulates the office holder (the chaplains) from arbitrary removal by diocesan bishop or religious superior. Appropriate qualifying courses to train chaplains for what can be seen to be a specialised task might also be predicted. The dysfunctions of bureaucratically administered organisations are well known but in so far as Weber was right in hypothesising that a bureaucracy was the most efficient form of administration, developments in the direction indicated might well be anticipated.

Secondly, Weber would direct us to consider the meanings which religion in general and institutional Catholicism in particular have for the Catholic student in higher education. It is necessary first of all to identify some of the characteristics of the student in higher education.[13] Overall only one-third of the students are female but the proportion varies very much from sector to sector. In universities one-third are female and about 70 per cent of college of education students are women. On the other hand, only one-fifth of those attending advanced courses in further education are women. Almost all students in higher education have the legal status of an adult. Overall only one student in eight is under the age of nineteen while nearly three-fifths of the men and two-fifths of the women are aged twenty-one or over. Considering full-time university students, only about one-fifth are pursuing postgraduate studies and about one in ten are from overseas. There are some differences in the subjects studied by undergraduates and postgraduates. Roughly two students in five are studying science, engineering or technology and one in five social sciences. One-fifth of the undergraduates are studying arts subjects while nearly one-fifth of postgraduates are studying education. There are bigger differences between the sexes. Nearly one-half of men undergraduates are studying science, engineering or technology compared to only one-fifth of the women while two-fifths of the women undergraduates are studying arts subjects compared to only one in seven of the men. Other differences occur between different institutions which reflect their different historical origins and charters. For example, one would expect the ex-CATS to have a higher proportion of men students and of scientists and engineers.

The religious beliefs and practices of Catholic adolescents in Catholic secondary schools have been discussed in detail above.[14] It was noted that in the Southwark diocese nearly half the fifteen-year-old boys and over one-third of the fifteen-year-old girls did not attend mass every Sunday and holiday of obligation. In the studies of fourth and fifth formers, parental religious adherence and practice were found to be key factors. In interviews with fourth formers there was evidence that religion was seen as childish, irrelevant and boring and that much lapsation appeared to be due to laziness in the absence of strong parental control, that is 'more drift than decision'.[15]

Apart from these studies Wright and Cox[16] reported recently on a replication in 1970 with a sample of 1574 sixth formers from 66 schools of a study of moral and religious beliefs carried out in 1963 with a sample of 2276 sixth formers from 96 schools. These authors found that

there have been highly significant changes in the moral beliefs of sixth form boys and girls in maintained grammar schools in England. The changes are greatest for sexual behaviour but extend to such issues as (the) colour bar and gambling. In general, the change is away from the uncompromising condemna-

tion of behaviour towards a more qualified, permissive or un-
decided position . . . (and) there were clear signs that girls had
changed more than boys.

These authors conclude that

> though strictness of moral belief is associated with religious
> commitment in both samples, *changes* towards a more permissive
> point of view are in no way delayed or impeded by such a
> commitment . . . though factually associated, religious and
> moral beliefs are not functionally related.

The adolescent years are perhaps those where sexual experimentation is particularly likely[17] and in view of the fact that the proportion of sixth formers who considered premarital sexual
intercourse 'always wrong' had declined from 56 per cent in 1963
to 15 per cent in 1970, it is interesting to note that Wright and Cox
observed that

> those who judged premarital sexual intercourse never wrong,
> nevertheless added that this was only so when the couple were
> in love or had a sense of responsibility towards each other. (Both
> samples condemned) 'sex for kicks' and indiscriminate promis-
> cuity. It seems plausible to argue that the change in rating
> represents a decided weakening in the link between sexual inter-
> course and marriage in the minds of the subjects, while the
> comments witness if anything to a strengthening of the link
> between sex and affection.

These then are some of the attitudes and values which school
leavers bring with them as they embark on courses in higher education, largely freed from the constraints of home, school and parish.
What sort of beliefs do they express in their early adult years?[18]
Pilkington and Poppleton[19] recently reported on a replication in
1972 of a study of religious beliefs, attitudes and practices among
students at Sheffield University, originally carried out in 1961. In
both years a proportionate, stratified, random sample of one in
every six students was taken within each faculty. Over this eleven-
year period the authors reported

> a massive and statistically significant movement away from
> religion on the part of the students . . . Particularly striking is
> the fact that, whereas in 1961 nearly threequarters of the students
> described themselves as having some form of religious belief, by
> 1972 this proportion had fallen to just over a half. Accompany-
> ing this decline in religious belief are equally heavy drops in the
> percentages of those reporting the saying of private prayers,

church attendance and active church membership. On the other hand . . . the erosion of religious belief and practice over the eleven years has been less serious among devout students than among those less committed to religion.

The decline in the religious attitude scale was particularly strong among the women. For Catholic students the proportion retaining active church membership declined dramatically from 86 per cent in 1961 to only 39 per cent in 1971. The general decline of religious attitudes was particularly striking among Catholic students and

it would seem that active members . . . now take less extreme positions on the attitude scale items than in 1961, reflecting a weaker adherence to traditional Christian beliefs . . .

It is interesting to note that the decline is strongest amongst first-year students and

in all, it seems likely that the important factors bringing about a movement away from religious belief and practice occur before students enter the university at all.

This has led Wright and Cox to suggest that

the social forces which are hostile to religion have not so much been increasing in strength . . . as reaching further down towards childhood.[20]

This finding is consistent with Bishop Mullins' view that

there is not a greater falling away from religion among Catholic students in higher education than there used to be, but that the Catholics in higher education are now far more representative of the total Catholic community than . . . 15 to 20 years ago.[21]

An interesting confirmation of the conclusions of Wright and Cox is found in Dr Tanner's mail questionnaire survey of Catholic students at London University in 1970;[22] 238 replies were received from 1007 students whose names had been forwarded to the Catholic Chaplaincy by their Catholic schools via the Catholic Education Council. The author comments that

possibly most surprising in the survey is the belief that the really radical change takes place in the last two years of secondary school.

Thus respondents suggested that mass attendance frequencies were unaffected by coming to the university. Continued attendance seemed to reflect religious conviction and personal need more than habit or the requirements of canon law. Most students feel that they had had an inadequate religious education—far too doctrinaire, and not related to the problems of contemporary living. It was widely referred to as indoctrination.

Very little religious reading appeared to be done and only one student in eight had read the scriptures in any way in the previous year. Ecumenism was strongly supported and students considered the hardest aspect of being a christian was 'practising what you preached'. By contrast the observance of religious rituals was found to be the easiest aspect. Only one-third of the students had had any contact with priests, religious or lay counsellors and of those only a half felt the contact had been helpful.

Finally, a small self-completion questionnaire survey of mass attenders at the University of Surrey was carried out by Fr F. Collins in the summer of 1975.[23] About three-quarters of the attenders replied. These mass attenders appeared to be a highly selected group coming disproportionately from practising homes and Catholic schools. About one-fifth of them came from outside the British Isles. Two-fifths of them reported they had Catholic boy/girl friends. Aspects of an appropriate spirituality were emphasised by about four-fifths of students including more emphasis on personal prayer, worship in small groups and ecumenism. Nine-tenths of these students had a favourable image of the priesthood, claiming to see it as an especially worthy vocation and to be on friendly terms with some priests. The contrast with the London students reflects the greater size and anonymity of the metropolis in contrast to the smaller, more compact arrangements in Guildford where most mass attenders would be resident on the university site less than 200 yards from the Cathedral chapel where mass is offered. For these students, too, the standard of living of priests was not considered to be excessive. A third cluster of attitudes related to Catholic education. Only three-fifths thought that Catholic schools helped teach Catholics their faith and the same proportion thought there was too much emphasis on teaching facts and doctrine rather than how to live and love as a christian. Nearly one-half thought there was too much coercion in the way religion was taught. A fourth cluster of attitudes related to the church's institutional concerns. About one-half of the students thought the church was detached from the needs and concerns of ordinary people and wanted the church to make more public statements on controversial issues. On the other hand, only one-third thought the church was too concerned with the maintenance of the plant or too concerned with sexual matters. Finally, nearly all the students rejected the notion that the church gave too much attention to social issues.

The third area where the insights of Weber would be fruitful for further study relates to his well-known typology of authority and his analysis of charisma. Related to this is his major distinction between the priest and the prophet. For Weber

> the personal call is the decisive element distinguishing the prophet from the priest. The latter lays claim to authority by virtue of his service in a sacred tradition, while the prophet's claim is based on personal revelation and charisma.[24]

In recent years there has been growing awareness of the gift of prophecy in the Catholic church, legitimated by the second Vatican Council.[25] A major study of the role of the university chaplains in the life of the Catholic church in England remains to be undertaken but my impression would be that they have had a crucial influence in encouraging a view of the church as the 'people of God' rather than a bureaucratically administered structure, in liturgical experimentation and promoting a more lively participation in the liturgy, in encouraging shared prayer and ecumenical activities, in deepening the faith and forming small but key groups of laity who are now active in the life of the church at both parish and national levels. It may be that this is elitism but if so it is based on the model of small group work carried out by our Lord with the apostles. Mission proceeds by the working of the leaven in the mass and students in higher education, because of their anticipated future favoured position as managers, professionals and administrators in the British class structure, are a key element of lay manpower. It is the major task of chaplains in higher education to promote their formation as committed christians.

A Durkheimian Perspective

The third great founding father of sociology was Emile Durkheim, who was emphatic about the *social* nature of religion and the expression of this in a moral community which he called a church. Religion was primarily concerned with the key distinction between the 'sacred' and the 'profane'. Ritual served to express and reinforce sentiments necessary for social integration and cohesion.[26] In his major study of the division of labour Durkheim was concerned to explore the changing basis of social cohesion in society. He contrasted what he called the mechanical solidarity which occurred when individuals shared a common set of beliefs, values and attitudes which were manifested in the detailed regulation of behaviour, with organic solidarity which arose wherever individuals were related to each other through their interdependence in a complex division of labour.[27] While repressive forms of punishment were necessary in order to emphasise shared values and sentiments in the former case, the system of social control tended to be restitutive or reparative under conditions of organic solidarity.

Basil Bernstein has recently applied this conceptualisation of Durkheim to the study of social change in the schools, arguing persuasively that there has been a shift in the principles of social integration in the schools from mechanical to organic solidarity.[28] It might be hypothesised that the same shift is taking place in the Catholic church in this country at the present moment. The relatively closed system of the homogeneous Catholic community with its enforced pattern of endogamy, its defensive structures of Catholic schools and close-knit parochial and social life orchestrated by the local Catholic priest to whom due deference and authority were given automatically, has rapidly given way to a system where exogamy is increasingly tolerated, and there is a breakdown in the strong mechanical links between home, schools and parish. The expansion of educational opportunities inevitably promoted these changes, as Joan Brothers shrewdly observed over a decade ago.

The evidence reviewed above suggests that this shift is well under way during secondary education but it is likely to be even more pronounced in higher education with its clear break with the constraints of childhood and the opportunities for anonymity if desired. Inevitably there is a privatisation of religion. The danger is that of anomie, the Durkheimian word for a lack of moral regulation, in terms of religious, moral and social behaviour. What is required is a new basis of social cohesion which is based on the divinely complex interdependence of gifts to replace the older legalistic framework of the past.

Concluding Observations

In this chapter an attempt has been made to empathise with a Marx, a Weber and a Durkheim in the task of commenting usefully on Catholic students in higher education. It has been argued that a Marxian perspective would direct us fruitfully to recognise the extent to which Catholic students come disproportionately from middle class homes and the extent to which our chaplaincy provision is geared overwhelmingly in favour of the elite university sector. A Weberian perspective would direct us in particular to search for the meanings which religion and the institutional church have for Catholic students at the present time. It is clear from the evidence reviewed that significant changes have taken place in the past decade and that there has been a noticeable decline in religious belief and practice. A Durkheimian perspective would lead us to interpret these shifts in terms of major structural changes in the Catholic community and, in particular, in the basis of its social cohesion.

Two final observations are relevant. In the first place, in reading the deliberations about Catholics in higher education in the issues of *The Dublin Review* in the late 1950s and early 1960s one is struck by the emphasis on the *cognitive* dimension of faith and the need to teach Catholic students more theology. It seems that in recent years the emphasis has shifted more to the *affective* and *conative* dimensions and that this shift is a healthy one. This view is well put by Bishop Huyghe, who is quoted by Cardinal Suenens in his recent book:[29]

> It's one thing to speak about Jesus Christ, quite another and infinitely more important to speak *to* Jesus Christ and to listen to His Spirit . . . Young people will not come to faith through the teaching of dogmas, but by personal experience of God in Jesus Christ.

Suenens then comments:

> This is how it was at the beginning. It was not the truth *about* Jesus but the truth *of* Jesus which was at the basis of conversion.

There is a need for Catholic students to radiate joy and love in their lives so that their neighbour will be attracted by the sight of Catholics loving one another. It is a major task of Catholic chaplains to promote this process. In this matter the influence of the charismatic movement is likely to be particularly important.

Secondly, the importance of small group liturgies, shared prayer and discussion might be noted. In recent years small group work has been recognised by many to have considerable advantages in education. The effectiveness of small groups seems to be enormously enhanced where they are able to meet together in some communal setting, sharing eucharistic worship, prayer, discussion, eating and living together for a few days at a time. It is interesting to note the number of key lay leaders now who were fired by their experiences on Student Cross or at Union of Catholic Student Conferences in the 1950s. It consequently seemed to me to be a serious loss when UCS collapsed in the late 1960s. The re-establishment of a national structure, now known as the Catholic Student Council (CSC), the rebirth and growth of new forms of Student Cross and the development of contemporary forms of self-catering Catholic student regional and national conferences[30] is therefore heartening and worthy of every possible support and encouragement.

8

Catholic Schooling in the United States and Australia

The last four chapters of this book have been concerned to describe some of the qualitative outcomes of Catholic schools in England today. The research base for making any generalisations is remarkably thin, given the size of the Catholic school system and the proportion of available resources devoted to its expansion especially in the post-war years. Nevertheless, in the belief that some knowledge is better than none, such few studies as are available have been presented in the hope that they will contribute to the understanding of processes of religious socialisation occurring in Catholic schools, and to more informed policy making. This is particularly important at the present time, as the Catholic community adapts not only to the consequences of a dramatic drop in the birth rate of the Catholic population since the mid-1960s and the present economic recession, but also to the quest for pastoral strategies more appropriate to the needs of the last quarter of the twentieth century.

Although the empirical base for generalising about Catholic schools in England is so slight, there have been a number of studies in other countries which are relevant to the consideration of the outcomes of what Greeley and Rossi called 'value-oriented education'.[1] These studies lend support to our own findings and also point the way to the future, in indicating lines of enquiry which would lead to greater knowledge and understanding of the processes of religious development among young people, and in saying something about the nature of social interaction *within*-schools and the causal processes which result in such enormous *between*-schools variations in religious (and other social) outcomes.

The best known empirical study of Catholic schools is undoubtedly that undertaken by Greeley and Rossi in the United States in 1963.[2] At this time the American Roman Catholic Church administered over 300 institutions of higher education, 2500 secondary schools and 10,000 elementary schools. Its 200,000 teachers, two-thirds of whom were priests, nuns and brothers, were teaching over six million students or some 14 per cent of the school population.[3] Apart from the sheer size of this system it is important to remember a major difference from the Catholic system of education in England. Whereas in this country all the teachers' salaries and all but 15 per cent of the capital costs for maintained schools are paid from public funds, in the United States Catholic schools are all private and almost entirely financed through tuition fees paid by the students and by private contributions.[4] Furthermore, in some areas Catholic schools are not available so that it is not surprising, therefore, that only about two-fifths of American Catholic children attend Catholic schools[5] compared with around three-fifths in this country.[6]

Greeley and Rossi aimed to study eight key issues:[7]

(1) The extent to which Catholic schools produced 'better' Catholics in terms of church and sacramental frequency, and doctrinal and ethical orthodoxy; and
(2) Involvement in Catholic organisations;
(3) Whether Catholic schools were in any way 'divisive';
(4) Whether or not those who had attended Catholic schools were more 'authoritarian' or prejudiced than other groups;
(5) Whether or not Catholic schooling hindered 'this-worldly' economic advancement;
(6) The extent to which support for the separate Catholic school system was being maintained;
(7) The relative effectiveness of the different levels of Catholic education; and
(8) Generational differences, in order to judge the likely responses to the profound changes taking place in the Roman Catholic church which were articulated through the second Vatican Council.

In order to pursue these research aims Greeley and Rossi surveyed a multistage area probability sample of 2071 Catholics between the ages of twenty-three and fifty-seven and a comparable group of 530 Protestants.[8] Additional data were obtained from 550 Catholic adolescents and a comparable group of 183 Protestant adolescents at high school[9] and 460 readers of *Commonweal*, representing the 'liberal Catholic elite'.[10] In the course of their analysis the authors constructed a number of scales of religious behaviour including sacramental, church-as-teacher, religious knowledge, doctrinal orthodoxy, ethical orthodoxy, and sexual mores indices and a measure of organisational membership. Generally speaking partial correlational analysis, using the Goodman-Kruskal gamma coefficient, was employed to measure the strength of the relationship between the various indices of religious behaviour and the amount of Catholic schooling, controlling for such variables as the religiousness of the home, social class, ethnicity, and so on.[11]

As a result of this analysis the authors are able to conclude that:

> there is a moderate but significant association . . . between Catholic education and adult religious behaviour, an association which survives under a wide variety of socio-economic, demographic and religious controls.[12]

This finding leads the authors to observe that:

> the Catholic experiment in value-oriented education has been a moderate (though expensive) success, and that therefore there is some reason to think that value-oriented education can affect human behaviour and attitudes in matters that are invested with heavy symbolic importance.[13]

A number of other findings are of particular interest here. First of all, the association between Catholic schooling and religious behaviour:

> is strongest amongst those who come from very religious family backgrounds . . . (and) those who went to Catholic colleges

which seems to indicate the presence of some sort of 'multiplier effect' in both cases.[14] Secondly, a comparison of the relative strengths of the four predictor attributes: religiousness of parents, educational level, sex, and Catholic schooling, shows the influence of the Catholic school to be the weakest predictor for the sacramental and ethical orthodoxy indices and organisational membership, weaker than educational level for the church-as-teacher and religious knowledge indices, and weaker than both educational level and parental religiosity for the doctrinal orthodoxy index.[15] Thirdly, very little relationship was found between religious behaviour and attendance at religious instruction classes for those not attending Catholic schools,[16] a finding which must be noted when considering alternatives to Catholic schools for the religious socialisation of young Catholics. Fourthly, 'no confirmation was found for the notion that Catholic schools are "divisive" ',[17] a finding clearly pertinent to the debate about the 'dual system' in England and Wales but also about segregated schooling in Northern Ireland.

Eleven years after this study was undertaken, Greeley and his co-workers replicated it and interviews were achieved with a national probability sample of 927 Catholics, 18 years of age and older, living in households within the 48 contiguous United States.[18]

It is, perhaps, important to note that apart from the replication of the earlier study, this research aimed to evaluate the various changes which had taken place in American Catholicism in the intervening years. Apart from the various changes emanating from the Vatican Council, the publication of the papal encyclical *Humanae Vitae* and those changes within American society itself associated with the Viet Nam war and the Civil Rights movement had radically affected the church in the United States. It is not my purpose here to comment on Greeley's interpretation of these changes, in terms of the relative impacts of the Vatican Council and *Humanae Vitae*, which has provoked considerable controversy.[19] Our concern at this point is to note those findings which relate specifically to the question of the influence which Catholic schooling has on subsequent adult religious behaviour.

In the eleven years since the Greeley-Rossi study considerable strides were made both in the conceptualisation of value-oriented education and in the analytical procedures available for the determination of its effectiveness and for the study of social change. The authors of this major study

assume that value-oriented education is concerned with maintaining and promoting organisational involvement, transmitting the ethical values and the doctrinal knowledge of the institution that maintains it, sustaining the basic world-view, explicit or implicit, of that organisation, and developing those social attitudes and that sort of organisational loyalty which the institution deems appropriate. Under these circumstances, the successful value-oriented educational enterprise is one which produces frequent organisational activity, acceptance of the official ethical values, capacity to repeat the official views the organisation endorses, acceptance of the underlying world-view of the organisation, commitment to its social attitudes and values, and a high level of organisational loyalty.[20]

In the operationalisation of these variables the authors not only use the same scales as in the 1963 study but also construct a number of new scales measuring, for example, support for the changes of the Vatican Council, support for changes in the priesthood, and also various styles of activism.[21]

The earlier study had employed an implicit four-variable model to explain adult religious behaviour but had been unable to say how much religious behaviour was explained by it. In the second study, apart from the original variables: sex, parental religiosity, educational level, and Catholic school attendance, two further variables, age and spouse's church attendance, were added. Furthermore, in the later analysis multiple regression techniques and path analysis were employed and the 1963 data re-analysed along with the 1974 data. The religious behaviour model in terms of these variables explained 31 per cent of the variance in activism in 1963 and 38 per cent in 1974. It was also found that over this period the religiosity of the spouse as measured by church attendance had become much more important.[22]

Summarising the results of the detailed analyses of all these factors the authors concluded that:

> Far from declining in effectiveness in the past decade, Catholic schools seem to have increased their impact. In a time of general decline in religious behaviour, the rate of decline for those who have gone to Catholic schools is much slower. The correlation between Catholic school attendance and religiousness is especially strong for those under thirty . . . In terms of the future of the organisation, Catholic schools seem more important for a church in time of traumatic transition than for one in a time of peaceful stability.[23]

When one looks at the details it is shown that:

> The net correlations between years in Catholic school and sexual orthodoxy, doctrinal orthodoxy, and the church's right to teach, as well as with Mass attendance and confession, have declined. But the net correlations between Catholic school attendance and participation in Catholic activities, support for religious vocations, and contributions to the church have increased. And among certain sub-populations, so has the correlation between Catholic school attendance and private prayer . . . Catholic schools *do* have an impact which is net of education, parental religiousness, spouse's religiousness, age, sex, and educational attainment. With the decline of the importance of parental religiousness and educational level in 1974, Catholic education is second only to religiousness of spouse in predicting religious behaviour. So not only absolutely but also relative to other factors, the importance of Catholic education has *increased* since 1963 . . . Furthermore, the impact of Catholic education in 1974 was especially strong for three groups that would be critical for the institutional future of Catholicism—young people under thirty, men from very religious backgrounds, and members of those eastern and southern European ethnic groups whose level of religious practice has traditionally been at or beneath average . . . At a time when the institution is in severe crisis . . . parochial schools would seem to have an important role to play in training the people

who will eventually provide support for institutional rejuvenation and resurgence.[24]

A particularly imaginative analysis relates to the ultimate value of 'hopefulness' which the authors regard as most clearly embodying the teachings of the Roman Catholic church:

> The 'hopeful' respondents are those who display some understanding of the existence of evil, while at the same time holding to their belief that the situation will end in a way that is ultimately positive and influenced by a benevolent reality . . .[25]

The data indicate that Catholic schooling is more important than either educational level or parental religiosity in fostering hopefulness.[26] This is important because

> The hopeful people score highest on Catholic activism, use of the Sacraments, approval of various kinds of changes stemming from the Second Vatican Council, and . . . lowest on anti-clerical sentiment.[27]

This leads the authors to point out that

> If the Church wants to husband its hopeful people, it must recognise the magnified importance of the parochial school system. In terms of human resources, Catholic schools are a tremendous asset for the changing church. They tend to produce people who are change-oriented and flexible, but secure in both their worldview and their loyalty to past traditions and values. Parochial schools are also producing people who are more tolerant of others and better able to cope with our increasingly diverse society.[28]

Finally, as in the 1963 study, there was little evidence to show that religious instruction outside the schools was an adequate substitute, even though it may be useful as a symbol of the concern of the church for those who do not attend Catholic schools.[29]

In the absence of any evidence to the contrary, there is no reason to suppose that these findings do not hold substantially in England, even allowing for the historical, structural, and cultural differences. No data are presently available to explore the impact of changes since the Vatican Council though a study at the University of Surrey currently under way should provide comparative data for England and Wales and enable an analysis of the effectiveness of Catholic schools in this country to be carried out.[30]

The third study of Catholic schools in other societies which is of interest is that undertaken in 1972 by Brother Marcellin Flynn in

New South Wales, Australia.[31] Like others, Flynn was concerned
at the lack of research findings relating to the effectiveness of a
system involving over 20,000 Catholic teachers of almost half a
million Catholic children or some 17 per cent of all Australian
children in 1974.[32] His study is of particular interest because it
attempted to measure school atmosphere or climate. Whereas
previous studies had generally been concerned with academic
climates and their impact on student achievements,[33] Flynn en-
deavoured to relate the organisational and religious climates of his
21 research schools to student religious behaviour. Such studies are
important for the investigation of processes occurring within schools
which are related to massive differences in outcomes, for example
religious behaviour, between schools, which cannot be explained by
variations in school size or type or by a range of neighbourhood
variables or the social composition of the intake.[34]

In his study, Flynn specifically aims

> to explore the Catholic School in action by investigating the sixth
> formers' perceptions of a Catholic school and its influence on
> them, and, further, endeavours to enquire into the ways the
> school communicates its Christian Message and values . . . (It)
> also attempts to analyse the religious and educational outcomes
> of Catholic Education

and to study the inter-relationships between the perceptions of the
goals of the Catholic schools of the teachers, parents and students,
the climate and morale of Catholic schools, and the religious and
academic achievements of the students.[35] Data were obtained mainly
from questionnaires completed by 1393 sixth formers, 404 teachers,
619 parents and a comparison group of 598 Catholic students in
state High Schools.[36] Responses to questions on students' ideal and
actual school goals, school climate, religious beliefs, values and
practices, and leisure-time activities, and teacher and parent perceptions of ideal school goals were subjected to the techniques of
factor analysis and principal components analysis using varimax
rotation and 21 scales constructed.[37]

Some of Flynn's findings echo those reported above for three
English comprehensive schools.[38] Thus while for teachers and
parents the most important ideal goal of Catholic schools is the
provision of christian community, for students it is personal development. Similarly, while teachers and parents give high priority
to religious education, students consider it much less important.[39]
Many of the reported religious, moral and social attitudes of the
students are also similar to those reviewed above for fifth formers
in three English comprehensive schools.[40] Flynn employs the con-

cept of *goal discrepancy*, measured by the difference between students' assessments of school ideal and actual goals, as a measure of students' alienation in the school situation.[41] A second measure is a morale scale derived from his analysis of school climate.

It is in the attempt to measure school climate that, in my opinion, the book makes its most important contribution. For Flynn, the concept indicates:

> the total interacting patterns of communication, culture and life (of the school and not only) . . . the goals espoused, but the procedures which are adopted in its day to day administration . . . the kinds of things that are rewarded, celebrated and emphasised, as well as the style of life which is valued and expressed.[42]

Unlike previous writers[43] who have generally defined school climate in terms of teachers' and head's behaviour. Flynn stresses the importance of the student body. His data are derived from 59 attitude questions about their school and seven items from a school goals questionnaire answered by the students. The data were then factor analysed and the varimax rotated factor yielded three factors from which student morale, attitude towards the headteacher (principal), and adolescent freedom scales were constructed.[44]

Flynn's analysis is complex and not perhaps as clear as it could be. In particular it seems to me that he does not always identify precisely which are his dependent and independent variables or indicate clearly what is his implicit causal model. In other words, what causes what? Are the three school climate variables to be considered as intervening variables between the various measures of religious belief, attitudes and behaviour as the dependent variables, and the various background variables such as social class and parental religion as the independent variables? Assuming that this is the implicit model then Flynn's data are most valuable. They show, for example, that the religious outcomes are much higher where student morale is high and that the differences between students with high and low morale is statistically highly significant.[45] But what causes differences in morale? Flynn uses the analysis of Barakat[46] to argue that student alienation arises from two extreme forms of authority relationships within the school which he terms overcontrol and undercontrol.[47] In a comparison of two schools, one where 85 per cent of the students considered they were allowed sufficient freedom by the school authorities and the other where 96 per cent considered they were not allowed sufficient freedom, he shows that in both cases the students scored significantly below the mean on the measure of religious outcomes and that:

the 'overcontrol' students are much more alienated than the 'undercontrol' students, suggesting that overcontrol is potentially more destructive of student morale.[48]

This is a finding of great practical importance and it raises again the need to study the processes occurring within schools as mentioned above in the discussion of the findings from the Southwark schools survey.[49] This, however, is a 'political' matter which involves in particular the co-operation of the staffs of the schools. It is unfortunate, therefore, that Flynn found it necessary to promise not to make any comparisons between individual schools.[50] Two further comments on this important study are relevant. Flynn shows firstly that even when parental religiosity is controlled

there are significant differences in the religious development of students, depending on the religious climate in the school[51]

and secondly that

there are strong indications that a good religious school improves the religious development of students from non-religious homes; poor religious schools, on the other hand, appear to weaken the influence of even good religious homes and so to act as a 'modifier' of the good religious values of the home.[52]

The five chapters of part III of this book have attempted to summarise some relevant findings relating to the qualitative outcomes of Catholic schools, with particular reference to the situation in England. Given the strength of the ideology of the Catholic school in institutional Catholicism,[53] it is a major task and contribution of the sociologist to subject such claims about the effectiveness of Catholic schools in the processes of religious socialisation or the pursuit of specified goals as are either explicitly, or more frequently implicitly empirical, to rigorous scrutiny and empirical testing in a spirit of scientific scepticism.[54] What appears to have happened is

the familiar process of *displacement of goals* whereby 'an instrumental value becomes a terminal value'[55]

where the Catholic school as a means to the achievement of religious goals has become an end in itself. Consequently the empirical claims of Catholic schools have not been subject to rigorous testing, not merely in this country but also in the United States and Australia.[56] In part III of this book the attempt has been made to make up for some of these deficiencies by reporting a number of relatively small-scale empirical studies of Catholic schooling in

England, to outline briefly a number of pertinent studies abroad which address similar research questions, and to suggest the direction in which future research might best go.

Since there is undisputed evidence that schools differ in their climate or atmosphere and that these differences are systematically related to the religious outcomes of the schools even when controlling for home background variables, there is a clear case for monitoring the situation in schools and identifying those which deviate significantly in terms of their religious achievements. Whether they are unusually successful or unsuccessful, it is important to explore further the causal processes involved if corrective measures are to be taken and general standards raised. What is certain, though, is that the pursuit of these goals will be seen as threatening by many teachers involved, and researchers will need to tread warily in areas where various interests have the power to frustrate the purposes of their work. Research tends to be acceptable to many people as long as existing power relationships or legitimating ideologies remain unchallenged. This is particularly the case where there are clear policy implications in the research findings. In part IV of this book two such matters relating to the structure and goals of the Catholic system of education in England and Wales, the area of continuing education and the provision of educational advice to the Bishops' Conference, will be briefly discussed.

PART IV

Some Policy Implications

9

Education—A Continuing Process

Sociological perspectives on education[1] have generally been derived from the contributions of Durkheim and Weber. From Durkheim's search for the social function performed by education in the promotion and maintenance of social integration we learn that

> education is the influence exercised by adult generations on those that are not yet ready for social life. Its object is to arouse and to develop in the child a certain number of physical, intellectual and moral states which are demanded of him by both the political society as a whole and the special milieu for which he is specifically destined.

In other words, 'education consists of a methodical socialisation of the young generation'.[2] Weber's contribution must be seen in the context of his concern for the historical process of rationalisation[3] and its concomitant the increasing bureaucratisation of social life and dominance of legal-rational forms of authority.[4] Thus he sees the struggle between 'the specialist type of man' against the older type of 'cultivated man' being

> determined by the irresistibly expanding bureaucratisation of all public and private relations of authority and by the ever-increasing importance of expert and specialised knowledge.[5]

Thus the functions of educational institutions are essentially two-fold:

1 The socialisation of members of a society or group into the dominant norms, values and beliefs of the society or group. For Catholics in England this would include not only the values of democracy, equality of opportunity and tolerance which are supposed to characterise the wider society but also those specific to the Catholic community, for example, the essential articles of religious faith and the norms of religious worship.

2 The training necessary to participate fully as adults in the complex division of labour of an advanced industrial society.

With industrialisation there has been a process of structural differentiation[6] so that these functions which were formerly carried out mainly by the family are now largely delegated to specialised agencies, notably the schools, colleges of education, universities and so on. For Catholics parochial institutions, especially the homily during Sunday mass, are particularly important, but other institutions such as youth clubs, discussion groups, societies and organisations clearly play a part in the on-going process of religious socialisation.

Unfortunately there is a strong tendency for organisational arrangements to rigidify so that, as Merton points out

adherence to the rules, originally conceived as a means, becomes transformed into an end-in-itself; there occurs the familiar process of *displacement of goals* whereby 'an instrumental value becomes a terminal value' . . . This may be exaggerated to the point where primary concern with conformity to the rules interferes with the achievement of the purposes of the organisation.[7]

It is therefore important constantly to redefine our educational goals and to re-appraise the various means employed in their pursuit. In the consideration of education as a continuing process four themes might usefully be distinguished:

1 The notion that education as defined above is a continuing life-long process, which commences at birth with early childhood socialisation, is most strongly institutionalised during the years of compulsory schooling, but continues afterwards throughout adult life until death. With this realisation it becomes more apparent that the school is but one, though clearly a major, means to the achievement of the goals which we as a Catholic community define for this life-long process.

2 The appraisal of the Catholic contribution to this process. In a very particular way the process of religious socialisation is life-long and concerned with the final end of man so that

the quintessential left by a Catholic education is a lasting consciousness of the fact and the meaning of death.[8]

3 The theme of interdependence and the need for co-operative participation in this life-long process of education. Two aspects are relevant:

(a) the relations between all those concerned with the formal educational processes in schools and colleges: professional teachers, parents, children, officials, other schools and communities and so on; and

(b) the relations between the specialised agencies of formal education and other institutions concerned with the on-going and life-long process of education, and particularly religious education, especially the family, parish, lay societies and organisations, special interest groups and so on.

4 A consideration of the institutions which are most appropriate to the different needs of Catholics at the various stages in their life cycles.

These four areas are closely linked. The main value of considering education and particularly religious education as a life-long process is that it directs attention to the fact that a plurality of needs for a plurality of groups at different stages in the life cycle requires a plurality of approaches and institutional arrangements. In this process the contribution of Catholic schools is clearly of major significance but more importantly the contribution of Catholic teachers as professional educators is probably far more crucial to the success of programmes of religious education than we have ever imagined. It is important to consider the contribution which Catholic teachers can play in areas outside the school and for adult age groups as well as their contribution within Catholic schools for school children. This has important implications for the renewal of the church and the development of appropriate pastoral strategies relevant to the needs of the last quarter of the twentieth century.

A Continuing Process
Since the end of the second World War and the initiation of 'secondary education for all' there has been a relentless accumulation of educational research which has directed attention increasingly to the importance of home background, parental interest and involvement, and pre-school socialisation processes for the subsequent outcomes of formal schooling. There have been at least four elements in this discovery. First of all the dominant influence of parental interest on primary school achievement was indicated by the longitudinal study of a national sample of children born in 1946[9] and by the researches initiated by the Plowden Committee.[10] Secondly, the research of Bernstein in focusing on the importance of language differences[11] has directed attention to the pre-school years and the potential contribution of nursery school education. Thirdly, there has been a growing awareness that the massive expansion of educational provision has failed to reduce social class

inequalities of achievement and opportunities.[12] This has led to a search for policies of 'positive discrimination' in favour of the disadvantaged. Fourthly, prominent among strategies of compensatory education have been proposals for the more systematic provision of pre-school education.[13]

While the search for remedies for gross inequalities of educational opportunity has led to the increasing concern of professional educationalists with the pre-school years, the rapidity of social change and the growing awareness that scientific knowledge is doubling every few years led manpower planners increasingly to promote the continuation of self-learning and systematic re-training throughout working life rather than the mastery of a supposedly fixed deposit of knowledge.[14] In the post-war world change has become institutionalised and it is necessary to recall that only one lifetime ago there were no cars, aeroplanes, radios, televisions, moon flights, antibiotics, national schemes of social security, let alone aggiornamento. Clearly, an education suitable for the world of 1900 would be quite inappropriate today. In the same way there is no reason at all to believe that an education suitable for a sixteen-year-old school leaver will be appropriate to the needs of the thirty-year-old parent, the fifty-year-old middle-aged person or to the sixty-five-year-old retired person. This applies not only in the case of the changing skills required in the labour market but also to the religious education requirement of Catholics at different stages in their life cycles.

Thus it might, without too much exaggeration, be suggested that twenty-year-olds are concerned with formal education, relationships between the sexes, idealism and social injustice; thirty-year-olds with the tensions of over-crowded homes, small children, career development and family limitation; forty-year-olds with turbulent relationships with young adolescents and ageing parents and coming to terms with career peaks and frustrated ambitions; fifty-year-olds with the decline of physical and mental abilities and the shock of loneliness on the exodus of children; the retired with the radical adjustments which must be made to the rhythm of life and preparations for death. For Catholics in particular there is the belief that life is not an end in itself but a pilgrimage and preparation for the ultimate end of man, though the awareness of this inevitably varies throughout the life cycle.

Clearly, therefore, any serious study of education, and especially religious education, as a continuing process must take note of this plurality of needs for different groups. Some of these groups have been identified in terms of their position in their life cycle but the principle of the plurality of religious needs is wider than this and includes specialist occupational groups, for example students or doctors, as well as special interest groups, for example members of the Newman Association or the Latin Mass Society. It is obviously impossible for a single pattern of religious education or a single institution, such as the Catholic school, to cater adequately for this plurality of needs. Rather there must be a plurality of approaches and a plurality of institutions within the church. The task of evolving such plural structures is part of the wider process of renewal in the church as a whole and is linked with the reform of the liturgy and of the parish, diocesan and national organisations.[15] In this process of renewal the contribution of professional teachers is likely to be particularly important.

The Catholic Contribution

It is perhaps more difficult to appraise fairly the contribution of the Catholic community to education. A number of Catholic scholars have reviewed the historical development of Catholic education in this country and the turbulent fight for the dual system.[16] They have emphasised that the churches were the pioneers in the provision of education for the poor and that until a century ago there were no state schools in England. It has been claimed that the rights and duties of parents have been defended, and asserted that through a concern for the moral development of the child by a Catholic teacher in a Catholic school, attention has been directed to the educational need for an identity of aim between parents and teachers and that a major contribution has been made to society in the training of a morally responsible citizenry. To the sociologist such assertions may be seen, at least in part, as the ideological underpinnings of a system whose manifest function was to secure the life-long allegiance of the young Catholic child to the church by an effective process of religious socialisation.[17] Historically, many who opposed the dual system rejected what they saw as the tyranny of clerical control; in part this reflected the growing professionalisation of teachers and their demand for autonomy in the areas of their specialised role skills. Furthermore, they resented the divisiveness resulting from inter-denominational rivalry and suspicion and claimed that a latent dysfunction of the dual system was the postponement of educational reform and the development of an adequate national system of education.[18] The last quarter of a century has, however, seen the end of 'passionate intensity' over church-school matters as the various churches have increasingly come to see their common need to combat a pervasive secularism in our society.[19]

The legacy of the historical commitment of the Catholic community to Catholic schools is to be seen in the present provision of over 3000 schools, staffed by 44,000 teachers for some 900,000 pupils. Apart from the schools there are still over 7000 students in the Catholic Colleges of Education.[20] In an inflationary situation it is difficult to measure accurately the financial commitment to Catholic schools and colleges represented in the massive post-war expansion. However, there is no doubt that these have been very considerable[21] and by all these *quantitative* indicators, the contemporary contribution of the Catholic community to education in this country, overwhelmingly in the Catholic school, is clearly enormous.

It is, however, far more difficult to assess the *qualitative* contribution and to distinguish aggressive assertion from empirical evidence. What is it that comprises the supposedly distinctive atmosphere of a Catholic school? What are the particular goals of Catholic schools in terms of religious and secular knowledge, attitudes, beliefs, values and norms of behaviour? What sorts of commitments do the schools hope to promote? How central to their purposes is worship and the liturgical life of the church? How effective are the schools in achieving their aims? Is there a gap between the ideal and the reality of practice? If so, why is this so? How can the religious education of young Catholics be made more effective? And so on; the list of relevant questions is endless.[22] What little research evidence there is on these issues was reviewed above.[23]

A number of researchers have attempted to measure the effectiveness of Catholic schools in terms of long term adult behaviour well after the supportive influence of the school has been left behind. It can be argued, however, that in the absence of an adult environment favourable to the maintenance of earlier school influences, the relatively weak long-term outcomes of Catholic schools are not unexpected. What appears to be erroneous is the inference that Catholic schools are ineffective. Rather, it is necessary to direct our attention to the development of new or more effective institutions for school leavers and adults for the continuation of the process of religious socialisation commenced, apparently with some success, in Catholic schools.

The Catholic contribution to education in this country has perhaps been mainly in the schools and the colleges of education, which have in any case always been viewed as an essential part of the school-based strategy. But given the wider perspective of education considered as a life-long process, we must at least pose some further questions. Firstly, are we making the contribution we should to nursery education or are we inhibited unduly by beliefs that not only is woman's place in the home but also that the pre-school age child's place is also in the home? Secondly, do we really accept parents as major partners in the education of their children and have we developed appropriate strategies and institutions for co-operating with them in the different problems of different age groups? Thirdly, why have we failed so deplorably to make systematic and institutionalised arrangements for the religious education of Catholic children in county schools and how best can we make a contribution to this? Fourthly, given the changing structure of the system of higher and further education in this country, is it really desirable to insulate our professional educators not only from other professionals but also from those of other religious beliefs during their training? Is this the best way of training mature teachers for Catholic schools? How can the talents and experience of our colleges of education best be utilised? Fifthly, given that there is a disaffection with institutionalised religion by a very large proportion of young Catholics after leaving school, including those educated in Catholic schools, are we really showing the concern we should for the religious education of adults? Are we really satisfied to confine this in the main to the Sunday homily and the weekly liturgy? What special contribution can Catholic teachers make to remedying the existing deficiencies? Sixthly, what are the present day needs of Catholic teachers, given the wider terms of reference implied by the notion of a continuing process of Catholic education? How best can they be helped to contribute their professional skills to the religious education of Catholics of all ages? Seventhly, what contribution can be made by research in Catholic education to our knowledge, understanding and evaluation of the existing strategies and to the continuing process of change, development and improvement in the Catholic contribution to education at all stages and levels?

The Implications of Interdependence

Who then is involved in this continuing process of education in which so much Catholic effort is invested? Traditionally most Catholic children of compulsory school age have been taught by professional Catholic teachers in parochial schools. Frequently these teachers have been appointed according to particularistic criteria by a parochial clergy. Traditionally the largely working class Catholic parents, a high proportion of whom were first or second generation Irish immigrants, were allowed no say in the formal education of their children. While shades of these traditions remain, by and large the position has changed since the end of the war. This reflects social changes in the wider society which have drawn attention to the fact of interdependence and the need to

E

adapt to it if reasonable levels of social integration are to be maintained.

First of all the Catholic school can no longer simply be identified with the single parish. Following the growth of the multiparish grammar school several decades ago, we are now becoming more familiar with the multiparish first or middle school. Inevitably this has necessitated a sharing of decision-making power by priest chairmen of managers and governors with other clergy and with lay managers and governors. One suspects, however, that in the vast majority of cases these managers are still sponsored by clergy rather than elected by representative lay groups. Secondly, this process of increasing involvement of the parents has been promoted by the general participation by Catholics in the post-war expansion of educational opportunities at the secondary and higher education stages. Joan Brothers explored the implications of this in Liverpool more than a decade ago.[24] As a consequence of the expansion of educational opportunities a considerable proportion of Catholics have experienced upward social mobility to professional and managerial status[25] and have articulately demanded that their formal rights as parents be more substantially recognised. Thirdly, the well publicised emphasis on the importance of good home-school links[26] and the growth of influential middle class educational pressure groups[27] has contributed to the demand for PTAS and for parental representation on managing and governing bodies. Fourthly, educational research has pointed to the problems of culture conflict[28] and the importance of the community school concept as a viable approach to the problem of educational disadvantage and the vicious cycle of deprivation.[29] The explicit aim of the community school is 'to obliterate the boundary between school and community, to turn the community into a school and the school into a community'.[30] The history of the post-war world, too, has emphasised the reality of interdependence. Internationally this country has had to come to terms with its decline of power and status and its dependence on others has been only too clear in the recent oil crisis. At home the increasing complexity of modern industry has resulted in the fragile interdependence of large numbers of specialised groups,[31] an interdependence which becomes painfully obvious with every major industrial dispute.

This interdependence must be paralleled in our provision for the life-long educational needs of the Catholic community. Thus in the formal educational system of schools and colleges it is necessary to recognise the essential contributions not only of teachers and administrators but also of parents, pupils and students. Christ stressed the dignity of every human being. Why should we be so hesitant to apply this in our educational institutions? Why should assistant teachers not be involved in all decision-making where their professional skills are relevant? Why should there not be teacher representatives on school and college governing and managing bodies? Why should there not be parental representatives on these managing bodies? Why should college of education students not be accorded full rights as autonomous adult citizens? Why should they not participate in decision-making committees of colleges to the same extent as undergraduate students in many universities? Why should we find it so very difficult to accept that children, too, have rights? Why should they not have more choice over their curricula? Why should they not participate more in school decision-making? Why cannot some Catholic schools be among the innovators with senior pupils on their governing bodies? It seems to me that all these questions are raised by the serious and systematic consideration of the implications of interdependence and by the theme 'working together'. And why should there be so many demarcation disputes over the shared use of facilities? Why should school facilities and playing fields not be more readily available for use by the community in out-of-school hours, at weekends and during holiday periods? As an indication of pride, commitment and identification the term 'my school' is appropriate but as a property claim it is an objectionable rejection of the fact of the interdependence of many in the joint enterprise of education. Let us consider, too, some other possibilities of working together. The sharing of school facilities, playing fields or science teachers and laboratories with less fortunate schools would be examples. In an age of tentative ecumenism let us also consider seriously the opportunities offered by ecumenical schools or sixth form colleges and by the sharing of chaplaincies in colleges or universities.

Apart from the relationships between all those concerned with the formal educational processes in the schools and colleges, it is also relevant to consider the relations between these specialised agencies of formal education and other institutions concerned with the continuous and life-long process of education, and especially religious education. Mention has already been made of the need for close links between the school and the family, but it is important also to foster those mutually advantageous relationships with all those parishes which service the schools and with their clergy, diocesan catechetical advisers and so on. It is a deficiency in our system of religious education that we have so far paid so little attention to the conflicts which arise not only between the school and the home but also between the parish and the school. What, for example, is likely to be the impact of an imaginative form-based, participating liturgy on the uncertain adolescent from a parish with a rigid and non-participating liturgy? And what is likely to be the impact on an impressionable child of major differences of interpretation on matters of belief or moral judgments between his religious education teacher and his parish clergy?

There seems little doubt that a considerable process of disaffection with the institutional church, and possibly and more seriously with the whole area of religious belief, occurs for many secondary school children well before they leave school. At least half of the children who have been to Catholic schools cease to go to mass regularly but why this happens we do not know. Here is an area of major importance where research needs to be undertaken. The framework of such research should include not only the schools but also the home and the nature of the local community as well as the parish, including the styles of liturgical worship and teaching by the clergy. Since the peer group is a major factor at this stage it must also be included in such a framework, together with those influences on it, including local youth groups of whatever complexion. It is important to realise that such research would be relevant not only to the schools but also to the renewal of pastoral strategies at all levels.[32]

The implication of education as a continuing process is the involvement of a multiplicity of institutions apart from the school, and especially the family, the parish and lay organisations of all kinds. Thus a short answer to the question 'who is involved in the renewal of Catholic education?' must be 'the whole Catholic community' since this education must be a life-long process and not be confined to the dozen years or so of compulsory schooling in formal organisations staffed by an elite of professional educators.

The Renewal of Structures

If the analysis so far has been correct, the implication of the recognition of education and especially religious education as a continuing process throughout life, is not only the interdependence of teachers, clergy, parents, pupils, students and parishioners in this process but also a need to renew our structures and strategies. I would like here to offer some suggestions based on the conclusion that a plurality of groups with a plurality of needs requires a plurality of structures and strategies. These suggestions are tentatively framed in terms of the various stages throughout the life cycle.

The first stage is that of the pre-school years. It has already been stressed that the findings of educational research over the past decade have directed attention increasingly to the provision of pre-school education in an attempt to reduce persistent social class inequalities of educational opportunity and achievement.[33] I suspect that Catholics have been unduly hesitant about promoting nursery schools or classes because of a dominant belief system which has simplistically assumed that the interests of the child were inevitably best served by a non-working mother looking after the child in the home for all twenty-four hours of every day right up to the compulsory school age. The evidence in no way supports such an extreme position[34] and the Catholic community should become more sensitive to the potential contribution it could make in these formative years. It is certain that some very important religious orientations have their origins in these years and it makes no sense to exclude the influence of professional teachers at this stage.

The second stage is that of compulsory schooling in first, middle and senior schools. It has already been emphasised that there must be more recognition of the interdependence of school, family, parish and youth group. In particular, there is an especial need for sufficient flexibility in parish liturgies to meet the different needs of children in their teens.[35] Two additional suggestions might be offered. In the first place more pupils are likely to remain at school until the age of eighteen or nineteen, when they will legally have adult status and be entitled to vote and marry. This trend must bring home the prime need to educate in the schools for the free exercise of independent judgment by this age. The school must increasingly become a democratic community of jointly participating teachers and pupils. Those pupils whose aspirations for independence are inadequately met by the schools will increasingly seek to complete their full-time education in colleges of further education where appropriate chaplaincy arrangements must be made. The second suggestion is that the most successful religious education provision for adolescents, in terms of its long-term influence, may well be the short, concentrated, residential retreat or conference in one of the increasing number of pastoral centres. This is an area where a diocesan pilot scheme might well be promoted and properly evaluated. One such weekend in a small group for all fifth formers and Catholics in local authority schools or colleges of further education might even have a more lasting effect in terms of real long-term religious commitment than any other form of provision for religious education which we might make.

The third stage is that of further and higher education where there is a need for imaginative, committed and dedicated chaplains. The full story of the innovativeness of university chaplains has yet to be told but there is little doubt that they have been responsible for some of the most meaningful worship in the contemporary church in this country. The structure of provision needs to be extended throughout further education and again the most lasting influences are likely to be grounded in intense religious formation in small groups of peers and in pastoral and retreat centres.

Beyond the early twenties, and the mid-teens for early school leavers, institutionalised religious education for Catholics is practically non-existent. For the one-third who attend Sunday mass there is the weekly liturgy and ten-minute homily and very little else apart from the programmes arranged for example by Newman Association circles. It is in the sphere of adult education that we need to do most thinking and experimenting. Here there is a need to develop plural and flexible strategies involving professional teachers, catechists, special interest groups, the seminaries, and groups at the parish level. The emphasis is likely to be on small groups.[36] Two institutions which could be further developed are the family group praying and studying together[37] and the diocesan pastoral centre.

It is important to realise that adult education provision is concerned with no less than the last three-quarters of the life span of the average Catholic. Any adequate provision must recognise the different needs of those at different stages in the half-century between completing formal education and death. I would tentatively suggest there will be at least five recognisably distinct stages in this pilgrimage: firstly, preparation for marriage; secondly, child-bearing; thirdly, child rearing; fourthly, family disintegration with the exodus of children from the home and death of parents; fifthly, retirement and death of the partner. As mentioned earlier these stages in the family life cycle correspond to parallel stages in the occupational life cycle of both parents. I would suggest that the dominant concerns and needs of people vary according to their place in the family and occupational life cycles, and that any adequate religious education provision must meaningfully address itself to these dominant concerns and needs.

Summary and Conclusion

This chapter has ranged widely and sometimes speculatively around its theme. It has assumed that it is important to consider the implications of the view that education is a continuing process throughout life for Catholics in general and for Catholic teachers in particular. This is important not only because of the pervasiveness of social change but also because religious education must be directed towards man's final end.

Recent research has focused attention on the pre-school years and the dominant influence of the family in determining the outcome of formal education. At the same time there has increasingly been an awareness that change is a major feature of our industrial and social life and that it no longer makes sense to assume that a fixed body of knowledge taught in schools and colleges is appropriate to the needs of adults throughout their full life span. Similarly, for Catholics it is increasingly apparent that post-school religious education based exclusively on the weekly Sunday sermon, for that minority who hears it, is quite inadequate for the needs of a mature, adult christianity appropriate to the demands and problems of a highly complex industrial, urban, secular society. These considerations led to the conclusion that there are in fact a plurality of needs for religious education which must be met by a plurality of approaches. Among these approaches the Catholic school staffed in the main by Catholic teachers is likely to continue to have a central place, in the absence of any revolutionary political change in this country.

Nevertheless, a number of major changes in the Catholic contribution to education and particularly to religious education may be anticipated. Firstly, within the school itself there is likely to be an increasing involvement of assistant teachers, parents and pupils in all decision-making. Secondly, there is likely to be decreasing boundary maintenance between the school and the community. Thirdly, there is likely to be more experimentation, for example, more ecumenical schools, and formally recognised chaplaincies in sixth form colleges and local authority schools. Fourthly, there is likely to be an increasing exploitation of small group strategies of religious education in family groups, at pastoral and conference centres, weekend retreats and so on. Catholic teachers have important skills to contribute to these developing strategies. Fifthly, there is likely to be an increasing use of different approaches to religious education corresponding to the different needs of particular interest groups, especially occupational groups and families at different stages in their life cycles. Sixthly, all these anticipated changes presuppose a parallel renewal in related institutions, notably the parish and diocese.

With these and other changes, renewal in religious education may become more of a reality. As professional educators Catholic teachers have a crucially important role to play in initiating, encouraging, leading and participating in such developments.

Educational Advice in the Church

The first-ever weekend conference[1] of bishops, priests and lay members of the Bishops' Commissions in England and Wales took place in 1975 at Birmingham, to evalute the work of the various commissions and advisory bodies and to discuss the theme 'evangelisation'. While the conference generated a stimulating exchange of views on various pastoral approaches it was extraordinary that there was at no stage a serious appraisal of the prime pastoral strategy of 'a place for every Catholic child in a Catholic school staffed by Catholic teachers trained in Catholic colleges of education'. One would have thought that the recent controversies over plans for secondary school reorganisation, the direct grant schools and the colleges of education might have been sufficiently important to have warranted some consideration. In fact the only public comments on Catholic schools were made by members of the Racial Justice Commission who alleged that in places they were discriminating against black children.[2] Perhaps on this occasion too many people were on their best behaviour; it was more important for the bishops and laity to get to know one another and discover their common interests than to debate controversial issues. Yet the issues of Catholic education are enormously important; the separate system of Catholic schools and colleges consumes a considerable proportion of the available resources of manpower, money and energy of the Catholic community.

This chapter is written in the belief that the present structures of advice and decision-making on educational matters in the church in this country are inadequate and need reform.[3] What are these present structures? First of all there is an Education Commission, one of the dozen bodies set up by the Bishops' Conference following the Vatican Council to advise it on a wide range of matters including ecumenism, international justice and peace, the liturgy, social welfare and so on.[4]

These commissions are directly responsible to the Bishops' Conference and report directly to it, usually through their presidents who are bishops. But the Education Commission differs from all the other commissions. It comprises the Catholic Education Council, the Department for Catholics in Higher Education, the Department for Catechetics and the Catholic Youth Service Council. There is also a Standing Committee 'whose function is to co-ordinate the work of Catholic Education and to promote discussion with the various specialised groups and associations involved'.[5] There is no lay representation on this committee at all, its members being five bishops, including the episcopal chairmen of the four constituent bodies.

Far and away the most powerful of these bodies is the CEC, which is concerned with the whole field of Catholic schools and colleges of education. Since the 1944 Act it has been responsible for the massive expansion of the Catholic system so that the number of Catholic children in maintained Catholic schools has doubled in the past quarter of a century to three-quarters of a million. The government grant available for school building programmes has been raised from 50 per cent to 85 per cent in a number of stages, as a result of quiet diplomacy and the professional competence of the CEC secretariat. The net cost to the Catholic community is difficult to estimate but must be in the region of £50 million. Generations of Catholics will owe those responsible for these achievements a very considerable debt of gratitude.

It might be suggested, however, that the time is ripe, with the recent rapid drop in the birthrate, with several dioceses apparently near bankruptcy in meeting debt repayments, and with raging inflation, for a pause and a reappraisal. Has the Catholic community allowed a means, the building of Catholic schools, to become an end in itself? How effective are these schools in producing committed Catholics? If only half the children who attend Catholic schools continue to practise is this an inevitable consequence of the total social environment and only to be expected? If so, what is the goal of the Catholic school? If not, how can these schools become more effective? What is their relative effectiveness in terms of measurable social, educational and religious attainments, given their inputs of manpower and finance, compared to actual or potential alternative strategies of religious education? What about the post-school years anyway, which are five or six times as long as the average school life-time? Would religious education in small, parish or work-based groups have more lasting influence? Should the Catholic community not shift its focus from the quantitative expansion of school buildings to the qualitative processes of learning in them?[6]

Although a number of individuals may be asking these questions it also seems important that some group systematically attempt to question the long-term strategies of religious education. It seems that the CEC has become preoccupied with the administrative task of servicing and extending the separate school system and the monitoring of actual and proposed legislation, so that there is no single group of people in the church in this country whose remit is to act as a 'think tank' over the whole area of religious education. There is no Education Commission with terms of reference analogous to the Laity Commission and this is a source of no little frustration to members of the latter commission. It is also an astonishing gap in the renewal of the church in this country, especially given the enormous commitment which there has been to the dual system by the Catholic community.

Six years ago the bishops in this country reviewed the work of their provisional commissions[7] and rejected the idea of an Education Commission with a 'think tank' function although they admitted that 'the relationship between those engaged in the work of the constituent councils has been almost nominal'. This rejection can only be legitimated in terms of what the provisional Laity Commission called 'a static notion of the church as a pyramid'[8] and a rule-based ideology which emphasised the importance of starting from first principles and applying them to particular situations. In the area of education the argument seems to run along the following lines:

> Education is primarily concerned with the teaching of immature young by knowledgeable teachers. In the area of Catholic education the recognised teachers are the bishops. Hence all matters relating to education are in a peculiar way reserved to the bishops who have ultimate responsibility for decisions regarding policy. Hence the Education Commission cannot operate in the same way as the Laity Commission and other commissions as a 'think tank'.[9]

Many Catholics would reject these views and claim that a dynamic model of the church which emphasised the full participation of the laity in all areas of the church's life had been given authoritative support at the Vatican Council. They would also prefer a situation-based ideology which stressed the necessity of starting from the real situation, judging it in the light of the scriptures and the church's latest understanding of Christ's teachings, and then working out an appropriate response to the real current situation. This was the view of many lay members of the Laity Commission whom Penny Mansfield and I interviewed in 1974 in connection with a study of change in the Catholic community in England, financed by the Social Science Research Council.[10] These members were frustrated at the largely abortive attempts to arrange fruitful discussions with the Catholic Education Council on the questions of parental involvement and participation in the education of their children and the appointment of school managers and governors.[11] They were also concerned to improve the quality of Catholic schools and colleges of education and to 'reach' those who had left the schools. Younger members made critical remarks about their own recent experiences while older members with children in the schools were alarmed at the growing signs of rejection of the Catholic faith by large numbers of the products of the Catholic schools, including their own children. Given the dominant situation-based ideology of the members, there was frustration that these observable phenomena were not being rigorously judged and evaluated.

Criticism was also levelled at the content of Catholic education in Catholic schools. One member observed that Christ's teaching had primarily been addressed to adults and that it seemed as though once the church had become involved in the education of children, it had forgotten that they grew into adults. Another member commented:

We do a superb job with little children, with infants; the baby Jesus *means* something to babies. I always remember when I was a kiddie, I really loved the baby Jesus. I used to want to go and see him . . . If my spiritual development had carried on at the same rate as my secular development within the school situation, I'd be an entirely different Catholic. In other words, we've got to blast through the baby Jesus into the adolescent Jesus and the man Jesus and what this implies, and I honestly don't think that we've thought this one through.

It was the 'thinking through' process which these national lay leaders and representatives saw as a task of a 'think tank' commission, and their disappointment and frustration at the avoidance of this task by all the official Catholic bodies dealing with educational matters, including the Education Commission, was real, intense and concerned.[12]

At first sight it is surprising that the Catholic Educational Council appears to be unable to pursue this task of offering advice to the Bishops' Conference on all educational matters. It is true that 'it acts as an advisory body to the hierarchy on all matters affecting Catholic Primary and Secondary Schools and Colleges of Education', a task which while clearly bounded is nonetheless enormous in its potential. But the objects of the Council also allow that 'in addition it undertakes such tasks in the field of Catholic education as it may be charged with by the hierarchy'.[13] Of course, it may be that the Bishops' Conference has not charged it with any tasks, but really lively advisory bodies are usually bold in their offering of advice on various issues even in advance of its being commissioned. Why is it that the CEC has been unable to fulfil these 'think tank' functions?

An indication of its work can be gleaned from a cursory glance at its published annual reports. The seventieth report for 1974 lists seventy-one members including four members of the secretariat. Apart from the secretariat there were only twenty-five lay members. The proportion was particularly low among the diocesan representatives; each of the nineteen dioceses is entitled to send two representatives but currently there are only nine lay representatives. Apart from the full council there is an executive committee of twenty-eight members, only five of whom are lay people. Finally, there are forty-two Diocesan Schools Commissioners, only four of whom are lay people, listed in the biennial Catholic Education Handbook; nineteen of these are also members of the executive committee. It appears that the executive committee meets twice yearly and that the quarterly meetings of the Diocesan Schools Commissioners take place earlier on the same days that the full council or executive committee meets. It is not surprising therefore that there is a considerable degree of overlapping of the business, that the meetings of the Council have substantially the appearance of rubber-stamping affairs, that discussion is cursory and there is little in the way of policy making, although there is policy confirmation. Meetings rarely last longer than $1\frac{1}{2}$ to 2 hours and with eighteen or so items on the agenda it is clear that there is practically no scope for serious debate on any controversial issues at these meetings.[14]

In a comparative analysis of the various advisory bodies set up by the Bishops' Conference since the Vatican Council, it was argued that the organisational consequences of these bodies were substantially determined by the nature of their task (whether diffuse or specific) and the nature of the membership (whether representative or expert). With the two variables dichotomised in this way, four types of outcome were indicated. One of these was described as follows:

When a commission or advisory body has a predominantly representative membership but also a task which is very specific, we would suggest that there is a tendency for Michels' Iron Law of Oligarchy[15] to operate and for key administrators to be overwhelmingly influential in the pursuit of an outcome which we would term administration. Because of its largely representative membership and the maintenance or infrequent modification of existing balances of power between the various interests represented on the commission, the outcome is likely to be a relatively cohesive commission and an absence of frustration because of the efficient pursuit by competent administrators of a task, the limits of which they become (often by default) largely responsible for defining.[16]

While theoretically the CEC constitution allows broad scope in the pursuit of the diffuse aim of offering advice to the Bishops' Conference on all educational issues, in practice it has become overwhelmingly concerned in the post-war years with the specific task of extending and maintaining the Catholic system of schools and colleges and of monitoring actual or potential legislation which might have implications for this system. Given this actual, specific task and its largely representative membership, it appears that the CEC is the type of organisation described above as having 'administration' outcomes. It does not appear to be capable, therefore, in its present form, of providing comprehensive educational advice to the bishops. Lest the point is still unclear, let me stress again that this conclusion derives from a comparative analysis of the structures of different advisory types of organisation and not from an analysis of the performance styles of key role players within the organisations.

A number of proposals for reform can be deduced from the same analysis and they concern the modification of the two determining characteristics of such bodies: the definition of the organisational goals and the nature of the membership, particularly in terms of their representative or technical qualifications and sponsorship. The proposals, then, include the clearer definition of the tasks of the CEC, its executive committee, and the Diocesan Schools Commissioners, and the prevention of unnecessary overlap. The membership composition should be reduced to a more workable size and with proportionately a much larger lay representation than at present. It should set up more working parties, with power to co-opt technical experts and consultants, whose task would be the presentation of detailed reports and working papers to the full meetings of the council. These meetings would last at least 24 hours on the pattern adopted by the other bishops' commissions and advisory bodies so that there would be time for extended discussion and debate on controversial issues and the benefits of the informal exchange of ideas.[17]

Such a reformed CEC, with the necessary additions to its staffing, would then be in a better position to perform two existing goals:

(a) the *administration and servicing* of the on-going system of Catholic education in England and Wales at the national level, including the evaluation of standards in the schools and the promotion of improved practice, and

(b) the *monitoring* of relevant or potential legislation or regulations which may have implications for the Catholic education system.

At the national level, however, and probably also at the diocesan level, there is a need to perform two further goals:

(c) *representation* of all the relevant interests in Catholic education, including teachers, parents and the laity generally, managers and governors, religious orders and dioceses; and the different levels of education: schools, further and higher education, youth and those involved in catechetics, and so on; and

(d) *forward planning*, including the identification of problem areas in the light of existing social trends, the reappraisal of educational priorities and goals, the promoting of innovation in the light of changing needs, and so on.

The purpose of representation is the political one of providing a platform for the achievement and articulation of consensus and the co-ordination of different parts of the system in the pursuit of the goals so agreed, and the communication of these to the various constituencies at the grass roots. At the moment lay representation is limited and many structural prerequisites for the mobilisation of the lay constituencies at parish and diocesan levels do not yet exist. Hence there is very little two-way communication with the main clients and source of finance, Catholics at the grass roots level.

It is, however, in the pursuit of the forward planning goals that, I believe, the biggest weakness lies. It seems at present as though the Catholic community in this country tends to respond pragmatically and in an ad hoc way to situations as they arise. The only body specifically in a position to overview the total educational needs of the Catholic community and to consider questions of priorities and the allocation of scarce resources of manpower and finance is the Standing Committee of the Bishops' Education Commission. There is no body specifically charged with the needs of five or fifteen years ahead.

It would seem that forward planning is essentially a technical exercise requiring independent specialists who are not primarily representative of particular interests. It is a task which requires good research and statistical servicing. While a forward planning group might be given specific tasks by the proposed representative body, for example, a new Education Commission, it would be important to insulate it from short-term 'trouble-shooting' demands and to enable it to focus more specifically on the 'signs of the times' and medium- and long-term needs and developments. The proposed Forward Planning Group would present its reports to the representative body which would have the major task of reconciling the various interests involved, achieving a reasonable consensus on the decisions arising from the deliberations, and communicating that consensus to the various constituencies represented. Because organisations pursuing the goals of representation and forward planning appear to require two different types of membership, some means of reconciling the conflicting needs is necessary. There are good reasons for doubting that all four goals can be pursued satisfactorily by a single organisation with a mixed membership. The likelihood is that representative members would be unable to contribute on technical matters while technical members would be frustrated by the political negotiations involved in achieving some measure of consensus between conflicting interests. Since it could be argued that any decisions, no matter how technically sound, eventually have to be accepted by various constituencies (bishops, priests, teachers, parents or laity generally, dioceses, religious orders, etc), it would seem to be desirable for the proposals of any Forward Planning Group to be deliberated upon by a representative national Education Commission.

In summary, therefore, the need for sound educational advice would seem to require

(a) an Education Commission, representative of all relevant interests, especially the laity, with terms of reference covering all aspects of formal education;

(b) an independent Forward Planning Group responsible for the consideration of long-term trends and needs and the distribution of resources for the system as a whole; and

(c) a secretariat responsible for the administration and servicing of the existing system, the monitoring of standards and of legislation.

Such a framework might be expected to improve the quality of advice on formal educational matters offered to the Bishops' Conference, but there remain a number of difficulties. It is by no means clear which technical experts should be appointed, but they should probably include a demographer or social statistician, a sociologist familiar with social trends in British society and the education system, an accountant familiar with the financial resources of the church, and educationalists with recognised expertise at all levels of formal education.

A second objection is that the scope for independent decision-making at the national level in the dual system is limited, and in many cases Catholics can only respond to policy changes determined in the wider society. This was probably the case with comprehensive reorganisation of secondary education and the recent closures of colleges of education. Nevertheless, within these constraints, there is and has been some scope for choice, for example in such matters as the provision of ecumenical schools and sixth-form colleges or in resisting the closure of St Mary's College of Education at Fenham (a decision which might well have serious repercussions for the other colleges).

A third objection is that the Catholic education system is not national in the sense that there is practically no central fund of manpower or financial resources which can be redeployed on the basis of centralised decision-making. Rather, decisions are generally made by individual dioceses and religious orders. While true, this criticism can be overstated and simply provide an excuse for maintaining the status quo and resisting institutional reform. It could also be argued that in fact the major decisions regarding the response by the Catholic community to government proposals in such matters as comprehensive reorganisation of secondary education and college of education closures were taken at national level, even if detailed implementation of these decisions was left to individual dioceses. In practice national trends, such as the decline of the birth rate or the preference for sixth-form studies in separate colleges, or national concerns, for example for social or racial equality of opportunity or for standards of achievement or for curriculum development, require a national response on the part of the Catholic community. I would therefore anticipate a growing bureaucratisation of the Catholic education system in England and Wales in response both to social change in the wider society and to the demands for national pastoral strategies within the Catholic community itself.[18] Given these trends, the need for reformed structures of educational advice is apparent.

PART V

11

Conclusions

This book originated from the observation that, in spite of its size and historical importance in the 'dual system' of state education in England and Wales, there is a conspicuous lack of information about the structure, organisation, legitimating ideologies, goals and achievements of the Catholic system. It aimed, therefore, to identify the essential features of this 'value-oriented education' system,[1] trace its growth in the post-war years, report some research studies of the qualitative achievements of Catholic schooling, discuss the available evidence on the effectiveness of Catholic schools, comment on some policy issues confronting Catholic decision-makers in this transition period at the end of three decades of continuous growth, and urge the case for further research in this neglected area of Catholic education.

It was argued that on both the educational grounds of ensuring that the values of home and school reinforce each other, and the political grounds of the rights of a distinctive minority group in a pluralist society to control the religious socialisation of its younger generations, there was a strong case for such a separate Catholic school system. Criticisms of the divisiveness of such schools and their limited achievements were shown to be without foundation.

Although one child in eleven attends a Roman Catholic school in England and Wales, this number represents only three-fifths of the numbers of baptised children in the appropriate age group. There are signs that this proportion could increase as school numbers fall so that the impact of the declining birth rate over the next decade would be softened. It may well be that this flexibility, together with what many in inner-city areas see as the favoured position of Catholic schools in not taking their proportionate share of immigrant children because of religious differences, and an apparent readiness on the part of Catholic headteachers to increase the proportion of non-Catholic children in their schools, will result in some antagonism from local authorities and teachers who do not have such flexibility in the competition for scarce pupil numbers. In the three years from 1974 to 1977 there was a decline of 54,000 in the five and under-twelve age group in Catholic schools, only partly balanced by an increase of 21,000 in the twelve and over age group.[2] The implications could well be serious for small Catholic secondary schools in the 1980s and lead to further experiments with ecumenical schools and possibly sixth-form colleges.

In the continuous expansion of the Catholic school system from the end of the war until 1974, the dominant concerns of the Catholic community were essentially *quantitative*, ensuring that it obtained at least its fair share of the school building programmes in line not only with the big expansion of the Catholic population (partly as a result of increased immigration, especially of Irish Catholics) but also the needs of the parishes in the new suburbs, housing estates and new towns. These experienced a big influx of Catholics moving out of the traditional inner-city parishes as a result of the various processes of urban redevelopment and upward social mobility due to post-war affluence, full employment and educational achievement. As a consequence of the administrative imperatives of meeting the demand for more Catholic schools and the prevailing ideology which saw the building of Catholic schools as a self-justifying goal, little attention was paid to the *qualitative* outcomes of Catholic schools. Nevertheless, increasingly insistent pleas for a demonstration that the financial burdens of the Catholic school building programmes were worthwhile in terms of the effectiveness of Catholic schools, either in encouraging greater institutional loyalty to Roman Catholicism (ie high weekly mass attendance or 'practice' rates and low 'leakage' rates) or in facilitating, or at least not hindering, the dominant secular goals of educational achievement with its recognised link to occupational status and economic rewards, were heard. With the growing awareness of the implications of the rapid decline in the birth rate and the depressed economic climate of the mid-1970s, there has been a shift of focus and there is now a greater awareness of the need to justify the very large proportion of Catholic resources (both manpower and financial) which are devoted to the Catholic school system.

Part III of this book offers some contributions in this area. Several small-scale studies are reported which enable a number of tentative conclusions to be drawn about the effectiveness of Catholic schools in this country. While it cannot be claimed that the findings of these studies would necessarily hold for Catholic schools generally, there is no reason to suppose that they would not be replicated in broad outline in other parts of the country. Indeed a number of similar studies, not only in this country but also in the United States and Australia, confirm that our findings are very similar to those reported elsewhere. There seem to be reasonable grounds, then, for believing that they have more general validity. In summary, the main conclusions of this section of the book are:

(1) There is evidence that the Catholic school can be an important agency for the religious socialisation of the young. Significant differences between the religious outcomes of Catholic schools and other schools were found, and within the Catholic school itself there were convergences between Catholic and non-Catholic pupils at least in the short term. In Greeley's terms it appears that

> the Catholic experiment in value-oriented education has been a moderate . . . success, and that therefore there is some reason to think that value-oriented education can affect human behaviour and attitudes in matters that are invested with heavy symbolic importance.[3]

(2) Nevertheless, there was evidence of considerable heterodoxy of doctrinal beliefs, ethical values, and religious observances and considerable deviation from the official norms of the institutional church on the part of a large proportion of young Catholics in the Catholic schools studied. While there was evidence of some conformity to church laws and rituals, there appeared to be a general absence of a deep christocentric religious conviction and commitment and a highly critical valuation of the institutional church on the part of a large majority of the Catholic adolescents surveyed.

(3) There was clear evidence of the strong influence of the home background of senior pupils on their reported religious beliefs and practices. Particularly important were parental and familial religious identification and behaviour.

(4) Students in Catholic schools generally considered that there was too much emphasis on the religious goals of the school which they complained were 'rammed down their throats', and that too little attention was paid to personal growth and development goals.

(5) Ritualism, anti-intellectualism and traditionalism do not appear to be inevitable features of a Catholic schooling but characterise only some types of school regime. In the studies reported in this book they were strongest in an independent convent school.

(6) Some two-fifths of fifteen-year-olds attending Catholic schools in the Southwark (mainly South London) diocese were not attending mass at least weekly. There is clear evidence that the process of lapsation from this institutional

requirement is well under way in the early years of secondary schooling. Interviews with fourth formers (fourteen- and fifteen-year-olds) indicated that, especially in non-practising homes, many children were allowed by their parents to choose whether or not to attend Sunday mass from the age of twelve.

(7) There are significant differences between schools in the religious outcomes of their students which cannot be explained by a wide range of ecological variables such as neighbourhood characteristics or the demographic composition of the student body. There are strong grounds for believing that there are processes occurring within schools which are responsible for generating these different outcomes. It is probable that these processes are largely determined by the nature of personal relationships, and especially authority relationships, prevailing within the schools.

(8) Studies of school organisational and religious climates are likely to elucidate the causal patterns in the generation of these processes.

(9) Four themes emerged as important in the interpretation of the religious socialisation of the young Catholic:

1 the struggle of the adolescent for the personal autonomy of the adult;
2 the antagonism or indifference to the 'official' religion of the institutional church[4] and the existence of a more privatised form of religion;
3 the impoverished conceptualisation of God and religion leading to its rejection as 'childish' in adolescence; and
4 in the absence of structural support from family or peer group much lapsation appears to be due to laziness and 'drift' rather than conscious choice and decision.

(10) While there is clear evidence that the religious attitudes and behaviour of university students have changed significantly in the past ten or fifteen years, part of the change is probably a reflection of the changing composition of the Catholic student body with the expansion of educational opportunities over this period. It also appears that much of the change is due to the different beliefs and practices which students bring with them to the university, in line with the evidence of processes of religious disaffection well under way early in the secondary school years.

(11) The findings of the various studies reported for Catholic schools in England are consistent with the findings of other

studies by Greeley in the United States[5] and Flynn in Australia.[6] There may be a common thread in all three Catholic schools systems, such as the common self-protectionism of Irish Catholic immigrants in Anglo-Saxon Protestant-dominated societies.[7]

One of the themes of this book is that 'the party is over' and that the three decades of continuous expansion necessitated by the high birth and/or immigration rates since the 1944 Act and facilitated by the continuous economic expansion and prosperity over this period are now at an end. Not only has the birth rate declined dramatically in the past decade but the country is experiencing its most serious economic recession since the 1930s. Whereas the Catholic community was previously able to support the continuous expansion of its school system and took considerable pride in its *quantitative* achievements, now it is beginning to experience the altogether new phenomenon of stagnation and even some rapid contraction, for example of its colleges of education. Whereas previously the dominant concerns were the administrative ones of expanding and servicing the school system with little concern for its effectiveness, there has recently been a gradual shift of emphasis and increasing interest in the *qualitative* nature of the Catholic schools system, identifying its distinctive features, disseminating knowledge about recognised exemplars, and promoting better practice and higher standards. Whereas previously the Catholic school was recognised not only as an important means to the achievement of religious goals but also as an essential and officially unchallenged goal, now there is an increasing awareness that the Catholic school is only one, even though an important one, of a range of alternative means to the achievement of the efficient religious socialisation of young Catholics. Whereas previously there was practically no concern for the complex inter-relationships between the Catholic school and the parish and the homes of its children, and no systematic study of how these relationships could be manipulated in order to optimise the religious outcomes of the interlocking web of Catholic institutions, now there is a growing awareness of the interdependence of these institutions and that they are important sources of mutual support and reinforcement for each other. This growing openness to other institutions is also reflected in the experimentation in a few places with 'ecumenical' schools.

The dramatic changes necessitated by the ending of the long period of expansion in the post-war years will involve the Catholic community in major policy choices, however much government policies and other external changes constrain the range of choice.

The two chapters in part IV of this book addressed a number of these relevant policy issues. In particular it was argued that there is a need to consider the whole area of continuing education beyond the statutory period of formal education. For Catholics this will mean stressing, far more than in the past, the provision of adult religious education which is sensitive to the different groups of people at different stages in their family or career life cycles. Rather than uncritically assuming that the provision of a sufficiency of places in Catholic schools is an adequate achievement in itself, these must be a recognition of the fact that 'a plurality of needs for a plurality of groups at different stages in the life cycle requires a plurality of approaches and institutional arrangements'. In order to meet these changing demands there must be satisfactory institutional arrangements for the provision of competent advice on educational matters so that decision-makers are fully informed of the various options open to them. To this end a number of suggestions were made for the reform of the Catholic Education Council and for a new and more representative Education Commission with a new and strategically vital forward planning group of technical experts charged with the responsibility of advising the Catholic community on the planning needs for the medium and long-term futures.

With the emergence of the Catholic community from its immigrant, urban ghettos there is also a decline in its defensiveness and introspection and a growing self-confidence. Whereas at one time Catholics would aggressively mobilise themselves to assert and claim their political rights as a minority in a pluralist society which had institutionalised the 'dual' system, there is now a growing awareness that there may be certain social problems on which, because of the particular location of Catholics in society and their web of educational, social and religious institutions, they may be particularly well qualified to speak. At the moment this potential contribution remains latent and largely unrecognised but it is there nonetheless. For example, there are rich possibilities in the knowledge and experience of the Roman Catholic Church in the declining inner-city areas where there exist not only Catholic schools but also the enormously supportive parochial institutions with priests, sisters, parish clubs and welfare organisations, mutual care for the weak, ill, old and young, and the support of various agencies of social control in such tight-knit communities.[8] In practice this potential requires harnessing and frequently may not be realised. Nevertheless, there is a potential here which is increasingly recognised by some of the religious orders of sisters, for example in some inner-city areas in Liverpool. In so far as this potential does exist for constructive social intervention on behalf of deprived groups in our society, it is important that the Catholic community exploit it as its contribution on behalf of the wider society. Given the web of Catholic institutions at the local level and given the recent interest in community schools[9] it is perhaps time that the Catholic community played a more active part in the public arena in contributing to the development of informed policy-making on these matters.

The final theme of this book has been the need for further research about the Catholic education system in England and Wales because it represents, as Greeley has pointed out,[10] a special case of 'value-oriented education'. It is important, therefore, as an example of the potential, as well as the limitations, of school-based systems of socialisation into the norms, values, beliefs and behaviour of specific social groups which have their own structures of mutual support and mechanisms of social control within a pluralistic form of society. As such its successes and failures are of interest to other ethnic or religious minority groups.

Apart from the intrinsic importance of such research, I would also argue that sociological research can contribute to processes of decision-making by the institutional leadership of the Roman Catholic church. Broadly speaking such research can contribute to the formulation of policies and educational strategies in three main ways.[11] Firstly, it can provide better *knowledge* of relevant facts, for example about the distinctive features of Catholic school climates or the religious beliefs and practices of Catholic pupils. It can also map resource mobilisation and utilisation, the extent of religious education provision for Catholics in local authority schools, and help identify areas of special need and attention such as immigrant children, inner-city schools, and so on. Secondly, it can contribute to the *understanding* of the various processes involved, for example, in the religious socialisation of young Catholics in a modern, industrial, urban, mobile, affluent society. In particular there seems to be a need for longitudinal studies of the religious development of young Catholics not only through the secondary school years, but from the formative years in the primary schools as well as follow-up studies during the early years of work, courtship and marriage. There is also a need for more in-depth explorations of religious meanings for young Catholics. It has also been suggested in this book that there is a need for greater understanding of what it is in a school that generates a 'Catholic atmosphere' which is related to high achievements of religious beliefs and commitment. Thirdly, research can contribute to the *evaluation* of alternative educational strategies, for example by comparing the relative effectiveness of Catholic primary and secondary schools, parish-based provision for the religious education of children in local authority schools, institutionalised short-term conferences in non-school environments (eg diocesan pastoral centres) and so on. Given the need to improve the efficiency with which the institutional church pursues its stated goals, some research input which subjects all existing means used in the pursuit of these goals would seem to be essential. The evaluation of experiments with ecumenical schools and sixth-form colleges, or with new curricula and so on, would also be relevant here.

Policy-makers must, however, be realistic about the cost of such research. Because the salaries of teachers in Catholic maintained schools are paid out of public funds, and also because practically all the administration of the Catholic schools system at the diocesan level is undertaken by priests, there is a tendency to underestimate the real costs of Catholic education. Consequently even the salaries of only two research officers are perceived as being prohibitively expensive.[12] The result seems to be that proposals for research into a system which employs over 44,000 teachers of over 900,000 children have been dismissed in the past without due consideration. It is here suggested that such decisions have been short-sighted and premature and have not fully taken into account the advantages which could accrue from the enhanced knowledge, understanding, evaluation and feedback to the Catholic education system which such research could contribute.

In any future agenda for research into Catholic schooling more attention should be paid to the theoretical insights to be found in recent writings in the sociology of education.[13] In the past decade there has been a marked shift away from the study of the class distribution of educational opportunities and academic achievements and towards the content of education and the social organisation of educational knowledge. In Bernstein's classic formulation:

> how a society selects, classifies, distributes, transmits and evaluates the educational knowledge it considers to be public, reflects both the distribution of power and the principles of social control. From this point of view, differences within and change in the organisation, transmission and evaluation of educational knowledge should be a major area of sociological interest.[14]

Ten years ago Bernstein, following Durkheim, analysed the implications of the contemporary shift of emphasis in the principles of social integration from mechanical solidarity (where individuals shared common beliefs and sentiments which produced a detailed regulation of conduct and where repressive punishment served to revivify these shared values and sentiments) to organic solidarity (where individuals were related to each other in a complex inter-dependence of specialised social functions and where the system of social control was concerned more with reconciling conflicting claims than with punishment).[15] Bernstein observed that there were now much less rigid boundaries both within the schools and externally, where they were now more open to neighbourhood and societal influences. Authority relationships within the schools were less formal and generally there was a movement away from the 'purity of categories' to a 'diversity of categories'.[16] There are problems, however, in this shift from a 'closed' school to an 'open' school. In particular, both teachers and pupils are likely to experience a sense of loss of structure, clarity over boundary definition, continuity and order and a general shift from certainty to ambivalence. What makes Bernstein's analysis particularly relevant here, though, is his concluding hypotheses:

> This problem of the relationship between the transmission of belief and social organisation is likely to be acute in large scale 'open' church schools. It may be that the open school with its organic modes of social integration, its personalised forms of social control, the indeterminacy of its belief and moral order (except at the level of very general values) will strengthen the adherence of the pupils to their age group as a major source of belief, relation and identity. Thus, it is possible that, as the open school moves further towards organic solidarity as its major principle of social integration, so the pupils may move further towards the 'closed' society of the age group. Are the educational dropouts of the fifties to be replaced by the moral dropouts of the seventies?[17]

These hypotheses are clearly of particular interest in the case of Catholic schools because they have emphasised the importance of inculcating distinctive religious beliefs and moral values. I am not aware that they have yet been tested in Catholic schools but especially in the light of the evidence of significant levels of religious disaffection on the part of Catholic pupils from Catholic schools,[18] it would seem to be important to do so and explore further the implications of a societal shift in the organisation of schooling.

Related to this theme is Bernstein's important formulation of the concepts of the classification and framing of educational knowledge.[19] He defines classification in terms of the 'degree of boundary maintenance' between educational contents (eg subjects) and framing in terms of 'the strength of the boundary between what may be transmitted and what may not be transmitted, in the pedagogical relationship' between the teacher and the pupil. He then distinguishes two broad types of curriculum, the collection and integrated types, mainly in terms of the strength of classification. He goes on to suggest that the nature of the knowledge code affects the power structure in the school and the nature of authority relationships between teachers and pupils. This leads to an analysis of the problem of order in the school, and the suggestion that, whereas in the case of collection knowledge-codes social order is generally unproblematic and arises out of the prevailing hierarchical authority relationships, in the case of integrated codes, order may be problematic if a number of conditions are not met. In particular it is essential that there is consensus about the integrating idea which must be explicitly formulated, and also that the linkage between this idea and the individual contents is systematically and coherently worked out. In a footnote Bernstein suggests that integrated codes rest upon a closed, explicit ideology and stand a better chance of success where there exist 'strong and effective constraints upon the development of a range of ideologies'. This has clear relevance in Catholic schools where formally there is a coherent religious world-view which is explicitly defined and related to all aspects of the social organisation of the school. Again, however, it would seem that the empirical testing of these hypotheses remains to be carried out.

In a contribution to the study of the social management of knowledge, Davies[20] has stressed the importance of culturally defined goals, values, norms and beliefs and that formal education 'involves both the creation and transmission of values'. In modern industrial society the relationships between values, norms and knowledge is extremely complex. The normative aspects of education depend partly on school rules and partly on rules operating generally in the wider society. In the case of Catholic secondary schools in England:

Some of these rules may derive from Catholic values (presumably those relating to worship) but most do not. The values of the school are presumably Catholic, and therefore different from those operating in the rest of the country but mediated through the school structure which is hardly specifically Catholic. The attempt will be made, however, to legitimise the rules by reference to Catholic values. On the other hand much of the knowledge transmitted will again be independent of Catholic values: curricula, exams, and even teaching syllabuses are set by central secular bodies. But even if the content is intended to be independent of Catholic values it is again mediated through a Catholic system. What does the value system do to the knowledge? In some measure this must be related to the social backgrounds of pupils and also to the ways that Catholic teachers resolve their role-conflicts. If the school is drawn from the children of manual workers, the ascriptive communal aspects of Catholicism may be stressed in preference to the individualistic aspects inherent in the examination selection process. On the other hand if the school is predominantly middle-class, one might expect that knowledge might be stressed as a Catholic value. The basic questions for research are therefore the extent to which the Catholic values are adapted to meet particular social exigencies, the extent to which these values intrude in the transmission of knowledge, and the degree to which the normative situation in the school takes precedence over them both. In all of this, the relationship of the school both to the immediate social catchment area and to the dual pressures of Church hierarchies and state educational authorities must be seen as a set of interactive levels influencing the school's 'behaviour'. It is only within this framework that the 'common sense knowledge of social structures' of both the teachers and the pupils can be studied usefully.[21]

Again, we have a detailed set of hypotheses which remain to be tested systematically.

A major concern of post-war sociology of education has been the extent to which education has provided enhanced opportunities for upward social mobility for working-class children. In recent years Bourdieu[22] has developed important insights into the process for the 'reproduction', that is the transmission and legitimation, of a culture through the education system. He has explored the degree to which the transmission of 'cultural capital' has replaced the inheritance of economic capital as a key determining variable in industrial societies and has developed a set of propositions concerning the relationships between the wielders of 'symbolic violence' and systems of 'cultural arbitraries'. Although Bourdieu is primarily concerned with the reproduction of class relationships by the school system, his work potentially has relevance for the analysis of the extent to which religious belief and value systems (cultural arbitraries) can be reproduced by Catholic teachers in Catholic schools legitimated by Catholic priests (arbitrary powers), and the extent to which the beliefs and values of the homes of the children (cultural capital) are important antecedent variables in the process.

The failure of many attempts to reduce social class inequalities of educational opportunities and the particular problems of developing nations have led in recent years to a number of radical critiques of formal education and its institutions. Hargreaves has usefully distinguished between the 'deschoolers', primarily concerned with educational institutions at the macro- or societal-level and with radical change, and the 'new romantics', who are primarily concerned with education at the micro- or classroom-level and with reform of the nature of teacher-pupil interaction.[23] From the point of view of Catholic educators it is, perhaps, important to be sensitive to the insights which can be gleaned from this mushrooming literature.[24] Hargreaves identifies the key points of the deschoolers, with particular reference to the work of Illich, as a criticism of our excessive reliance on institutions such as schools which are economically unfeasible, highly inefficient and socially divisive; a certification process which is irrelevant to the real needs of employment; and schools which wrongly create the illusion that all learning is the product of teachers who must be professionally qualified. While there is some merit in these criticisms they are highly selective, one-sided and exaggerated, and overlook the massive expansion of educational achievements at least in the industrialised nations. Furthermore, Illich's prescriptions are not very helpful in that they avoid the central issues of power and the political, social, economic and technical feasibility of his solution, which in any case contains the germs of a further process of bureaucratisation of his networks of learning. There is also no good reason to suppose that the access of working-class children to educational facilities will be improved by a process of deschooling which fails to recognise the complexity of the inter-relationships between educational and other social institutions such as the family and the economy.[25] Nevertheless, it is important to note the suggestion made by Illich and improve the access of learners to resources other than those encompassed within the school system. Apart from such insights there is little else of concrete value for the existing Catholic education system.

More useful are the writings of the 'new romantics' such as Holt, Kohl, Postman and Rogers. In his analysis of their writings, Hargreaves identifies four main assumptions about the learning process: that learners are naturally motivated and that lack of interest on the part of pupils is a consequence of the cumulative damage of schooling; that the learner should be free to choose his own curriculum, methods of working and pace of work; that traditional teacher-directed learning promotes defensive strategies of 'getting by' on the part of the pupils; that there needs to be a redefinition of the role of the teacher as a fellow-learner; and that traditional conceptions of teacher authority and control need to be reformulated with a stress on trust, honesty, openness and pupil self-evaluation. Finally, Hargreaves predicts that one consequence of a growing dissensus about education is that conflicts will increase in severity and diversity.[26] In a number of places in this book it has been suggested that major differences of school outcomes might be systematically related to differences in the authority regimes. This hypothesis finds support in the impressionistic writings of the 'new romantics' but it remains to be tested in controlled research.

Among the critics of formal schooling, Freire, who distinguishes between education as domestication and education as liberation,[27] is likely to be of most value to Catholic educators with a post-Vatican Council orientation which is sensitive to the existence of world-wide social injustice and has a concern to socialise its young in freedom to be witnesses in the real world of today to the gospel imperatives of love.[28] For Freire the task of the educator is to enter into dialogue with the pupil about concrete experienced situations. This dialogue is to be 'nourished by love, humility, hope, faith and trust' and in the process culture is created and recreated and the world transformed.[29] A key concept is that of *conscientisation* which

> refers to the process in which men, not as recipients, but as knowing subjects, achieve a deepening awareness both of the socio-cultural reality which shapes their lives and of their capacity to transform that reality[30]

and means

> learning to perceive social, political, and economic contradictions, and to take action against the oppressive elements of reality.[31]

In the dialogical process of action which Freire advocates, *witness* is one of the principal expressions of the cultural and educational character of the transformation of society and consists of the following essential elements:

> *consistency* between words and actions; *boldness* which urges the witness to confront existence as a permanent risk; *radicalisation* . . . leading both the witness and the ones receiving that witness to increasing action; *courage to love* (which, far from being accommodation to an unjust world, is rather the transformation of that world on behalf of the increasing liberation of men); and *faith* in the people, since it is to them that witness is made.[32]

Given the proclaimed goals of the Roman Catholic church to act on behalf of the poor, deprived and oppressed peoples, races and classes of the world,[33] it is an important research question to

describe the extent to which its educational institutions are promoting the sorts of witness to 'this-worldly' concerns of social justice, and to understand more fully the pedagogical processes which generate those forms of witness which express themselves in social action to transform social structures in favour of the less-privileged groups in society.

Finally, reference should be made to a recent study of the beliefs of young people in England today by Martin and Pluck on behalf of the Church of England General Synod Board of Education.[34] This study is particularly interesting not only for its valuable description of the religious beliefs and practices of 100 young people in the age range 13–24 and including appropriate sex, social class and urban/rural quotas, but also for its preliminary theoretical interpretations derived from the sociology of religion of Berger and Luckmann.[35] Martin and Pluck report a massive amount of heterodoxy of beliefs and practices, extensive evidence of inconsistency and incoherence of beliefs, conventionality, and forms of 'common religion' very similar to those reported for Catholics.[36] Young people reported a privatised form of religion, stressed the importance of openness, sincerity and commitment rather than belief but an almost complete absence of an attachment to any of the institutional forms of christianity. The authors report that a moderate hedonism was considered to be a normal and legitimate aim in life. Religious education was perceived as boring and irrelevant, and religion as childish. Young people also commented on the strength of peer group ridicule in constraining attachment to institutional religion, on their laziness with regard to any form of religious affiliation, and frequently legitimated their views in terms of a simplistic scientism. Every one of these characteristics was also reported above for Catholic adolescents, though the intensity of them may have been somewhat muted in the case of the Catholic children who were attending Catholic schools. This study thus provides a useful indication that the types of religious beliefs reported for Catholic adolescents reflected in large measure those for young people in England generally.

What is potentially more important, however, is the attempt by Martin and Pluck to explain these beliefs in the light of the recent work of Berger and Luckmann on 'plausibility structures' of meaning of the social world. They note that as long as people have group support they seem to be able to tolerate apparent inconsistencies. With the observed emphasis on open-mindedness, individuality and the private nature of belief there is a tendency for a sacred, cosmic reference to be found redundant. Martin and Pluck suspect that what they noticed from their interview transcripts was not just the bequest of modernity so much as a non-conformist stress on individual sincerity as superior to institutional conformity. They conclude by suggesting five analytic models of religiosity in terms of the various dimensions indicated by Glock and Stark.[37] The first model stresses ritual behaviour and was found to be relevant in the estimates of other people's religion by Martin and Pluck's respondents. The second model derives from Catholicism and stresses the ideological and intellectual as well as the ritual dimensions. The third model is essentially Protestant and shifts the focus away from external social controls towards individual response. The authors suggest this model can be detected in some aspects of post-Vatican II Catholicism. Fourthly, there is the rational-scientific model and finally a model which deals in the traditions of folk magic. Martin and Pluck conclude their challenging exploratory study by observing that in their sample of young people

> we caught some glimpses of the rituals of family and folk magic, but this we suspect is just the tip of the iceberg. Could it be that the major vehicles of symbolic and ritual expression for the young never really surfaced in our interviews because they are not conventionally associated with religion? We suspect that the three major areas which could throw light on the symbolic life of the young are pop music, football and cars and motorcycles. Any broader study of beliefs and values would need to take them seriously. The secret, private world of the disco, coffee bar and youth club may be more resistant to the erosion of the symbolic dimension than apparently the public world of education and church has been.[38]

What we have here, then, is a plausible theoretical framework for analysing the whole range of beliefs about life, death, existence and purpose and the nature of the universe. There are strong grounds for suspecting that the plausibility structures of Roman Catholics are as varied as those for the young people interviewed by Martin and Pluck. Future research will need to take into account not only institutional religion but also the ways in which Catholic youth construct their plausibility structures and the relationship of these to different family, community, peer group, school and parish supports.

At the end of this review of Catholic education in England since the war, we can conclude by observing that while the achievements in terms of the expansion of the size and scope of the system have been considerable, the challenges in the present transitional period are great. Now that the period of expansion is at an end, a re-

F

appraisal of the system may well lead to a better husbanding of scarce manpower and financial resources in the pursuit of the more efficient religious socialisation of young Catholics. At the same time there is the possibility that a more self-confident and 'open' Roman Catholicism will become conscious that its system of 'value-oriented education' will be highly regarded in a society characterised by value dissensus and normlessness. A large number of research problems remain, but there are rich possibilities for enhanced understanding to be found in recent work in both the sociology of education and the sociology of religion.

Notes

The Bibliography gives full details of books referred to here simply by author and date.

Chapter 1

1 I am grateful for helpful comments on an earlier draft of this chapter from M. Shipman.
2 The size and characteristics of the Catholic system of education in England and Wales will be discussed more fully in chapter 2 of this book.
3 See eg A. C. F. Beales 1963; V. A. McClelland 1973; G. A. Beck (ed) 1950, chs 10–13.
4 J. Murphy 1971, ch 9.
5 See eg A. Tropp 1957.
6 *The Case for Catholic Schools* Catholic Education Council, 2nd edition 1955.
7 See chapter 2. This increase is largely explained by the growth of the Catholic population generally, mainly as a result of Irish and European immigration.
8 J. E. Floud, A. H. Halsey and F. M. Martin 1956, 137.
9 S. Wiseman 1964, 68, 183–5.
10 J. B. Mays 1962; J. B. Mays et al 1968.
11 J. B. Mays 1962, 51; J. B. Mays 1964, 63.
12 J. B. Mays 1964, 67.
13 J. B. Mays 1965, 153.
14 G. R. Grace 1972, 63–4.
15 N. Bennett 1976, 150, 152.
16 C. Lindsey 1970, 43, 72, 118–19.
17 C. Benn and B. Simon 1970, 278–83. The same point is also made by A. Corbett 1968, 792–4.
18 A. Little et al, 1972, 205–12.
19 DES 1972, chs 9–12 and 189.
20 J. W. B. Douglas 1967; Central Advisory Council for Education (England) 1967.
21 For example, Pope Paul has been reported as claiming that the turbulence and dissent in the Roman Catholic church today 'tends to be produced with a new method, that of the sociological survey';

The Times 4 December 1969. Cardinal Heenan was also alarmed by the demand for surveys; *The Tablet* 16 September 1972. For an interesting example of the strong resistance to action research in Catholic schools in Liverpool, see E. Midwinter 1972, 83–4.

22 Pius XI 1929; G. A. Beck 1955. The Vatican Council reaffirmed 'the Church's right freely to establish and to run schools of every kind and at every level'; 'Declaration on Christian Education' in W. H. Abbott (ed) 1966, section 8. More recently a new document, 'The Catholic School', has been issued from the Vatican by the Sacred Congregation for Catholic Education 1977.

23 J. Westergaard and A. Little 1970.

24 Pius XI, op cit, paras 95–8.

25 'Declaration on Christian Education', op cit, paras 7–9.

26 'The Catholic School', op cit.

27 The contribution of research in Catholic education will be considered more fully in chapter 11 of this book.

28 H. O. Evennett 1944, 124–6.

29 G. A. Beck 1955, 5.

30 Ibid, 7.

31 A. C. F. Beales 1950, 407.

32 J. Brothers 1964.

33 See eg L. Bright and S. Clements (eds) 1966, espec chs 8 and 15; P. Jebb (ed) 1968; B. Tucker (ed) 1968; A. E. C. W. Spencer 1971; J. Callaghan and M. Cockett 1975.

34 See eg the concern expressed at the £6·5m debt in the Westminster diocese and estimates of £700,000 interest payments in 1977 alone, mainly as a result of the massive school-building programme initiated in the 1960s. *Catholic Herald* 11 February 1977 and 29 April 1977.

35 See eg R. Dowden 1977. In an outline of some of the results of a survey of *CH* readers, 9341 of whom returned completed questionnaires, it was reported that 'of those responding to the survey 81 per cent think that it is important that a school is Catholic, and 62 per cent think it "very important" '.

36 A. M. Greeley and P. H. Rossi 1966; A. M. Greeley, W. C. McCready and K. McCourt 1976.

37 M. Flynn 1975.

38 See Catholic Information Services 1976.

Chapter 2

1 Anon 1971, 4–5. More recently the annual Catholic contribution has been put at £6 million.

2 Ibid. See also H. O. Evennett, ch 2; A. C. F. Beales 1950, ch XIII; E. Mahoney in G. A. Beck 1955, 15–19.

3 Precise estimates of this growth for the period 1938 to 1960 are difficult to make, partly because of the major changes in school

designation and the confusion between schools and departments and partly because the systematic collection of school statistics was not commenced until the 1950s. Two estimates are, however, indicative of renewed growth in the early post-war years. A. C. F. Beales reports that there were 363,000 children in 1382 (maintained) schools in 1949, op cit, 408; and in *The Case For Catholic Schools* figures indicated a growth in the number of pupils on registers in Catholic Public Day Schools from 377,000 in 1938 to 395,000 in 1950 and 429,000 in 1953, op cit, 78.

4 This figure is based on an estimate of around 50,000 children in convent schools in W. J. Battersby 1950, ch XII, and around 19,000 boys in boarding and grammar schools in 1948 in W. J. Battersby 1950, ch XI. There are no comprehensive estimates in Evennett's review, op cit.

5 DES 1976, table 16.

6 The remainder of this chapter is based largely on statistics published in *Catholic Education: A Handbook* by the Catholic Education Council in 1960–61, 1962–3, 1964–5, 1967, 1969, 1971, 1973 and 1975. I am much indebted to R. F. Cunningham, Secretary, and P. M. Blake, Assistant Secretary, for allowing me access to the latest data for 1976 and 1977, which are to be published in the 1978 edition of the *Handbook*, and for their helpful comments while drafting this chapter. The responsibility for the interpretation of the figures is, of course, entirely my own.

7 See eg H. O. Evennett, op cit; W. J. Battersby, op cit.

8 *Houghton Report* 1974.

9 See eg the assumptions in the terms of reference given to the Public Schools Commission in 1965 which included the objectives 'to create a socially mixed entry . . . and to reduce the divisive influence which they now exert'. Donnison First Report 1968, vii and ch 1. Not all Catholics accepted these criticisms. For example Fr Patrick Barry, Headmaster of Ampleforth, when chairman of the Headmasters' Conference, referred to 'underhand campaigns', 'discriminatory legislation' and 'squalid guerrilla warfare against independence in education'. Norman St John-Stevas, the Catholic Conservative spokesman on education, likened the campaign against the independent schools to the dissolution of the monasteries by Henry VIII. See *The Times* 24 and 25 September 1975. Neither commentator addresses the socially divisive functions of independent education in British society. All the same, it is perhaps important to note that many Catholic independent schools, often run by religious orders originally expelled from France, provided for generally modest fees the only available Catholic education in areas where the Catholic population density was too low to support the provision of maintained schools. Thus the Donnison Report recorded that there was a much higher proportion of free or assisted places taken up by the local authorities in Catholic independent and direct grant schools which take a much higher proportion of their pupils from

the homes of semi-skilled or unskilled workers. See Donnison Second Report 1970, espec paras 112–16, 130, 132, 146 and 336.

10 The Sacred Congregation for Catholic Education 1977, paras 23, 75 and 89.

11 Catholic Education Council for England and Wales *Report for the Year 1975*, 10.

12 DES Press Notice, 27 January 1976, reported in *The Times* 28 January 1976.

13 The proportion of full-time pupils in all direct grant and independent schools in January 1975 was 5·7 per cent. See DES 1976, table 1.

14 Since 1964 the Catholic birth rate has declined more rapidly than that of the population as a whole. By 1975 Catholic baptisms had declined to 52 per cent of the peak figure in 1964 whereas total births had declined only to 69 per cent of the 1964 figure. The proportion of Catholic baptisms, which was approximately 16 per cent of live births in 1964, had declined to under 13 per cent by 1975. While it is possible that Catholic fertility rates had declined more rapidly than those of the population as a whole during this time, a major contributory factor is thought to have been the fall in the scale of immigration from Ireland after the early 1960s. See eg R. F. Cunningham *News Bulletin No 15* Catholic Education Council 1971, 24–5.

15 Catholic Information Services 1976.

16 A. C. F. Beales 1950, 408.

17 In particular, they do not adequately reflect the concentration of the Catholic population in urban areas within largely rural dioceses or the substantial provision of independent education in 1949, which was mainly in the south.

18 These changes will be analysed further in a forthcoming book by M. P. Hornsby-Smith, R. M. Lee and P. A. Reilly who have been carrying out a study, financed by the Social Science Research Council, on 'Tradition and Change in the Roman Catholic Community in England'.

19 See eg G. A. Beck 1950, chs XII and XIII.

20 Catholic Education Handbook 1960–1; Catholic Education Council for England and Wales *Report for the Year 1960*, 39.

21 Catholic Education Council for England and Wales *Report for the Year 1971*, 26–7.

22 Catholic Education Council for England and Wales *Report for the Year 1976*, 16–17. The number of students in this year had declined to 7720, a drop of 15 per cent compared to the previous year.

23 R. F. Cunningham, 'Catholic Birthrate in Recent Years' *News Bulletin No 15*, CEC 1971, 25. The CEC has also recently reported that the number of six-year-old pupils in Catholic schools as a proportion of the relevant baptismal rate was 60·8 per cent in 1970 and 57·5 per cent in 1973. Since then the proportion has increased steadily to 62·9 per cent in 1977.

24 Other factors tending to limit the proportion of baptised children attending Catholic schools include mortality between baptism and compulsory schooling, net emigration, attendance at ESN schools and the unwillingness of parents to send young children to Catholic schools where considerable travelling is involved.

Chapter 3

1 An earlier version of this chapter was published in *The Month* 5(10) October 1972, 298–304.
2 G. A. Beck 1955, 1–15.
3 R. F. Cunningham, Catholic Education Council for England and Wales *News Bulletin No 15* 1971, 25.
4 A. E. C. W. Spencer 1971.
5 See eg P. Jebb (ed) 1968; B. Tucker (ed) 1968.
6 A. M. Greeley and P. H. Rossi 1966.
7 Fr A. Greeley gives a good example of this in his article 1972, 48–53.
8 I share Fr Greeley's predisposition in the article referred to 'that diversity is part of the human condition and . . . that it would be unfortunate . . . if all cultural diversity were eliminated . . . It is only after men belong to something and are confident in that to which they belong that they can interact freely and trustingly with others' op cit, 53. Fr Greeley was referring to ethnic diversity; I would also apply it to religious diversity.
9 R. Rose 1971, 335 ff.
10 It may also be noted that Greeley and Rossi also found no confirmation for the notion that Catholic schools are divisive in American society, op cit, 220.
11 Pius xi 1929. 'All three, school, family and church—must constitute one temple of Christian education', para 93.
12 J. W. B. Douglas 1967, 87.
13 Central Advisory Council for Education (England) 1967; vol 1, 32–6 and vol 2, 181. A summary of relevant research has been given in A. Sharrock 1970.
14 M. Argyle 1958, ch 5.
15 D. Butler and D. Stokes 1971, chs 3 and 4.
16 See eg R. K. Kelsall and H. M. Kelsall 1971, 85; Central Advisory Council for Education (England) 1954; B. Jackson and D. Marsden 1966.
17 W. Kornhauser 1960, chs 3 and 13. Note also the defence of cultural diversity by Fr Greeley, already noted.
18 Ibid, 80.
19 In different ways two recent studies by Catholic sociologists provide evidence for these post-war developments. See J. Hickey 1967, and J. Brothers 1964. Since 1974 the author of this book has been engaged in a study of 'Tradition and Change in the Roman Cath-

olic Community in England' which has been financed by the Social
Science Research Council. Evidence of the post-war social mobility
of Catholics will be presented in a forthcoming book based on this
research.

20 J. Murphy, ch 9.
21 Archbishop G. P. Dwyer explicitly asserts the pluralist case in his
introduction to the Archdiocese of Birmingham *Building Fund
Report, 1952–1970*: 'It is good that we have a dual system. In
England and Wales we believe in a "plural society". With agreement on basic loyalties, we nonetheless see the acceptance of varied
cultural and religious groups as a bulwark of our liberties.'
22 These thoughts exactly parallel the conclusions of the Greeley-
Rossi study in the United States. These authors concluded 'being
for or against a school system with over five million students is
like being for or against the Rocky Mountains: it is great fun but
it does not notably alter the reality' (op cit, 231).
23 See eg A. E. C. W. Spencer 1971, 24. In some dioceses, for example
Westminster in 1977, this was creating considerable problems.
24 G. A. Beck op cit 1955, part 4. See also G. A. Beck *The Cost of
Catholic Schools* 1955.
25 R. F. Cunningham, private communication.
26 Diocese of Arundel and Brighton Newsletter 1971.
27 R. F. Cunningham made the same point in Catholic Education
Council for England and Wales *News Bulletin No 14* 1967, 16.
28 An attempt to provide some relevant data for England will be made
in a national Gallup survey of Roman Catholics to be carried out
in 1977–8 at the University of Surrey.
29 Pius XI op cit.
30 G. A. Beck 1955, 1–2.
31 H. O. Evennett 1944, 125.
32 W. M. Abbott (ed) 1966, 634–55, section 8.
33 Ibid.
34 A. E. C. W. Spencer 1971, 8.
35 Ibid 8–10.
36 A. E. C. W. Spencer 1968, 165–221.
37 M. Lawlor 1965.
38 A. M. Greeley and P. H. Rossi, op cit. See also A. M. Greeley,
W. C. McCready and K. McCourt 1976.
39 See eg E. L. McDill and L. C. Rigsby 1973.
40 A pioneering study has been undertaken by Bro Marcellin Flynn
in Catholic schools in Australia. See M. Flynn 1975.
41 A. E. C. W. Spencer 1968, 207.
42 A. E. C. W. Spencer 1971, 14.
43 Catholic Education Council for England and Wales *News Bulletin
No 14* 1967, 23–9.
44 A. M. Greeley and P. H. Rossi 1966, 225. See also P. H. Rossi and
A. S. Rossi 1957, 168–99; A. M. Greeley 1963; A. L. Rhodes and
C. B. Nam 1970, 253–67.

45 Op cit.
46 A. E. C. W. Spencer 1968, tables 8, 12 and 14.
47 A. M. Greeley and P. H. Rossi 1966, 221–3.
48 A. M. Greeley, W. C. McCready and K. McCourt 1976, 306.
49 U. Bronfenbrenner 1971.
50 J. W. B. Douglas, op cit; The Plowden Report, op cit.
51 J. S. Coleman et al 1966. The major survey covered over 645,000 children of varying ages and in 4000 public (ie state) schools and its findings have provoked a vigorous debate because they challenge much conventional wisdom and because of the crucial policy implications. For an introduction to this debate see Harvard Educational Review 1969; C. Jencks et al 1972.
52 Coleman Report, op cit, 325.
53 E. L. McDill and L. C. Rigsby, op cit, 128.
54 G. A. N. Smith and A. Little 1971; E. L. McDill et al 1969; DES 1972. (See also four additional volumes relating to specific EPA projects).
55 A. E. C. W. Spencer 1968.
56 A. M. Greeley and P. H. Rossi 1966. The authors comment that 'any expectations that formal education will accomplish miracles of conversion or personality change are naïve', 229.
57 Ibid, 219.
58 Ibid, 47, 85–9. The importance of school-community rapport is stressed by McDill and Rigsby who report 'our study indicates that those institutions with substantial school-community rapport have a partnership which is important to high productivity by the schools', op cit, 124.
59 M. N. Berridge 1968: 'the essential period for providing a stable, supportive environment, so that children can form a solid basis of Catholic beliefs, attitudes and values is at the primary stage, particularly from 9 to 12'. However, during adolescence when 'young people need to restructure and test out the reality and validity of what they have learnt' she believes that Catholic secondary schools are in danger of 'producing a false conflict in many of our children by confusing the role of authority in a completely Catholic setting with that of the teaching and sacramental role of the church'. It would be most helpful 'if Catholic teachers could be present in a guiding capacity and not solely as authority figures' (93–4).
60 A. M. Greeley and P. H. Rossi 1966, 181–2.

Chapter 4

1 See eg L. Bright and S. Clements (eds) 1966, especially chs 8 and 15; P. Jebb (ed) 1968; B. Tucker (ed) 1968; A. E. C. W. Spencer 1971; J. Callaghan and M. Cockett (eds) 1975. More recently Shirley Williams, the Secretary of State for Education and Science, speaking as a Roman Catholic, said that many Catholic schools did not equip their pupils for the outside world which was largely

secular. 'I find many of them do not know how to defend their
beliefs,' she said. 'It is no good for children to go out with a rigid
set of values which collapse when they meet the outside world';
Catholic Herald 18 February 1977.

2 Catholic Education Council Report for 1968, 13, 20; 1969, 11, 21;
1970, 11, 30; 1971, 15; 1972, 18, 21.

3 Catholic Education Council Reports for 1971, 15, 19; 1972, 17, 24;
1973, 15, 23; 1974, 13, 20; 1975, 12; 1976, 18.

4 See the following publications of the Catholic Education Council
which have arisen from this work: *Insights Into Catholic Secondary
Education* 1972–3; *Further Insights Into Catholic Secondary Education* 1973–4; *Further Insights Into Catholic Secondary Education* 1975; *The Primary School* 1975; *The Catholic Primary School*
1976.

5 See eg J. A. Hughes 1976; N. K. Denzin 1970.

6 Catholic Education Council Reports for 1972, 24; 1973, 15; 1974,
13.

7 K. F. Nichols (ed) 1974.

8 Ibid, ix; Catholic Education Council Report for 1972, 25.

9 R. K. Merton 1957, ch 1.

10 This section is a revision of an article which first appeared in *The
Tablet* 9 December 1972.

11 Especially in John xxiii 1961 and 1963; and in Paul vi 1967 and
1971.

12 Justice in the World; Statement of Synod of Bishops in Rome, 1971.

13 See eg *Gaudium et Spes* in W. M. Abbott (ed) 1966, 181–316.

14 R. Rose 1971. See also ch 3 in this volume.

15 See ch 2 in this volume.

16 This has been acknowledged by the Racial Justice Commission of
the Bishops' Conference of England and Wales. See *Where Creed
and Colour Matter: A Survey on Black Children and Catholic
Schools* Catholic Information Office 1975.

17 M. Argyle and B. Beit-Hallahmi 1975, 82, 91, 94–7.

18 See eg P. Adams et al 1972; The School of Barbiana 1970; P.
Delooz 1976.

19 M. Lawlor 1965.

20 R. Lambert et al 1968 and 1970; see also R. Lambert 1966 and 1968.

21 This policy of providing convent education for the daughters of
the non-Catholic middle classes might well be resulting in the
'neutralising of apostolic influence' as has recently been suggested
by M. M. Winter 1973, 47. On the other hand, it could be that the
policy is a missionary endeavour of major importance. The important point to note is that Fr Winter's hypothesis is one which could
be tested by appropriately designed empirical research. A comparison of the responses of the Catholic and non-Catholic pupils in the
convent school of this present study is clearly pertinent and has
policy implications for the many independent convent schools in
England and the women religious who teach in them.

22 These details were first reported in M. P. Hornsby-Smith 1974. A more complete discussion is given in M. P. Hornsby-Smith and A. H. Thomas 1973.

23 These details were first published in M. Hornsby-Smith and M. Petit June 1975, 261–72.

24 R. K. Merton and P. L. Kendall 1956.

25 M. P. Hornsby-Smith April/June 1976, 2–4. See also ch 6 in this volume.

26 M. P. Hornsby-Smith and J. M. Fitzpatrick 1976, 2–5. See also ch 6 in this volume.

27 R. Lambert et al 1968, 28–9.

28 R. Lambert et al 1970, 284–5 and 1968, 60, 89–91. One item from Lambert's list, on the abolition of beating, was excluded as being irrelevant in the case of girls.

29 R. Lambert et al 1968.

30 On academic achievement see eg J. W. Douglas 1967, 87; Central Advisory Council for Education (England) 1967, vol 1, 32–6 and vol 2, 181; J. S. Coleman et al 1966, 325. On religious outcomes see eg A. M. Greeley and P. H. Rossi 1966, 47, 85–9. A fuller discussion of these sources is given in ch 3 of this volume.

31 A. Etzioni 1961.

32 See eg W. Waller 1932; P. W. Jackson 1968; School of Barbiana, 1970; D. H. Hargreaves 1972, espec ch 6.

33 J. H. Westergaard and H. Resler 1975.

34 This is a major concern of the book by M. M. Winter, op cit. There is a further discussion of the implications of continuing education in ch 9 of this volume.

Chapter 5

1 This section was first reported in M. P. Hornsby-Smith, A. H. Thomas and M. Petit 1977, 2–6.

2 R. Lambert 1966 and 1968; R. Lambert et al 1968 and 1970.

3 C. Lindsay 1970.

4 R. K. Merton 1957, chs 4 and 5.

5 R. Lambert et al 1970, 121 ff, 294–6.

6 This section was first reported in M. P. Hornsby-Smith and M. Petit June 1975, 261–72.

7 C. Y. Glock and R. Stark 1965; R. Stark and C. Y. Glock 1968.

8 S. Labovitz 1967, 151–60; and 1970, 515–24.

9 A. McKennell 1970, 227–45.

10 See eg M. Seeman 1959, 783–91; R. Blauner 1964.

11 This section was first reported in M. P. Hornsby-Smith and M. Petit March/April 1975, 2–6.

12 For a simple introduction to Factor Analysis see D. Child 1970. Details of the SPSS computer programs are given in N. H. Nie et al 1970.

13 A. McKennell, op cit.
14 The results of the study of 'Tradition and Change in the Roman Catholic Community in England' which has been financed by two grants from the Social Science Research Council and carried out at the University of Surrey, will be published in a forthcoming book.
15 M. Lawlor 1965.

Chapter 6

1 The Lawrence Report 1974, 72; R. Brech 1972, 35; Catholic Information Services 1973, 9.
2 R. F. Cunningham, Catholic Education Council for England and Wales News Bulletin No 15, 1971, 25.
3 This paragraph first appeared in M. P. Hornsby-Smith May/June 1975, 5–10.
4 This section was first reported in M. P. Hornsby-Smith April/June 1976, 2–4.
5 This section was first reported in op cit May/June 1975.
6 C. Y. Glock and R. Stark 1965, 91, 93; R. Stark and C. Y. Glock 1968, 28–9, 33.
7 R. Lambert et al 1968 and 1970; R. Lambert 1966 and 1968; see also ch 5 in this volume.
8 R. Lambert et al 1970, 121 ff, 294–6. See also ch 5 in this volume.
9 R. K. Merton 1957, chs 4 and 5.
10 Collapsing the retreatism, ritualism and rebellion modes, chi square $= 8.44$, 2 df, $p = 0.015$.
11 A number of spelling corrections and minor punctuation or grammatical adjustments have been made in the illustrative quotations.
12 All three comprehensive schools had recently been created by the amalgamation and extension of formerly single sex grammar or independent schools. This appeared to have given rise to considerable transitional problems and some resentment, especially in the case of two of the schools. The transition appeared to have given rise to fewer problems in the case of the school run by a religious order.
13 According to The Church 2000, in nearly two-thirds of marriages solemnised in the church in 1970, one partner was not a Catholic; Catholic Information Services 1973, 9.
14 chi square $= 6.32$, 1 df, $p < 0.02$. It should be noted that this finding conflicts with other evidence which suggests that lapsation rates are higher among working class Catholics. This is discussed further in M. P. Hornsby-Smith, R. M. Lee and P. A. Reilly 1977.
15 This section was first reported in M. P. Hornsby-Smith and J. M. Fitzpatrick July/Sept 1976, 2–5.
16 These views were also put by C. D. P. McDonald 1976, 2–3.
17 D. Matza 1964.

18 This section first appeared in M. P. Hornsby-Smith, R. M. Lee and P. A. Reilly op cit 1977.

Chapter 7

1 This chapter is a slightly revised version of an article which first appeared in *The Month*, 9 (6) June 1976, 191–8, and which was based on a talk given at a Conference of Chaplains, La Sainte Union College of Education, 17 December 1975. I am indebted to Bishop Mullins, Chairman of the Department of Higher Education of the Education Commission of the Bishops' Conference, for giving me access to previously unpublished data and for his very helpful comments on an earlier draft of this paper.

2 Committee on Higher Education 1963.

3 J. Brothers 1964.

4 G. A. Beck 1958, 101–7.

5 A. C. F. Beales 1959, 11–16.

6 M. P. Fogarty 1960, 100–5.

7 See eg M. F. D. Young (ed) 1971.

8 My study of lay members of the Bishops' Commissions and of religion in a commuter parish provides some evidence. One-third of the lay members of the Bishops' Commissions in 1974 appeared to belong to the 'new middle class'.

9 Department of Higher Education 1974. I am grateful to Bishop Mullins for permission to quote aggregate figures from this report.

10 It was reported that the annual collection for the National Catholic Fund would have to provide £140,000 in 1975; cf Catholic Information Office *Briefing*, 5(11) 12 April 1975, 10.

11 According to R. Cunningham, Secretary CEC: cf Catholic Information Office, Official Report of Sixth National Conference of Priests, 1–5 September 1975, 26.

12 M. Weber 1947, 328–41.

13 DFS *Education Statistics for the United Kingdom 1973*, HMSO 1975. In the absence of comprehensive demographic data for Catholic students in higher education it has been assumed that the averages for the national student population hold.

14 In chapters 4 to 6. Relevant findings were also given in my article 'Catholic Adolescents' September 1975, 918–21.

15 See also J. J. Gaine 1975, 1221–2.

16 D. Wright and E. Cox 1971, 332–41.

17 M. Schofield 1968.

18 Early reviews of the religious beliefs and practices of university students were given by P. Black 1960, 105–25; J. B. Brothers 1964, 71–82.

19 G. W. Pilkington et al, nd.

20 D. Wright and E. Cox 1973, quoted in ref 19.

21 Bishop D. J. Mullins, private communication.

22　R. E. S. Tanner, nd.

23　I am grateful to Fr F. Collins for permission to quote these results.

24　M. Weber 1966, 46 (first published in 1922).

25　See eg *Lumen Gentium* in W. M. Abbott (ed) 1966, 14–96.

26　E. Durkheim 1915 (first published 1912). The implications of the breakdown of barriers between the 'sacred' and the 'profane' in the contemporary church remain to be explored. One key example concerns the relationship between the priest and the layman (eg the chaplain and the student). The sociological implications of an incarnational theology also remain to be explored in the light of the Durkheimian insights.

27　E. Durkheim 1964 (first published 1893).

28　B. Bernstein 1975, ch 3.

29　L. J. Suenens 1975, 51–2.

30　See, for example, recent issues of CSC *News*, the newsletter of the Catholic Student Council.

Chapter 8

1　A. M. Greeley and P. H. Rossi 1966.

2　Ibid.

3　Ibid, 1–2.

4　Ibid, 1.

5　Ibid, 270.

6　See chapter 2 of this book.

7　A. M. Greeley and P. H. Rossi, op cit 9–15.

8　Ibid, appendices I and II.

9　Ibid, chapter 8.

10　Ibid, 211–14.

11　Ibid, especially chapter 4.

12　Ibid, 219.

13　Ibid, 222–3.

14　Ibid, 223.

15　Ibid, 105.

16　Ibid, 227.

17　Ibid, 224.

18　A. M. Greeley, W. C. McCready and K. McCourt 1976, appendix I.

19　See eg the reviews of the book by C. L. Johnston et al 1976, 806–8; and M. A. Neal, summer 1977, 181–4.

20　A. M. Greeley et al, 13.

21　Ibid, chapter 6 and appendix V.

22　Ibid, chapter 6. In 1974 the path coefficients (beta) between spouse's church attendance and Catholic activism, church's right to teach, doctrinal orthodoxy, financial contribution, sacramental reception, mass attendance, communion and confession as dependent variables were greater than those with any of the other religious behaviour model variables. Sex (female) had the largest coefficient with private

prayer and age with sexual orthodoxy and was as strong as spouse's church attendance with financial contribution (ibid, 169).
23 Ibid, 310.
24 Ibid, 306–7.
25 Ibid, 285.
26 Ibid, 290–1.
27 Ibid, 293.
28 Ibid, 301.
29 Ibid, 211.
30 I am carrying out the analysis of this survey with Raymond M. Lee, a Research Fellow in the Department of Sociology, University of Surrey.
31 M. Flynn 1975.
32 Ibid, 6–7, 284. It is interesting to note that whereas in 1950 only 5 per cent of the staff were lay teachers, this proportion had risen to two-thirds in 1974 and was 54 per cent in the research schools; ibid, 91–2.
33 E. L. McDill and L. C. Rigsby 1973.
34 For some studies indicating the existence of major differences between schools see eg M. J. Power et al 1967; D. Reynolds 1976, 124–37; M. P. Hornsby-Smith April/June 1976, 2–4.
35 M. Flynn 1975, 2–3.
36 Ibid, 39–43.
37 Ibid, 44–46.
38 See chapter 5 in this book.
39 M. Flynn 1975, 115–16.
40 Ibid, chapter 8; see also chapter 5 of this book.
41 M. Flynn 1975, 113, 136.
42 Ibid, 119–20.
43 For example, A. W. Halpin and D. B. Croft 1963.
44 M. Flynn, op cit, 133–5.
45 Ibid, 137–42; p less than 0·001.
46 H. Barakat 1969, 1–10.
47 M. Flynn, op cit, 123–5, 135–6.
48 Ibid, 142–7.
49 See chapter 6 of this book.
50 M. Flynn, p iv of appendix A in his covering letter to the students.
51 Ibid, 185.
52 Ibid, 186.
53 See eg *Gravissimum Educationis*, in W. M. Abbott (ed) 1966, 634–55, especially sections 5 and 8; and The Sacred Congregation for Catholic Education 1977. See also chapter 1 of this book.
54 A similar point was made by Greeley and Rossi, op cit, 7.
55 R. K. Merton 1967, 199.
56 A. M. Greeley et al, op cit, 10; M. Flynn, op cit, 6–7. A useful and critical review of some of the criticisms of Catholic schools in England and Wales up to the early 1970s was given in A. E. C. W. Spencer 1971.

Chapter 9

1 This chapter is an amended version of a paper read at the annual Study Conference of the Catholic Teachers' Federation at Madeley College of Education on 2 January 1974, and subsequently published in *Catholic Education Today*, *8*, 1974 (2) Mar/Apr, 4–6, (3) May/June 18–21, and (4) Jul/Aug 10–13.

2 E. Durkheim 1956, 71.

3 See for example R. A. Nisbet 1970, 141–50, 292–300.

4 See for example M. Albrow 1970, chapters 2 and 3.

5 H. H. Gerth and C. W. Mills 1948, 243.

6 N. J. Smelser 1959, 2.

7 R. K. Merton 1957, 199.

8 H. O. Evennett 1944, 125.

9 J. W. B. Douglas 1967, 87.

10 Central Advisory Council for Education (England) 1967; vol 1, 32–36 and vol 2, 181.

11 B. Bernstein 1971–1975.

12 For a review of the literature see, for example, J. Westergaard and A. Little 1970, and R. K. Kelsall and H. M. Kelsall 1971.

13 A. H. Halsey (ed) 1972, chapters 6–8. Note, however, B. Bernstein 1971, ch 10.

14 See, for example, Department of Education and Science 1968; Council for Scientific Policy 1968; D. J. Price 1963; Committee on Higher Education 1963, paras 258–72.

15 See for example Catholic Information Services 1973; M. Winter 1973; Catholic Information Services 1976; The Lawrence Report 1974.

16 H. O. Evennett, op cit; G. A. Beck (ed) 1950, especially chapters 10–13; A. C. F. Beales 1963; J. Murphy 1971; V. A. McClelland 1973; M. Gaine 1968; G. A. Beck 1955.

17 The effectiveness of this process has increasingly been challenged by Catholics themselves; see for example P. Jebb, op cit, B. Tucker (ed) 1968; A. E. C. W. Spencer 1971. My own view is that all the published research shows a positive, if slight, association between Catholic schools and the achievement of religious goals, but that further research is urgently needed in order to understand more clearly the processes which take place in schools and to ensure more effective strategies of religious socialisation. I developed this in chapter 3 in this volume.

18 A. Tropp 1957.

19 J. Murphy, op cit, chapter 9.

20 See chapter 2 in this volume for details.

21 For estimates of the financial contribution by Catholics since the war, see chapter 3 in this volume.

22 For recent statements of the aims of Catholic education see for example F. Bottomley 1973, 227–34; K. Nichols 1972, 4–7.

23 See part III of this book.

24 J. Brothers 1964.
25 R. Brech 1972. The Social Science Research Council has recently financed a study of 'Tradition and Change in the Roman Catholic Community in England' at the University of Surrey. In a forthcoming book on this research my colleagues and I will report on the social mobility of Catholics in the post-war years.
26 J. W. B. Douglas, op cit; The Plowden Report, op cit.
27 For example, the Advisory Centre for Education and the Confederation for the Advancement of State Education.
28 See for example B. Jackson and D. Marsden 1966.
29 See for example A. H. Halsey, op cit, chapters 9–12.
30 A. H. Halsey, op cit, 189.
31 The French sociologist, Emile Durkheim, was particularly concerned to explore the implications of this process and the changing nature of social cohesion from mechanical to organic solidarity; see E. Durkheim 1964. The relevance of this analysis for the schools has recently been considered in B. Bernstein 1975, ch 3, and for management structures in industrial organisations in T. Burns and G. M. Stalker 1966. It remains to explore the implications of social change for the nature of social cohesion in the Catholic community in England. It might be hypothesised that it is increasingly shifting to one of organic solidarity based on the recognition of the interdependence of clergy and laity, and of teachers, clergy, parents and pupils.
32 See for example *The Church 2000* op cit; M. Winter, op cit; *A Time for Building*, op cit.
33 A. H. Halsey, op cit, chapters 6–8.
34 See for example S. Yudkin and A. Holme 1963; R. Davie et al 1972, 42–47.
35 M. P. Hornsby-Smith Aug 1975, 518–24.
36 M. Winter, op cit, forcefully argues the case for pastoral strategies based on small groups. This chapter has generally accepted this view but some caution is necessary. A strategy successful in Latin American circumstances may not necessarily be appropriate in the complex urban industrial societies.
37 Some suggestive material for such groups is now available. See for example O. and A. Pratt 1967 and 1973; Sister Monica Mary 1972.

Chapter 10

1 This chapter originated with my article 'Educational Advice' which appeared in *The Tablet*, 25 October 1975, 1027–29. At the time it aroused considerable antagonism partly because it was thought improper for me to be critical of the Catholic Education Council while a member of that body, and partly because it was considered that I was critical of individuals. Nevertheless, I repeat and

attempt to develop my argument here because it is still a matter of importance for the Catholic community in England and Wales and because my concern is with structures of advice, not with individuals. I believe a close reading of the text will confirm this. It is up to others to judge the propriety of publishing this chapter while remaining a member of the CEC. My view is that it is part of my potential contribution as a sociologist to write and promote discussion of important policy matters. Providing the focus is on structures and policies and not individuals it can contribute to the renewal of structures in the contemporary Roman Catholic church. Furthermore, all the material used in the writing of this chapter can be found in published reports.

2 National Catholic Commission for Racial Justice *Where Creed and Colour Matter: A Survey on Black Children and Catholic Schools* Catholic Information Office 1975.

3 It should be pointed out that both the working procedures of the Catholic Education Council and the structure of the Bishops' Education Commission are currently under review.

4 Report of a Review Committee of the Bishops' Conference of England and Wales 1971.

5 *The Catholic Directory of England and Wales* 1977, 22.

6 A cursory glance at the recent annual reports of the CEC suggests that it has in fact done so to some extent.

7 Ref 4.

8 *Report to the Laity* 1971, 48.

9 I do not intend to imply by this that the bishops on the Education Commission do not consult widely before making decisions. This is certainly not the case. But it remains true that there is no institutional base for informed and representative consultation, debate and negotiation about policies across the whole educational spectrum 'from the cradle to the grave' and embracing a concern for the complex interrelationships between home, school, parish and the wider society. It also remains true that the exclusion of lay participation from the main level of advice and consultation for the Bishops' Conference, the level at which policy recommendations are made, priorities determined and interests reconciled, is unique among the bishops' commissions. This is a social fact which requires some explanation.

10 M. P. Hornsby-Smith and Penny Mansfield, March 1975, 84–9.

11 The CEC version of these negotiations can be found in the *Annual Reports* for 1969, 23; 1971, 14–23; 1972, 12.

12 M. P. Hornsby-Smith and Penny Mansfield 1974.

13 *Catholic Education: A Handbook* 1975, 8.

14 The CEC has a working party considering these matters and plans longer meetings to promote more intensive discussion of major policy issues.

15 R. Michels 1962.

16 'Overview of the Church Commissions', op cit.

17 'Educational Advice', op cit. Several of these proposals are being or are soon to be adopted.
18 Catholic Information Office 1976. I have discussed some implications of national pastoral strategies in M. P. Hornsby-Smith, August 1977, 742–3, and Autumn 1977, 13–16.

Chapter 11

1 The phrase derives from the two studies of American Catholic schools by A. M. Greeley and P. H. Rossi 1966, and A. M. Greeley, W. C. McCready and K. McCourt 1976.
2 *Catholic Education: A Handbook*, Catholic Education Council 1975, tables 4.1 and 4.2, and CEC preliminary tabulations for 1977.
3 A. M. Greeley and P. H. Rossi, op cit, 222–3.
4 See also M. P. Hornsby-Smith, R. M. Lee and P. A. Reilly October 1977; and also their booklet 1977.
5 A. M. Greeley and P. H. Rossi, op cit; A. M. Greeley et al, op cit.
6 M. Flynn 1975.
7 I am grateful to Martin Redfern for this suggestion.
8 I am grateful to Norbert Winstanley for this observation.
9 See eg Department of Education and Science 1972, especially chapters 9–12 and 189–90.
10 A. M. Greeley and P. H. Rossi, op cit; A. M. Greeley et al, op cit.
11 M. P. Hornsby-Smith and G. Dann August 1975, 340–9.
12 For a wider discussion of the weaknesses of the manpower and financial accounting procedures in the Roman Catholic Church in England and Wales, see M. P. Hornsby-Smith August 1977, 742–3; and Autumn 1977, 13–16.
13 See especially M. F. D. Young (ed) 1971; R. Brown (ed) 1973; J. Karabel and A. H. Halsey (eds) 1977.
14 B. Bernstein 1975, ch 5, 85–115 (also chapter 2 in M. F. D. Young, op cit, and chapter 13 in R. Brown, op cit).
15 B. Bernstein 1975, ch 3, 67–75. The concepts of mechanical and organic solidarity derive from E. Durkheim 1964; they have been employed in a study of organisational change by T. Burns and G. M. Stalker 1966.
16 Bernstein attributes this distinction to M. Douglas 1970.
17 B. Bernstein 1975, ch 3, 74–5.
18 See chapter 6 in this book.
19 B. Bernstein 1975, ch 5.
20 I. Davies 1971, 267–88.
21 Ibid, 279–80.
22 P. Bourdieu and J-C Passeron 1977. See also P. Bourdieu 1973, 71–112, and J. Karabel and A. H. Halsey, op cit, 487–511.
23 D. H. Hargreaves 1974, 186–210.
24 See for example I. D. Illich 1973; E. Reimer 1971; P. Goodman 1971; J. Holt 1964; P. Freire 1972 [1] and [2]; P. Freire 1976; I. Lister 1974.

25 D. H. Hargreaves, op cit.
26 Ibid.
27 P. Freire 1974.
28 See eg Paul vi 1967 and 1971.
29 P. Freire 1974 [2] 45–7, and 1972 [2] 60–6.
30 P. Freire 1972 [1], footnote 51.
31 P. Freire 1972 [2], footnote 15.
32 Ibid, 143–4. Also relevant here is the new liberation theology; see in particular: G. Gutierrez 1974; J. L. Segundo 1977; M. A. Neal 1977
33 Paul vi, op cit. See also W. M. Abbott (ed) 1966, 181–316; John xxiii 1961 and 1963; and *Justice in the World*, Third International Synod of Bishops 1972.
34 B. Martin and R. Pluck 1977.
35 See P. L. Berger and T. Luckmann 1971; P. L. Berger 1973; T. Luckmann 1970.
36 B. Martin and R. Pluck, op cit. For Catholic secondary school pupils see chs 5 and 6 in this book. For analyses of the religious beliefs and practices of adult Catholics based on the interviews with random samples of Catholics in four parishes in London and Preston, see M. P. Hornsby-Smith, R. M. Lee and P. A. Reilly 1977; October 1977; and December 1977, 406–9.
37 C. Y. Glock and R. Stark 1965; R. Stark and C. Y. Glock 1968.
38 B. Martin and R. Pluck, op cit, 59.

Tables

Table 2.1: Number of Catholic Schools by Type of School, 1960–1977

TYPE OF SCHOOL	1960	1964	1968	1972	1974	1977
Maintained All Age	478	193	22	—	—	—
Total Maintained Primary	1704	1776	1894	2039	2111	2148
Maintained Modern	276	363	366	272	208	151
Maintained Grammar and Technical	67	62	69	56	52	39
Maintained Comprehensive and Bilateral	12	21	56	157	218	280
Total Maintained Secondary	357	465	535	531	528	530
Total Maintained	2061	2241	2429	2570	2639	2678
Direct Grant (Grammar)	42	56	56	56	56	43
Independent Efficient	na	328	314	287	282	244
Total Independent	590	574	497	385	347	311
Total all Schools	2748	2929	3042	3072	3094	3071

(SOURCE: Catholic Education Handbooks.)

Table 2.2:
Growth of Catholic Maintained Comprehensive School Provision, 1964–77

ITEM	1964	1968	1972	1974	1977
Total Secondary Schools	465	535	531	528	530
Total Comprehensive Schools	11	56	171	234	317
Total Pupils at Secondary Schools × 1,000	186	227	266	313	342
Total Pupils at Comprehensive Schools × 1,000	9	35	107	161	235
% Pupils at Comprehensive Schools	4·6	15·3	40·4	51·3	68·8

(SOURCE: Catholic Education Council.)

Note: Comprehensive Schools including Secondary Middle, Comprehensive and Sixth Form Colleges.

Table 2.3:
Number of Pupils in Catholic Schools by Type of School, 1960–1977
(in thousands)

TYPE OF SCHOOL	1960	1964	1968	1972	1974	1977
Maintained all Age	127	49	5	—	—	—
Total Maintained Primary	402	434	476	498	500	461
Maintained Modern	97	138	135	108	102	70
Maintained Grammar and Technical	31	30	34	32	30	23
Maintained Comprehensive and Bilateral	7	15	35	102	155	222
Total Maintained Secondary	136	186	227	266	313	342
Total Maintained	538	621	703	764	813	803
Direct Grant (Grammar)	25	36	38	38	39	30
Independent Efficient	na	83	81	76	78	72
Total Independent	115	117	107	91	87	83
Total all Schools	684	779	854	899	944	919

(SOURCE: Catholic Education Handbooks.)

Table 2.4: Age Distribution of Pupils in Catholic Schools, 1964–1977

AGE GROUP	NUMBERS (× 1,000)			% CHANGE	
	1964	1974	1977	1964–74	1974–77
Under 5	20·1	36·4	43·6	+81·1	+19·8
5 and under 8	225·5	225·7	203·6	+0·1	−9·8
8 and under 12	277·1	334·2	302·2	+20·6	−9·6
12 and under 16	227·8	288·9	308·7	+26·8	+6·9
16 and over	28·4	59·2	60·6	+108·5	+2·4
TOTAL	778·9	944·4	918·7	+21·2	−2·7

(SOURCE: Catholic Education Handbooks.)

Table 2.5:
Non-Catholic Pupils in Catholic Schools by Sex and Type of School,
1960–1977 (%)

TYPE OF SCHOOL	1960		1968		1977	
	BOYS	GIRLS	BOYS	GIRLS	BOYS	GIRLS
Maintained Primary	0·7	0·9	0·7	0·8	2·6	2·7
Maintained Secondary	0·5	2·8	0·5	1·4	1·8	2·9
All Maintained	0·7	1·4	0·7	1·0	2·3	2·8
Direct Grant (Grammar)	1·9	15·8	1·9	8·6	4·7	7·8
Independent Efficient	na	na	13·2	39·5	21·9	45·4
All Independent	18·7	44·7	16·7	41·3	24·5	46·7
All Special and Approved	9·9	20·4	7·7	17·7	33·9	38·7
All Schools	2·8	11·6	2·2	8·0	3·9	8·1

(SOURCE: Catholic Education Handbooks.)

Table 2.6:

Analysis of Teachers in Catholic Schools by Religious Status, Academic Status, Sex and Type of School, 1964–1976

TYPE OF SCHOOL	YEAR	ALL TEACHERS									
		Secular Clergy	Men Religious	Women Religious	Catholic Laymen	Catholic Laywomen	Non-Catholic Men	Non-Catholic Women	All Teachers	% non-Catholic	% Graduates
Total Maintained Primary	1964	—	3	1551	2719	8800	118	461	13652	4·2	4·2
	1976	—	2	1290	3750	12220	240	1382	18884	8·6	7·1
Total Maintained Secondary	1964	35	147	535	3920	2876	636	590	8739	14·0	31·2
	1976	39	157	703	6176	4956	3288	3093	18412	34·7	40·9
Total Maintained	1964	35	150	2086	6639	11676	754	1051	22391	8·1	14·7
	1976	39	159	1993	9926	17176	3528	4475	37296	21·5	23·8
Direct Grant (Grammar)	1964	21	143	220	495	695	65	183	1822	13·6	68·3
	1976	10	109	151	588	614	226	364	2062	28·6	71·6
Independent Efficient	1964	91	505	1425	539	1265	138	489	4452	14·1	44·2
	1976	56	295	703	543	996	398	804	3795	31·7	47·7
Total Independent	1964	146	676	2211	662	1636	162	635	6128	13·0	38·0
	1976	61	336	884	578	1163	417	916	4355	30·6	44·1
Total all Schools	1964	202	1014	4641	7921	14094	999	1880	30751	9·4	22·5
	1976	110	618	3085	11208	19030	4209	5799	44059	22·7	27·9

(SOURCE: Catholic Education Handbooks.)

Table 2.7:
Regional Distribution of Catholic Maintained Schools, 1949–1976

		1949[1]				1976[2]			
		Schools		Pupils × 1,000		Schools		Pupils × 1,000	
TYPE OF DIOCESE[1]		N	%	N	%	N	%	N	%
A	All but wholly rural	207	15·0	26·5	7·3	366	13·6	98·9	12·3
B	All but wholly maintained	522	37·8	195·1	53·7	1084	40·4	323·0	40·2
C	Mainly rural but responsible for 'urban' concentrations	372	26·9	89·4	24·6	664	24·7	187·2	23·3
D	Dioceses responsible for Greater London	281	20·3	52·2	14·4	569	21·2	193·9	24·1
TOTAL		1382	100·0	363·2	100·0	2683	99·9	803·0	99·9

SOURCES:

1 A. C. F. Beales in G. A. Beck, op cit 408

Group A dioceses were Menevia, Nottingham, Northampton, Portsmouth, Clifton and Plymouth.

Group B dioceses were Liverpool, Salford, Leeds and Hexham and Newcastle.

Group C dioceses were Lancaster, Middlesborough, Shrewsbury, Cardiff and Birmingham.

Group D dioceses were Westminster, Brentwood and Southwark (and for 1976, Arundel and Brighton).

2 Catholic Education Handbook.

Table 4.1: Characteristics of Research Schools

ITEM	Sch 1	Sch 2	Sch 3	Convent	Girls	Sec
Type of School	Maint Comp	Maint Comp	Maint Comp	Indep Girls	Indep Girls	LEA Sec
Religious Affiliation	RC	RC	RC	RC	Angli- can	None
No of Students in Sample	212	170	98	81	58	99
% Roman Catholic Students	94	84	80	36	na	3
% Both Parents Catholics	63	53	52	na	na	1
% Female Students	45	47	40	100	100	52
% Non-manual Fathers	58	68	91	99	97	20
% Mothers Working	56	54	41	na	na	62
Sex Segregation	YES	NO	NO	YES	YES	NO
Streaming	YES	YES	NO	YES	NO	YES
Year of Data Collection	1973	1973	1973	1972	1972	1973

Table 4.2: Pupil Aspirations by Type of School (%)

ASPIRATION TO BE AN OUTSTANDING	BOY BOARDERS 16–18		GIRLS 14–17	
	Public Schools	State/Inte- grated	Anglican School	Catholic School
Scholar	23·9	43·3	20·7	27·2
Head of School/House	20·8	12·1	13·8	16·0
Sportsman/woman	26·0	24·9	5·2	14·8
Writer, Actor, Musician, Artist	25·3	17·4	51·7	40·7
N (= 100%)	954	284	58	81

Table 4.3:
Acceptance of Traditional Values by School and Religious Affiliation (%)

SAMPLE	N	Date of Field Work	SCALE OF ACCEPTANCE			
			0–6	7–12	13–18	19–20
Boy boarders 16–18 in public schools	954	1966–7	12·2	57·1	28·9	1·0
Boy boarders 16–18 in state and integrated schools	284	1966–7	33·0	57·1	9·4	0·0
Girls 15–17 in Anglican school	58	1972	53·4	46·6	0·0	0·0
RC girls 14–17 in Convent school	29	1972	17·2	65·6	17·2	0·0
Non-Catholic girls 14–17 in Convent school	52	1972	19·2	69·3	11·5	0·0

(0 = no acceptance; 20 = complete acceptance of traditional values.)

Table 4.4:
Agreement with Six Attitudes or Values by School and Religious Affiliation (%)

ATTITUDE OR VALUE	% AGREEMENT								Significance between schools p less than
	Anglican School		Catholic Convent						
			RCs		NonCaths		All		
	%A	N	%A	N	%A	N	%A	N	
I Christian Morality	40	38	75	24	68	43	70	67	0·01
II Anti-Modern Culture	0	37	13	15	17	30	16	45	ns
III Anti-Traditional	21	29	45	20	31	35	36	55	ns
IV Anti-Intellectualism	0	45	23	26	15	40	18	66	0·01
V Anti-Youth Culture	9	44	19	26	17	47	18	73	ns
VI Woman's Traditional Role	4	55	35	26	31	48	32	74	0·001
Total Girls in Sample	58		29		52		81		—

(N = number of valid scales available.)

Table 5.1: Student Assessment of School Goals by School (%)

GOAL	ASSESSMENT	1 RC COMPR	2 RC COMPR	3 RC COMPR	4 RC CONVENT	5 ANGLIC GIRLS	6 LEA SECOND
1 Prepare students for a suitable job or career	A Tries	86	71	84	(44)	43	84
	B Should	43	49	38	(25)	78	36
	C Succeeds	45	33	30	(30)	16	32
2 Put into practice christian values	A Tries	79	80	76	(65)	83	59
	B Should	36	29	23	(4)	47	23
	C Succeeds	40	29	18	(31)	28	5
3 Get good O and A level results	A Tries	77	78	77	(51)	81	58
	B Should	39	35	34	(4)	52	38
	C Succeeds	61	40	23	(42)	86	42
4 Enable students to recognise what is right from wrong	A Tries	77	70	61	(47)	78	60
	B Should	42	37	40	(1)	57	41
	C Succeeds	34	31	32	(52)	45	18
5 Develop students' individual interests and talents	A Tries	42	29	33	na	na	44
	B Should	68	69	65			48
	C Succeeds	23	20	24			25
6 Prepare students for adult life	A Tries	66	48	44	na	na	71
	B Should	53	64	53			29
	C Succeeds	36	25	22			26
7 Teach christian doctrine	A Tries	70	65	73	na	na	44
	B Should	31	22	22			28
	C Succeeds	42	23	20			4
8 Encourage students to challenge traditional ideas and opinions	A Tries	34	31	35	na	na	32
	B Should	61	58	60			56
	C Succeeds	16	20	22			10
N = 100%		211	170	98	81	58	99

Note In the RC Convent Girls' School, students were wrongly advised to select one option for each goal. The results obtained are therefore not directly comparable to those for the other schools but are nevertheless indicative.

Table 5.2:
Rank Order of School Goals in Four Mixed Secondary Schools by
School Type and Sex

GOAL	GROUP	TRIES	SHOULD	SUCCEEDS
1 CAREER	3 RC comprehensives	1	4	2
	1 LEA secondary	1	5	2
	Male	1	4	2
	Female	1	4	2
2 CHRISTIAN	3 RC comprehensives	2	7	4
VALUES	1 LEA secondary	4	8	7
	Male	2	7	6
	Female	2	7	5
3 O AND A	3 RC comprehensives	3	6	1
RESULTS	1 LEA secondary	5	4	1
	Male	3	5	1
	Female	3	6	1
4 RIGHT AND	3 RC comprehensives	4	5	3
WRONG	1 LEA secondary	3	3	5
	Male	4	6	3
	Female	4	5	3
5 INTEREST	3 RC comprehensives	7	1	7
AND TALENTS	1 LEA secondary	6	2	4
	Male	7	1	7
	Female	7	1	7
6 ADULT LIFE	3 RC comprehensives	6	3	6
	1 LEA secondary	2	6	3
	Male	6	3	4
	Female	6	2	4
7 CHRISTIAN	3 RC comprehensives	5	8	5
DOCTRINE	1 LEA secondary	6	7	8
	Male	5	8	5
	Female	5	8	6
8 CHALLENGE	3 RC comprehensives	8	2	8
	1 LEA secondary	8	1	6
	Male	8	1	8
	Female	8	3	8

N in 3 RC comprehensives = 472; 1 LEA secondary = 96.
N in 4 mixed schools: male = 308; female = 260.

Table 5.3: Student Mode of Adaptation to Responsibility by School (%)

OPTION	MODE OF ADAPTATION	CUL-TURE GOALS	INSTIT MEANS	1 RC COMP	2 RC COMP	3 RC COMP	4 RC CONV	5 ANGL GIRLS	6 LEA SEC	MIXED SCHOOLS M	F	GIRLS INDEP SCHOOLS
1 Do your best	Conformity	+	+	57	38	53	40	47	52	39	62	43
2 Do as little as possible	Retreatism	−	−	2	7	0	1	2	8	5	2	1
3 Even if you don't like school policy, make sure everyone keeps the rules	Ritualism	−	+	15	8	9	33	18	8	12	9	27
4 Enforce only the rules you believe are valuable	Innovation	+	−	24	40	35	26	33	25	36	24	29
5 Don't worry about the rules; exploit the position for what it is worth	Rebellion	±	±	3	8	3	0	0	9	7	3	0
N = 100%				201	156	91	81	57	93	284	257	138

(Don't knows and multiple responses have been omitted; figures have been rounded. + = acceptance; − = non-acceptance by students of school goals and approved means for pursuing them.)

Table 5.4: Social, Moral and Religious Attitudes of Secondary School Students by School

STATEMENT	N	RC SCH 1	RC SCH 2	RC SCH 3	RC CONVENT	ANGLICAN INDEP	LEA SEC
		% agreement, omitting don't knows and no responses					
1 Religion is the basis of all true morality	584	56	40	62	82	59	28
2 Women are best kept in the home	693	17	14	19	42	3	19
3 Intellectuals can't be trusted	521	12	23	14	28	2	28
4 Parents know best	504	47	42	38	—	—	39
5 Pupils ought to obey their teachers without question	538	36	18	36	—	—	29
6 It is wrong to have sexual relations before marriage	664	25	15	20	45	40	18
7 Christianity is the highest form of religion	523	65	44	37	67	45	40
8 Families today should be limited to 2 or 3 children	548	36	50	49	—	—	44
9 You can't really read poetry for pleasure	630	30	33	26	34	16	58
10 School uniform should be abolished altogether	682	40	43	32	24	16	58
11 Politics should be left to the leaders	510	29	35	19	—	—	50
12 The use of contraceptives is wrong	528	12	14	9	—	—	6
13 Children should be brought up in a religion	516	76	68	82	—	—	33
14 Nationalisation is better than free enterprise	440	43	34	45	44	22	55
15 In order to run smoothly every institution needs laws and regulations	558	98	91	94	—	—	92
16 Schools should encourage children to make up their own minds on controversial matters	547	97	98	96	—	—	97

Table 5.5: Belief in God by School

STATEMENT	RC SCH 1	RC SCH 2	RC SCH 3	LEA SEC
		(% responses)		
1 I know God really exists and I have no doubts about it	23	19	14	9
2 While I have some doubts, I feel that I do believe in God	43	42	48	21
3 I find myself believing in God some of the time but not at other times	10	17	16	13
4 I don't believe in a personal God, but I do believe in a higher power of some kind	11	11	13	2
5 I don't know whether there is a God and I don't believe there is any way to find out	6	7	1	36
6 I don't believe in God	2	1	1	8
7 None of the above statements fit my belief in God	5	4	5	12
NO OF STUDENTS	205	159	91	92

Table 5.6: Belief in Divinity of Jesus by School

STATEMENT	RC SCH 1	RC SCH 2	RC SCH 3	LEA SEC
		(% responses)		
1 Jesus is the Divine Son of God and I have no doubts about it	23	18	20	11
2 While I have some doubts, I feel basically that Jesus is Divine	36	31	31	14
3 I feel that Jesus was a great man and very holy but I don't feel him to be the Son of God any more than all of us are children of God	6	12	5	11
4 I think Jesus was only a man although an extraordinary one	6	8	10	14
5 Frankly, I'm not entirely sure there was such a person as Jesus	9	9	6	31
6 None of the above statements fits my belief in Jesus	20	23	28	18
NO OF STUDENTS	205	160	94	90

Table 5.7:
Varimax Analysis of Adolescent Beliefs and Attitudes (Orthogonal)

| ITEM | ROTATED FACTOR LOADINGS | | | | | COM-MUNALITY |
	I	II	III	IV	V	
1 RELMOR	53*	40	11	07	−16	4843
2 WOMHOM	01	09	43	02	−14	2102
3 INTELL	−04	−12	53*	−00	00	2978
4 PARKBT	18	61*	04	01	05	4074
5 OBEYTR	01	65*	01	02	−06	4281
6 SEXREL	36	39**	−10	−03	13	3105
7 CHRHGH	37*	37	16	27	14	3884
8 FAMLIM	−10	02	03	00	−50*	2639
9 POETRY	−09	−06	47*	−17	18	2964
10 ABOLUN	−22	−32	37	00	10	2987
11 POLEAD	−05	22	46	−15	09	2916
12 CONTRA	18	35**	00	−10	28*	2418
13 CHIREL	57*	32	−15	06	01	4537
14 NATNSN	−03	05	15	09	21	0778
15 LAWREG	19	26	−08	50*	−02	3568
16 OWNMND	−09	−20	−11	52*	07	3337
17 BLFGOD	73*	01	−09	−03	11	5502
18 BLFJES	81*	06	−13	03	09	6932
LATENT ROOT	2·25	1·76	1·17	0·67	0·51	6·36
% VARIANCE	12·49	9·78	6·48	3·73	2·84	35·32

Decimal points omitted; items used in scale construction (*, **).

Table 5.8: Social, Moral and Religious Attitudes by School, Sex, Father's Occupation, Mother's Employment, Student and Parental Religion

SCALE	I	IIa	IIb	III	IV	V
ABBREV TITLE	CHRELN	DEFPTS	SEXMOR	ANTINT	INDFRM	CONMOR[2]
SCORE (INCL)	5–10	2–5	2–6	2–6	2–3	2–5
	(% low scorers; low scores represent high levels of agreement with items 1–16 and orthodox christian beliefs in God and Jesus)					
School 1	56·8	50·0	49·4	54·8	66·0 ⎫	55·2
School 2	29·9	40·7	37·7	66·4	59·9 ⎬ ***	41·3
School 3	44·2	47·5	48·8	59·2	56·1 ⎭	35·1
LEA Sec	30·3	45·9	34·9	86·2[1]	45·0***	39·5
Male	38·3	43·5	40·7	68·5*	65·9***	44·1
Female	49·0	49·5	46·9	58·7*	52·1***	45·2
Father non-manual	43·8	48·9	47·7	59·9**	60·4	42·7
Father manual	40·0	44·8	39·7	74·2**	58·4	43·1
Mother working	42·3	49·3	43·2	61·5	59·4	45·2
Mother not	46·7	44·1	47·8	63·3	60·8	45·3
Student RC	48·8	50·6	49·2	62·6	62·7	50·0***
Student other religion	36·3	42·1	39·0	71·8	53·6	32·7***
Both parents RC	49·6	48·0	50·0*	64·9	62·2 ⎫	51·5***
One parent RC	38·3	48·0	40·0	51·1	66·2 ⎬ ***	43·2
Other	36·3	43·4	37·9*	71·6	48·4***	34·7***
ALL	43·3	46·3	43·3	63·1	58·9	45·1
Avg N	213	420	441	400	472	452

* p <0·05   ** p <0·02   *** p <0·01   (comparing groups indicated).

1 Corresponding figures for convent school and anglican girls school were 77·2 per cent and 40·4 per cent respectively.

2 In the computation of CONMOR the directionality of FAMLIM has been reversed.

Table 5.9:
Characteristics of a Catholic perceived by Catholic Adolescents (%)

STATEMENT	NO OF REPLIES	VERY IMPOR-TANT	IMPOR-TANT	NOT VERY IMPOR-TANT	UN-IMPOR-TANT
1 Has a personal relationship with God	363	28·1	42·7	20·7	8·5
2 Prays regularly and frequently	398	8·3	43·2	38·4	10·1
3 Goes to mass weekly	400	15·3	41·8	29·3	13·8
4 Goes to confession at least once a month	393	4·6	20·4	47·1	28·0
5 Goes to mass occasionally when not of obligation	353	7·1	36·8	34·8	21·2
6 Says the rosary	387	0·8	7·5	44·2	47·5
7 Models his life on the example given by Christ in the new testament	375	11·5	32·8	28·0	27·7
8 Makes a firm effort to try again after personal sin and failure	390	39·7	50·0	5·1	5·1
9 Obeys the laws of the church	385	14·5	49·1	25·2	11·2
10 Keeps up to date with happenings in the church by reading Catholic papers etc	401	1·0	10·0	35·9	53·1

(Don't Knows and No Responses have been omitted.)

Table 5.10: Attitudes of Catholic Adolescents to Controversial Issues in the Church (%)

STATEMENT	NO OF REPLIES	STRONG-LY AGREE	AGREE	DIS-AGREE	STRONG-LY DIS-AGREE
11 Mixed marriages are wrong	403	2·7	3·7	32·5	61·0
12 The church is out of date in its attitude to birth control	371	42·0	38·8	14·0	5·1
13 Catholics ought to obey the laws of the church without question	392	3·3	12·0	57·9	26·8
14 The pope has too much power	320	10·3	19·7	57·2	12·8
15 Church and politics should not be mixed	359	27·0	48·2	19·2	5·6
16 Bishops should be elected by the laity	250	11·2	43·6	36·8	8·4
17 Priests ought to be allowed to get married if they wish	386	26·4	45·9	16·3	11·4
18 You should act according to your conscience and not just blindly follow the laws of the church	388	47·7	45·4	4·6	2·3
19 The mass ought to be more flexible	357	25·5	56·0	15·7	2·8
20 The unity of the christian churches is very important	355	30·4	54·6	11·5	3·4

(Don't Knows and No Responses have been omitted.)

Table 5.11: Varimax Analysis of Religious Attitudes (orthogonal)

		ROTATED FACTOR LOADINGS					COM-
ITEM	N	I	II	III	IV	V	MUNALITY
1 PERSGD	368	67*	−10	−02	08	04	4641
2 PRAYS	402	42*	−21	07	40	13	4084
3 MASSWK	404	23	−22	22	66*	07	5921
4 CONFMT	397	−06	−07	31	39	39*	4122
5 MASSX	355	09	06	−02	02	60*	3714
6 ROSARY	391	25	−09	44	21	38*	4530
7 CHRTNT	379	57*	−11	17	07	05	3691
8 FIRMEF	394	54*	−12	−23	30	12	4660
9 OBEYS	388	30	−12	20	66*	12	6015
10 RDPAPS	405	23	−10	20	19	36*	2653
11 MIXDMR	406	−05	−05	27	04	07	0838
12 BRCONT	374	−19	36*	−31	−19	−11	3099
13 CRCHLW	394	16	−02	43	38*	07	3626
14 POPWR	322	−25	52*	−07	−19	−18	4062
15 CHRPOL	361	−05	34	−01	14	07	1446
16 BSHELE	250	04	72*	05	−15	−02	5450
17 PRSMAR	390	−08	52*	−14	−23	−08	3534
18 CONSCI	392	07	18	−50	−11	10	3069
19 MSFLEX	360	−24	50*	−22	−10	14	3810
20 UNITY	358	41	−04	−23	13	26	3128
Latent Root		1·83	1·76	1·28	1·73	1·01	7·61
% Variance		9·17	8·78	6·39	8·63	5·03	38·00

Decimal points omitted.

Items used in scale construction *.

Table 5.12: High Scorers on Four Scales and Agreement with Four Statements by School, Sex, Father's Occupation, Mother's Employment and Parental Religion (%)

ITEM/SCALE ABBREV TITLE SCORE	I RELORN 4-8	II DEMPWR 5-10	III CONFOR 3-6	IV VOLUNT 4-8	11 MIXDRM 1,2	15 CHRPOL 1,2	18 CONSCI 1,2	20 UNITY 1,2
School 1	55·6	47·8	28·0	2·6	5·2	74·4	94·4	84·5
School 2	33·3	45·5	20·0	1·9	6·0	82·9	90·2	81·4
School 3	42·4	38·5	25·4	4·6	10·7	63·6	94·8	91·9
Male	41·3	47·8	27·2	3·3	6·7	79·3*	90·9	82·9
Female	49·7	40·3	21·4	2·1	6·2	69·2	95·8	87·8
Father non-manual	49·3*	41·2	24·7	2·6	5·1	71·3	92·1	87·2
Father manual	32·3	52·8	17·6	1·5	6·8	77·5	93·9	86·2
Mother working	47·3	44·4	29·6	3·4	6·9	78·0	94·5	88·5
Mother not	45·2	39·5	20·6	2·0	6·2	72·4	91·5	84·6
Parents RC	46·8	35·9**	25·1	3·5	6·4	72·5	93·8	86·4
Mother RC	43·7	56·0	27·2	2·3	6·7	78·8	93·2	84·2
Father RC	39·1	66·7	14·8	0·0	3·3	84·6	89·3	77·7
ALL	45·5	45·1	24·8	2·8	6·4	75·2	93·1	85·0
AVG N	292	167	321	296	365	328	353	324

* p <0·05   ** p <0·01 (compared to two other groups together).

Table 6.1: Self Reported Mass Attendance by Age and Sex (%)

RESPONSE	SEX	AGE GROUP							
		11	12	13	14	15	16	17	18
1	Boys	20	17	13	9	6	6	6	13
	Girls	14	10	6	6	5	6	9	7
2	Boys	63	61	58	53	49	61	59	61
	Girls	73	72	66	64	59	66	64	52
3	Boys	14	16	19	22	25	19	18	19
	Girls	11	14	20	18	21	17	17	19
4	Boys	4	6	10	17	19	14	18	8
	Girls	3	4	8	12	15	12	10	22
N = 100%	Boys	2,072	2,235	2,149	2,047	1,523	558	257	80
	Girls	2,214	2,141	1,974	1,977	1,717	630	352	27

(Percentages have been rounded.)

Table 6.2:
Mass Attendance weekly or more by Year and Ability Grouping (%)

SCHOOL	ABILITY GROUP	YEAR				
		1	2	3	4	5
Boys	UPPER	90	79	83	64	59
Comprehensive	LOWER	82	74	67	52	51
Mixed	ABOVE					
Comprehensive	AVERAGE	93	94	94	na	na
	AVERAGE	94	98	77	na	na
	BELOW					
	AVERAGE	92	91	73	na	na

(Percentages have been rounded.)

Table 6.3: Mass Attendance weekly or more by Age, Sex and Area (%)

SEX	AREA	AGE GROUPS							
		11	12	13	14	15	16	17	18
Boys	ILEA	86	81	74	62	55	74	69	73
	GLB	82	81	70	65	62	59	60	76
	Kent	70	62	59	48	45	52	38	—
Girls	ILEA	88	85	74	70	60	72	72	59
	GLB	87	83	74	75	73	76	74	—
	Kent	82	71	62	54	46	54	76	—

(Percentages have been rounded.)

Table 6.4: Number of Schools with High or Low Weekly Mass Attendance Rates for 15-year-old pupils, Average and Range Rates (%), by Sex, Forms of Entry, Type and Control of School and Area

Mass Attendance	SEX		SIZE (FE)		TYPE		CONTROL		AREA	
	Single	Mixed	Under 4	4 and over	Sec mod	Comp /gram	Relig order	Not	Kent	London
High (60% and over)	16	7	13	10	9	14	11	12	1	22
Low (under 60%)	12	9	15	6	14	7	7	14	6	15
School Mean (%)	61	51	56	59	52	64	65	52	43	60
School Range (%)	36	25	25	30	25	36	40	25	25	28
	84	72	84	75	84	83	84	72	64	84

Table 6.5: Belief in God by Religious Group (%)

BELIEF	DISAFFECT	RCS	NON-CATHS
1 I know God really exists and I have no doubts about it	8	23	13
2 While I have doubts, I feel that I do believe in God	19	50	40
3 I find myself believing in God some of the time but not at other times	14	14	13
4 I don't believe in a personal God, but I do believe in a higher power of some kind	47	7	19
5 I don't know whether there is a God and I do not believe there is any way to find out	3	5	11
6 I don't believe in God	8	1	4
N = 100%	36	350	47

(Figures have been rounded. Other responses have been omitted.)

Table 6.6: Belief in Divinity of Jesus by Religious Group (%)

BELIEF	DISAFFECT	RCS	NON-CATHS
1 Jesus is the Divine Son of God and I have no doubts about it	7	30	21
2 While I have some doubts, I feel basically that Jesus is Divine	16	47	37
3 I feel that Jesus was a great man and very holy but I don't feel him to be the Son of God any more than all of us are children of God	19	8	16
4 I think Jesus was only a man although an extraordinary one	29	7	11
5 Frankly I'm not entirely sure there was such a person as Jesus	29	8	16
N = 100%	31	287	38

(Figures have been rounded. Other responses have been omitted.)

Table 6.7: Ideal Efficiencies for School Goals and Indices of Disaffection
by Religious Group

SCHOOL GOAL	IDEAL EFFICIENCIES %			INDEX OF DISAFFECT
	Disaffected	RCs	Non-Caths	
1 Prepare students for a suitable job or career	59	91	71	65
2 Put into practice christian values	114	105	80	109
3 Get good 'O' and 'A' level results	94	131	110	71
4 Enable students to recognise what is right from wrong	40	86	82	46
5 Develop students' individual interests and talents	11	36	30	32
6 Prepare students for adult life	43	56	28	76
7 Teach christian doctrine	184	113	136	162
8 Encourage students to challenge traditional ideas and opinions	15	33	32	46

$$\text{Ideal Efficiency} = \frac{\% \text{ School succeeds in its pursuit of goal}}{\% \text{ School should pursue goal}} \times 100$$

$$\text{Index of Disaffection} = \frac{\text{Ideal Efficiency for disaffected Catholics}}{\text{Ideal Efficiency for Roman Catholics}} \times 100$$

Table 6.8: Modes of Adaptation to Responsibility by Religious Group (%)

ALTERNATIVE REACTIONS	MODE OF ADAPTATION	CULTURE GOALS	INSTIT MEANS	DISAFF	RCS	NON-CATHS
1 Do your best	Conformity	+	+	29	52	51
2 Do as little as possible	Retreatism	−	−	5	3	2
3 Even if you don't like school policy, make sure everyone keeps the rules	Ritualism	−	+	12	12	8
4 Enforce only those rules you believe are valuable	Innovation	+	−	48	29	35
5 Don't worry about the rules; exploit the position for what it is worth	Rebellion	±	±	7	5	4
N = 100%				42	355	51

(Figures have been rounded; Multiple responses and no responses have been omitted. + = acceptance; − = non-acceptance by students of school goals and means.)

Table 6.9:
Agreement with Controversial Statements by Religious Group (%)

STATEMENT	DISAFFECTED (a)	RCS (b)	NON-CATHS (c)	INDEX OF AGREEMENT (a/b) × 100
1 Religion is the basis of all true morality	26	55	54	47
2 Women are best kept in the home	9	18	15	52
3 Intellectuals can't be trusted	18	17	10	108
4 Parents know best	21	47	36	44
5 Pupils ought to obey their teachers without question	18	32	28	58
6 It is wrong to have sexual relations before marriage	5	23	17	21
7 Christianity is the highest form of religion	20	57	45	35
8 Families today should be limited to 2 or 3 children	59	41	52	143
9 You can't really read poetry for pleasure	30	32	19	95
10 School uniform should be abolished altogether	43	40	33	109
11 Politics should be left to the leaders	18	31	25	56
12 The use of contraceptives is wrong	7	14	4	51
13 Children should be brought up in a religion	56	78	60	72
14 Nationalisation is better than free enterprise	37	41	38	90
15 In order to run smoothly every institution needs laws and regulations	91	95	94	96
16 Schools should encourage children to make up their own minds on controversial matters	98	97	98	101

(Figures have been rounded; don't knows and no responses have been omitted.)

Table 6.10: Characteristics of Catholic by Religious Group (% important)

STATEMENT	DISAFFECTED (a)	RCS (b)	INDEX OF AGREEMENT (a/b) × 100
1 Has a personal relationship with God	66	72	92
2 Prays regularly and frequently	42	53	80
3 Goes to mass weekly	20	61	33
4 Goes to confession at least once a month	14	26	55
5 Goes to mass occasionally when not of obligation	29	46	62
6 Says the rosary	3	9	32
7 Models his life on the example given by Christ in the new testament	21	47	44
8 Makes a firm effort to try again after personal sin and failure	86	90	95
9 Obeys the laws of the church	26	68	39
10 Keeps up to date with happenings in the church by reading Catholic papers etc	6	11	50

(Figures have been rounded; don't knows and no responses have been omitted.)

Table 6.11: Agreement with Controversial Issues in the Church by Religious Group (%)

STATEMENT	DISAFFECTED (a)	RCS (b)	INDEX OF AGREEMENT $(a/b) \times 100$
11 Mixed marriages are wrong	3	6	42
12 The church is out of date in its attitude to birth control	92	80	116
13 Catholics ought to obey the laws of the church without question	3	17	16
14 The pope has too much power	55	27	205
15 Church and politics should not be mixed	73	75	97
16 Bishops should be elected by the laity	68	53	128
17 Priests ought to be allowed to get married if they wish	90	70	128
18 You should act according to your conscience and not just blindly follow the laws of the church	95	93	102
19 The mass ought to be more flexible	94	81	117
20 The unity of the christian churches is very important	71	87	82

(Figures have been rounded; don't knows and no responses have been omitted.)

Table 6.12: Reported Religious Outcomes by School, Sex, Ability, Social Class, Ethnic Group, Family Position, Family Practice, Parental Religion and Parental Practice (%)

RELIGIOUS OUTCOME	ALL CASES %	SCHOOL		SEX		ABILITY		SOC CLASS		ETHNIC GP		FAM POS		FAM PRAC		PAR RELIG		PAR PRAC	
		ST PET	ST PAUL	M	F	H	L	H	L	A–I	OTHER	YOUNG	OTH	ALL	OTHER	RC	MIXED	YES	OTHER
RE boring	41	25	53	40	43	50	37	44	21	50	37	50	38	20	55	41	43	25	53
Belief in Jesus	49	50	48	46	52	72	33	52	47	30	57	60	43	59	43	52	42	55	44
Belief in God	56	63	48	58	52	67	48	65	53	20	70	60	53	77	43	58	50	68	44
Mass weekly	56	67	46	64	48	53	59	52	71	50	61	69	50	100	28	61	42	88	25
Prays volunt	64	68	59	59	71	69	62	62	77	29	78	79	56	80	54	64	64	79	50
Communicant	69	79	57	61	77	78	63	82	60	50	83	75	66	94	54	72	62	86	52
Goes to confess	72	79	63	70	75	82	65	85	67	50	86	81	67	100	57	77	58	90	57
Max Cases	48	24	24	25	23	19	29	23	17	10	33	16	32	19	29	36	12	24	24

INDEPENDENT VARIABLE

Table 7.1: Estimates of Catholic Students in Higher Education and Chaplaincy Provision in England and Wales, 1975

Item	Universities	Catholic Colls of Education	Other Colls of Education	Polytechnics	Other major establishments	All Higher Education
No of institutions	38	13[1]	145[2]	30	595	821
Students on advanced courses ($\times$ 1,000)	205	10[1]	100[3]		203	518
Estimated RCs (%)[4]	8–12	85[5]	4–6		10–15	8–15
Estimated RC students ($\times$ 1,000)	16–25	7[5]	4–6		20–30	47–68
Estimated chaplains[6]	65	Most	0		54	120–140
Estimated chaplaincies[6]	39	na	0		0	39
Estimated income required (£/year $\times$ 1,000)[6]	209	?	?		?	500–750

Notes

1 CEC *Handbook* 1975, 23–7. This is likely to contract; for details see Catholic Information Office *Briefing* 22 November 1975.

2 Declining with amalgamations with polytechnics etc. The Dept Higher Education Office has details of Catholic school leavers going to 114 non-Catholic teacher training establishments in 1975.

3 Estimated from UK figures in DES *Education Statistics 1973* HMSO 1975.

4 Baptism/birth rates have declined in the past decade. Figures in Dept Higher Education, Education Commission of Bishops' Conference *Specialist Colleges Report* 1968 (3 vols) suggest 13 per cent ratio in the early 1950s was relevant for entrants into further education in the late 1960s. The CEC *News Bulletin*, 14, 1967, suggested that fewer Catholic school leavers than expected went to universities, but that more than expected went to colleges of education and further education establishments.

5 CEC *Annual Report* 1974, 24–5.

6 CEC *Handbook* 1975; National Catholic Fund for Chaplaincies in Higher Education *Report on the Present Situation of Chaplaincies* 1974.

Bibliography

ABBOTT, W. H. (ed.) *The Documents of Vatican II* London, Dublin, Chapman 1966.

ADAMS, P. et al *Children's Rights: Towards the Liberation of the Child* London, Panther 1972.

ALBROW, M. *Bureaucracy* London, Macmillan 1970.

ANON, 'Catholic Education 1870–1970', *News Bulletin no 15* Catholic Education Council for England and Wales 1971, 4–5.

ARCHDIOCESE OF BIRMINGHAM *Building Fund Report: 1952–1970*, 1970.

ARGYLE, M. *Religious Behaviour* London and Boston, Routledge 1958.

ARGYLE, M. and BEIT-HALLAHMI, B. *The Social Psychology of Religion* London and Boston, Routledge 1975.

BARAKAT, H. 'Alienation: A Process of Encounter Between Utopia and Reality' *BJS* 20(1) March 1969, 1–10.

BATTERSBY, W. J. 'Educational Work of the Religious Orders of Women: 1850–1950', ch XII in G. A. Beck (ed) *The English Catholics: 1850–1950* London, Burns Oates 1950.

BATTERSBY, W. J. 'Secondary Education for Boys', ch XI in G. A. Beck (ed) *The English Catholics: 1850–1950* London, Burns Oates 1950.

BEALES, A. C. F. 'Catholic Higher Education. I: Conclusions from a Conference', *Dublin Review* (No 479) Spring 1959, 11–16.

BEALES, A. C. F. *Education Under Penalty: English Catholic Education from the Reformation to the Fall of James II, 1547–1689* London and New York, University of London Press 1963.

BEALES, A. C. F. 'The Struggle for the Schools', ch XIII in G. A. Beck (ed) *The English Catholics: 1850–1950* London, Burns Oates 1950.

BECK, G. A. *The Case for Catholic Schools* London, Catholic Education Council 1955.

BECK, G. A. 'Catholic Higher Education: Our Present Problem' *Dublin Review* (No 476) Summer 1958, 101–7.

BECK, G. A. *The Cost of Catholic Schools* London, Catholic Truth Society 1955.

BECK, G. A. (ed.) *The English Catholics: 1850–1950* London, Burns Oates 1950.

BENN, C., and SIMON, B. *Half Way There: Report on the British Comprehensive School Reform* London, McGraw-Hill 1970.

BENNETT, N. *Teaching Styles and Pupil Progress* London, Open Books 1976.

BERGER, P. L. *The Social Reality of Religion (The Sacred Canopy)* Harmondsworth, Penguin 1973.

BERGER, P. L. and LUCKMANN, T. *The Social Construction of Reality: A Treatise in the Sociology of Knowledge* Harmondsworth, Penguin 1971.

BERNSTEIN, B. *Class, Codes and Control. Vol 1: Theoretical Studies Towards a Sociology of Language* London and Boston, Routledge 1971.

BERNSTEIN, B. *Class, Codes and Control. Vol 3: Towards a Theory of Educational Transmissions* London and Boston, Routledge 1975.

BERNSTEIN, B. 'A Critique of the Concept of Compensatory Education', ch 10 in *Class, Codes and Control. Vol 1* London and Boston, Routledge 1971.

BERNSTEIN, B. 'On the Classification and Framing of Educational Knowledge', ch 5 in *Class, Codes and Control. Vol 3* London and Boston, Routledge 1975.

BERNSTEIN, B. 'Open Schools—Open Society?', ch 3 in *Class, Codes and Control. Vol 3* London and Boston, Routledge 1975.

BERRIDGE, M. N. 'Integration and Commitment: The Task of Catholic Education Today', ch 2 in B. Tucker (ed) *Catholic Education in a Secular Society* London, Sheed and Ward 1968.

BLACK, P. 'The Religious Scene: Belief and Practice in the Universities', *Dublin Review* (No 484) Summer 1960, 105–25.

BLAUNER, R. *Alienation and Freedom: The Factory Worker and His Industry* Chicago and London, University of Chicago Press 1964.

BOTTOMLEY, F. 'Catholics and the Aims of Education', *The Month* 6(7) July 1973, 227–34.

BOURDIEU, P. 'Cultural Reproduction and Social Reproduction', ch 3 in R. Brown (ed) *Knowledge, Education and Cultural Change* London, Tavistock 1973.

BOURDIEU, P. and PASSERON, J-C., *Reproduction: In Education, Society and Culture* London and Beverly Hills, Sage 1977.

BRECH, R. *The Church: Joint Venture of Priests and Laity* London, Living Parish Pamphlets 1972.

BRIGHT, L. and CLEMENTS, S. (eds) *The Committed Church* London, Darton Longman and Todd 1966.

BRONFENBRENNER, U. *Two Worlds of Childhood: USA and USSR* London, Allen & Unwin 1971.

BROTHERS, J. B. *Church and School: A Study of the Impact of Education on Religion* Liverpool, Liverpool University Press 1964.

BROTHERS, J. B. 'Religion in the British Universities: The Findings of Some Recent Surveys", *Archives de Sociologie des Religions* (No 18) 1964, 71–82.

BROWN, R. (ed) *Knowledge, Education and Cultural Change* London, Tavistock 1973.

BURNS, T. and STALKER, G. M. *The Management of Innovation* London, Tavistock 1966.

BUTLER, D. and STOKES, D. *Political Change in Britain: Forces Shaping Electoral Choice* Harmondsworth, Pelican 1971.

CALLAGHAN, J. and COCKETT, M. *Are Our Schools Christian? A Call to Pastoral Care* Great Wakering, Mayhew-McCrimmon 1975.

Catholic Directory of England and Wales London, Universe Publications (published annually).

CATHOLIC EDUCATION COUNCIL FOR ENGLAND AND WALES *Catholic Education: A Handbook* London (published biennially).

CATHOLIC EDUCATION COUNCIL FOR ENGLAND AND WALES *News Bulletin* London (published periodically).

CATHOLIC EDUCATION COUNCIL FOR ENGLAND AND WALES *Report for the Year* London (published annually).

CATHOLIC EDUCATION COUNCIL FOR ENGLAND AND WALES *Insights into Catholic Secondary Education, 1972–73* London.

CATHOLIC EDUCATION COUNCIL FOR ENGLAND AND WALES *Further Insights into Catholic Secondary Education, 1973–74* London.

CATHOLIC EDUCATION COUNCIL FOR ENGLAND AND WALES *Further Insights into Catholic Secondary Education, 1975* London.

CATHOLIC EDUCATION COUNCIL FOR ENGLAND AND WALES *The Primary School* London 1975.

CATHOLIC EDUCATION COUNCIL FOR ENGLAND AND WALES *The Catholic Primary School* London 1976.

CATHOLIC INFORMATION OFFICE *Briefing* Abbots Langley (published at frequent intervals).

CATHOLIC INFORMATION SERVICES *The Church 2000: An Interim Report of the Joint Working Party set up to Discuss the Preparation of National Pastoral Strategy for England and Wales* Abbots Langley 1973.

CATHOLIC INFORMATION SERVICES *A Time for Building: Report of the Joint Working Party on Pastoral Strategy* Abbots Langley 1976.

CENTRAL ADVISORY COUNCIL FOR EDUCATION (ENGLAND) *Children and Their Primary Schools* (Plowden Report), 2 vols, London: HMSO 1967.

CENTRAL ADVISORY COUNCIL FOR EDUCATION (ENGLAND) *Early Leaving* London, HMSO 1954.

CHILD, D. *The Essentials of Factor Analysis* London, New York and Sydney, Holt Rinehart & Winston 1970.

COLEMAN, J. S. et al *Equality of Educational Opportunity* (Coleman Report) US Department of Health, Education and Welfare Washington, US Government Printing Office 1966.

COMMITTEE ON HIGHER EDUCATION *Higher Education* (Robbins Report) Cmnd 2154, London, HMSO 1963.

CORBETT, A. 'Catholics at School' *New Society* 28 November 1968, 792–4.

COUNCIL FOR SCIENTIFIC POLICY *Enquiry into the Flow of Candidates in Science and Technology into Higher Education* (Dainton Report) Cmnd 3541, London, HMSO 1968.

CRAFT, M. (ed) *Family, Class and Education: A Reader* London, Longman 1970.

CUNNINGHAM, R. F. 'Catholic Birthrate in Recent Years' *News Bulletin No 15* London, CEC 1971, 25.

DAVIE, R. et al *From Birth to Seven* London, Longman 1972.

DAVIES, I. 'The Management of Knowledge: A Critique of the Use of Typologies in the Sociology of Education', ch 9 in M. F. D. Young (ed) *Knowledge and Control* London, Collier-Macmillan 1971.

DELOOZ, P. *The Social Context of Youth Catechesis* Brussels, Pro Mundi Vita Bulletin 63; November 1976.

DENZIN, N. K. *The Research Act in Sociology: A Theoretical Introduction to Sociological Methods* London and Sydney, Butterworths 1970.

DEPARTMENT OF EDUCATION AND SCIENCE *Educational Priority. Vol 1; EPA Problems and Policies* (ed by A. H. Halsey) London, HMSO 1972.

DEPARTMENT OF EDUCATION AND SCIENCE Science Policy Studies No 3 *The Employment of Highly Specialised Graduates—A Comparative Study in the UK and the USA* (McCarthy Report) London, HMSO 1968.

DEPARTMENT OF EDUCATION AND SCIENCE *Statistics of Education: 1975 Vol 1, Schools* London, HMSO 1976.

DEPARTMENT OF HIGHER EDUCATION, EDUCATION COMMISSION OF BISHOPS' CONFERENCE, NATIONAL CATHOLIC FUND FOR CHAPLAINCIES IN HIGHER EDUCATION *Report on the Present Situation of Chaplaincies and Their Immediate and Long-Term Capital and Income Requirements* Cardiff 1974.

DEPARTMENT OF HIGHER EDUCATION, EDUCATION COMMISSION OF BISHOPS' CONFERENCE *Specialist Colleges Report* 3 vols, Cardiff 1968.

Diocese of Arundel and Brighton Newsletter Financial Supplement May 1971.

DONNISON REPORT *The Public Schools Commission First Report, Vol 1,* London, HMSO 1968; *Second Report, Vol 1, Report on Independent Day Schools and Direct Grant Grammar Schools* London, HMSO 1970.

DOUGLAS, J. W. B. *The Home and the School* London, Panther 1967.

DOUGLAS, M. *Purity and Danger: An Analysis of Concepts of Pollution and Taboo* Harmondsworth, Pelican 1970.

DOWDEN, R. 'Importance of a Catholic School' *Catholic Herald* 1 April 1977.

DURKHEIM, E. *The Division of Labour in Society* Glencoe, Free Press 1964 (fp 1893).

DURKHEIM, E. *Education and Sociology* New York, Free Press 1956.

DURKHEIM, E. *The Elementary Forms of the Religious Life* London, Allen & Unwin 1915 (fp 1912).

ETZIONI, A. *A Comparative Analysis of Complex Organisations* New York, Free Press 1961.

EVENNETT, H. O. *The Catholic Schools of England and Wales* London, CUP 1944.

FLOUD, J. E., HALSEY, A. H and MARTIN, F. M. *Social Class and Educational Opportunity* London, Heinemann 1956.

FLUDE, M. and AHIER, J. (eds) *Educability, Schools and Ideology* London, Croom Helm 1974.

FLYNN, M. *Some Catholic Schools in Action: A Sociological Study of Sixth Form Students in 21 Catholic Boys' High Schools* Catholic Education Office Sydney 1975.

FOGARTY, M. P. 'The Rising Tide: Growing Numbers of Catholic Students', *Dublin Review* (No 484) Summer 1960, 100–5.

FREIRE, P. *Cultural Action for Freedom* Harmondsworth, Penguin 1972.

FREIRE, P. 'Education: Domestication or Liberation?', ch 3 in I. Lister (ed) *Deschooling* London, CUP 1974.

FREIRE, *Education for Critical Consciousness* London, Sheed and Ward 1974.

FREIRE, P. *Pedagogy of the Oppressed* Harmondsworth, Penguin 1972.

GAINE, J. J. 'Young Adults' Faith' *The Tablet* 13 December 1975, 1221–2.

GAINE, M. 'The Development of Official Roman Catholic Educational Policy in England and Wales', ch 7 in P. Jebb (ed) *Religious Education* London, Darton Longman & Todd 1968.

GERTH, H. H. and MILLS, C. W. *From Max Weber: Essays in Sociology* London, Routledge 1948.

GLOCK, C. Y. and STARK, R. *Religion and Society in Tension* Chicago, Rand McNally 1965.

GOODMAN, P. *Compulsory Miseducation* Harmondsworth, Penguin 1971.

GRACE, G. R. *Role Conflict and the Teacher* London and Boston, Routledge 1972.

GREELEY, A. M. *Religion and Career: A Study of College Graduates* New York, Sheed & Ward 1963.

GREELEY, A. M. 'The Uses of Sociology', *The Month* 5(2) February 1972, 48–53.

GREELEY, A. M. MCCREADY, W. C. and MCCOURT, K. *Catholic Schools in a Declining Church* Kansas City, Sheed, Andrews & McMeel 1976.

GREELEY, A. M. and ROSSI, P. H. *The Education of Catholic Americans* Chicago, Aldine 1966.

GUTIERREZ, G. *A Theology of Liberation: History, Politics, Salvation* London, SCM 1974.

HALPIN, A. W. and CROFT, D. B. *The Organisational Climate of Schools* Chicago, University of Chicago Press 1963.

HARGREAVES, D. H. 'Deschoolers and New Romantics', ch 9 in M. Flude and J. Ahier (eds) *Educability, Schools and Ideology* London, Croom Helm 1974.

HARGREAVES, D. H. *Interpersonal Relations and Education* London and Boston, Routledge 1972.

HARVARD EDUCATIONAL REVIEW, *Equal Educational Opportunity* Cambridge Ma, Harvard University Press 1969.

HICKEY, J. *Urban Catholics: Urban Catholicism in England and Wales from 1829 to the Present Day* London, Dublin and Melbourne, Geoffrey Chapman 1967.

HOLT, J. *How Children Fail* Harmondsworth, Penguin 1964.

HORNSBY-SMITH, M. P. 'A Sociological Case for Catholic Schools', *The Month* 5(10) October 1972, 298–304.

HORNSBY-SMITH, M. P. 'Justice in Education', *The Tablet* 9 December 1972.

HORNSBY-SMITH, M. P., 'Education—A Continuing Process' *Catholic Education Today* 8 1974; (2) March/April, 4–6, (3) May/June, 18–21, (4) July/August, 10–13.

HORNSBY-SMITH, M. P. 'Young Disaffected Catholics', *Catholic Education Today* 9(3) May/June 1975, 5–10.

HORNSBY-SMITH, M. P. 'Plural Parish Liturgies' *Clergy Review* 60(8) August 1975, 518–24.

✕ HORNSBY-SMITH, M. P. 'Catholic Adolescents' *The Tablet* 27 September 1975, 918–21.

HORNSBY-SMITH, M. P. 'Educational Advice', *The Tablet* 25 October 1975, 1027–9.

HORNSBY-SMITH, M. P. 'Southwark Diocese Mass Attendance Survey' *Catholic Education Today* 10(2) April/June 1976, 2–4.

HORNSBY-SMITH, M. P. 'Catholic Students in Higher Education', *The Month* 9(6) June 1976, 191–8.

HORNSBY-SMITH, M. P. 'Ecclesial Strategy' *The Tablet* 6 August 1977, 742–3.

HORNSBY-SMITH, M. P. 'Resources and Priorities: Some Observations Arising Out of *A Time for Building, The New Sower* 3(1) Autumn 1977, 13–16.

✕ HORNSBY-SMITH, M. P. and THOMAS, A. H. *Do Catholic Schools Have a Distinct Atmosphere? A Comparative Study of Two Denominational Independent Girls Schools* University of Surrey 1973 (mimeo).

HORNSBY-SMITH, M. P. and MANSFIELD, M. C. *The Work of the Laity Commission: Some Reflections based on Interviews with Lay Members of the Laity Commission* University of Surrey 1974 (mimeo).

HORNSBY-SMITH, M. P. and MANSFIELD, M. C. 'Overview of the Church Commissions' *The Month* 8(3) March 1975, 84–9.

HORNSBY-SMITH, M. P. and PETIT, M. 'Religious Attitudes of Catholic Adolescents' *Catholic Education Today* 9(2) March/April 1975 [I] 2–6.

HORNSBY-SMITH, M. P. and PETIT, M. 'Social, Moral and Religious Attitudes of Secondary School Students', *J Moral Education* 4(3) June 1975 [II] 261–72.

HORNSBY-SMITH, M. P. and DANN, G. 'The Contribution of Sociology to the Catholic Church' *New Blackfriars* 56 August 1975, 340–9.

HORNSBY-SMITH, M. P. and FITZPATRICK, J. 'Conversations with Catholic Fourth Formers', *Catholic Education Today* 10(3) July/September 1976, 2–5.

HORNSBY-SMITH, M.P., THOMAS, A. H. and PETIT, M. 'School Goals and Student Adaptations in Secondary Schools' *Catholic Education Today* 11(1) January/March 1977, 2–6.

HORNSBY-SMITH, M. P., LEE, R. M. and REILLY, P. A. 'Orthodoxy, Heterodoxy and Common Religion Among Grass Roots Catholics in Four

English Parishes', paper read at the Annual Meetings of the Society for the Scientific Study of Religion and the Religious Research Association, Chicago 30 October 1977 [I].

HORNSBY-SMITH, M.P., LEE, R. M. and REILLY, P. A. *Out of Practice? The Process of Lapsation* Pastoral Investigation of Social Trends Working Paper No 12, Liverpool Institute of Socio-Religious Studies 1977 [II].

HORNSBY-SMITH, M. P., LEE, R. M. and REILLY, P. A. 'Lapsation and Ideology', *The Month 10*(2) December 1977 [III], 406–9.

HOUGHTON REPORT *Report of the Committee of Inquiry into the Pay of Non-University Teachers* Cmnd 5848 London, HMSO 1974.

HUGHES, J. A. *Sociological Analysis: Methods of Discovery* London and Melbourne, Nelson 1976.

ILLICH, I. D. *Deschooling Society* Harmondsworth, Penguin 1973.

JACKSON, B. and MARSDEN, D. *Education and the Working Class* Harmondsworth, Pelican 1966.

JACKSON, P. W. *Life in Classrooms* New York, Chicago and London, Holt Rinehart and Winston 1968.

JEBB, P. (ed) *Religious Education: Drift or Decision?* London, Darton Longman & Todd 1968.

JENCKS, C. et al *Inequality: A Reassessment of the Effect of Family and Schooling in America* New York and London, Basic Books 1972.

JOHN XXIII *New Light on Social Problems (Mater et Magistra)* London, Catholic Truth Society 1961.

JOHN XXIII *Peace on Earth (Pacem in Terris)* London, Catholic Truth Society 1963.

JOHNSTON, C. L. et al, review of *Catholic Schools in a Declining Church* in *Contemporary Sociology 5*(6) November 1976, 806–8.

KALTON, G. *The Public Schools: A Factual Survey* London, Longmans 1966.

KARABEL, J. and HALSEY, A. H. (eds) *Power and Ideology in Education* New York, OUP, 1977.

KELSALL, R. K. and KELSALL, H. M. *Social Disadvantage and Educational Opportunity* London, New York and Sydney, Holt Rinehart and Winston 1971.

KORNHAUSER, W. *The Politics of Mass Society* London, Routledge 1960.

LABOVITZ, S. 'Some Observations on Measurement and Statisics' *Social Forces 46* 1967, 151–60.

LABOVITZ, S. 'The Assignment of Numbers to Rank Order Categories' ASR *35*(3) 1970, 515–24.

LAMBERT, R. *Introduction* to G. Kalton *The Public Schools: A Factual Survey* London, Longmans 1966.

LAMBERT, R., 'Religious Education in the Boarding School', ch 6 in P. Jebb (ed) *Religious Education* London, Darton Longman & Todd, 1968.

LAMBERT, R. et al *A Manual to the Sociology of the School* London, Weidenfeld & Nicolson 1970.

LAMBERT, R. et al *New Wine in Old Bottles? Studies in Integration within the Public Schools* Occasional Papers on Social Administration No 28 London, Bell 1968.

LAWRENCE REPORT *Ground Plan: A Suggested Scheme for Roman Catholic Diocesan Boundaries* Abbots Langley, Catholic Information Office 1974.

LAWLOR, M. *Out of this World: A Study of Catholic Values* London, Melbourne and New York, Sheed & Ward 1965.

LITTLE, A. et al 'Class Size, Pupil Characteristics and Reading Attainment', in V. Southgate (ed) *Literacy at All Levels* London, Ward Lock 1972, 205–12.

LINDSEY, C. *School and Community* Oxford, Pergamon 1970.

LISTER, I. (ed) *Deschooling* London and New York CUP 1974.

LUCKMANN, T. *The Invisible Religion: The Problem of Religion in Modern Society* New York and London, Collier-Macmillan 1970.

MARTIN, B. and PLUCK, R. *Young People's Beliefs: An Exploratory Study Commissioned by the General Synod Board of Education of the Views and Behavioural Patterns of Young People Related to their Beliefs* London 1977.

MATZA, D. *Delinquency and Drift* New York, Wiley 1964.

MAYS, J. B. *Education and the Urban Child* Liverpool, Liverpool University Press 1962.

MAYS, J. B. *Growing Up in the City: A Study of Juvenile Delinquency in an Urban Neighbourhood* Liverpool, Liverpool University Press 1964.

MAYS, J. B. et al *School of Tomorrow: A Study of a Comprehensive School in a North-West Newtown* London, Longmans 1968.

MAYS, J. B. *The Young Pretenders: A Study of Teenage Culture in Contemporary Society* London, Michael Joseph 1965.

MCCLELLAND, V. A. *English Roman Catholics and Higher Education, 1830–1903* London, OUP 1973.

MCDILL, E. L. et al *Strategies for Success in Compensatory Education: An Appraisal of Evaluation Research* Baltimore and London, John Hopkins Press 1969.

MCDILL, E. L. and RIGSBY, L. C. *Structure and Process in Secondary Schools: The Academic Impact of Educational Climates* Baltimore and London, John Hopkins University Press 1973.

MCDONALD, C. D. P. 'Researching the Effectiveness of Catholic Religious Education', *Catholic Education Today* 10(1) January/March 1976, 2–3.

MCKENNELL, A. 'Attitude Measurement: Use of Coefficient Alpha with Cluster or Factor Analysis' *Sociology* 4(2) 1970, 227–45.

MERTON, R. K. *Social Theory and Social Structure* London and New York, Free Press 1957.

MERTON, R. K. and KENDALL, P. L. *The Focused Interview* Glencoe, Free Press 1956.

MICHELS, R. *Political Parties* New York and London, Collier Books 1962.

MIDWINTER, E. *Priority Education: An Account of the Liverpool Project* Harmondsworth, Penguin 1972.

MUNGHAM, E. and PEARSON, G. (eds) *Working Class Youth Culture* London and Boston, Routledge 1976.

MURPHY, J. *Church, State and Schools in Britain: 1800–1970* London, Routledge 1971.

NEAL, M. A., review of *Catholic Schools in a Declining Church* in *Sociological Analysis 38*(2) Summer 1977, 181–4.

NEAL, M. A. *A Socio-Theology of Letting Go: The Role of a First World Church Facing Third World Peoples* New York, Ramsey and Toronto, Paulist Press 1977.

NICHOLS, K. F. 'Christianity, Humanism and Education' *Catholic Education Today 6*(5) September/October 1972, 4–7.

NICHOLS, K. F. (ed) *Theology and Education* Slough, Association of Teaching Religious 1974.

NIE, N. H. et al *Statistical Package for the Social Sciences* New York, London and Sydney, McGraw-Hill 1970.

NISBET, R. A. *The Sociological Tradition* London and Melbourne, Heinemann 1970.

PAUL VI *The Great Social Problem (Populorum Progressio)* London, Catholic Truth Society 1967.

PAUL VI *Social Problems (Octogesima Adveniens)* London, Catholic Truth Society 1971.

PILKINGTON, G. W. et al 'Changes in Religious Beliefs, Practices and Attitudes among University Students over an Eleven Year Period in Relation to Sex Differences, Denominational Differences and Differences between Faculties and Years of Study', University of Sheffield (mimeo) nd.

PIUS XI *The Christian Education of Youth* 1929 (London, CTS 1949).

POWER, M. J. et al 'Delinquent Schools?' *New Society* 19 October 1967.

PRATT, O. and PRATT, I. *Let Liturgy Live* London, Sheed & Ward 1973.

PRATT, O. and PRATT, I. *Liturgy Is What We Make It*, London and Melbourne, Sheed & Ward, 1967.

PRICE, D. J. *Little Science, Big Science* New York, Columbia University Press 1963.

RACIAL JUSTICE COMMISSION OF THE BISHOPS' CONFERENCE OF ENGLAND AND WALES *Where Creed and Colour Matter: A Survey on Black Children and Catholic Schools* Abbots Langley, Catholic Information Office 1975.

REIMER, E. *School is Dead* Harmondsworth, Penguin 1971.

REPORT OF A REVIEW COMMITTEE OF THE BISHOPS' CONFERENCE OF ENGLAND AND WALES *Commissions: Aid to a Pastoral Strategy* London, 1971.

Report to the Laity: The Work and Experience of the Provisional Laity Commission 1967–1971 London, Living Parish Pamphlets 1971.

REYNOLDS, D. 'When Teachers and Pupils Refuse a Truce', in E. Mungham and G. Pearson (eds) *Working Class Youth Culture* London, Routledge 1976, 124–37.

RHODES, A. L. and NAM, C. B. 'The Religious Context of Educational Expectations", *ASR*, *35*(2) April 1970, 253–67.

ROSE, R. *Governing Without Consensus: An Irish Perspective* London, Faber 1971.

ROSSI, P. H. and ROSSI, A. S. 'Some Effects of Parochial School Education in America' *Harvard Educational Review* 27(3) *Summer* 1957, 168–99.

SACRED CONGREGATION FOR CATHOLIC EDUCATION *The Catholic School* Abbots Langley, Catholic Information Office 1977.

SCHOFIELD, M. *The Sexual Behaviour of Young People* Harmondsworth, Pelican 1968.

SCHOOL OF BARBIANA *Letter to a Teacher* Harmondsworth, Penguin 1970.

SEEMAN, M. 'On the Meaning of Alienation', ASR 24 1959, 783–91.

SEGUNDO, J. L. *The Liberation of Theology* Dublin, Gill and Macmillan 1977.

SHARROCK, A. *Home/School Relations: Their Importance in Education* London, Macmillan 1970.

SISTER MONICA MARY *Family Mass Themes* Diocese of Portsmouth Catholic Education Centre 1972.

SMELSER, N. J. *Social Change in the Industrial Revolution* Chicago, University of Chicago Press 1959.

SMITH, G. A. N. and LITTLE, A. *Strategies of Compensation: A Review of the Educational Projects for the Disadvantaged in the United States* Centre for Educational Research and Innovation Paris, OECD 1971.

SOUTHGATE, V. (ed) *Literacy at All Levels* London, Ward Lock 1972.

SPENCER, A. E. C. W. 'An Evaluation of Roman Catholic Education Policy in England and Wales: 1900–1960', in P. Jebb (ed) *Religious Education* Darton Longman & Todd 1968.

SPENCER, A. E. C. W. *The Future of Catholic Education in England and Wales* London, Catholic Renewal Movement 1971.

STARK, R. and GLOCK, C. Y. *American Piety: The Nature of Religious Commitment* Berkeley, Los Angeles and London, University of California Press 1968.

SUENENS, L. J. *A New Pentecost?* London, Darton Longman & Todd 1975.

TANNER, R. E. S. *A Survey of London Catholic Student Opinion on Religious Matters* Catholic Chaplaincy to the Universities in London nd.

THIRD INTERNATIONAL SYNOD OF BISHOPS *Justice in the World* London, Catholic Truth Society 1972.

TROPP, A. *The School Teachers* London, Heinemann 1957.

TUCKER, B. (ed) *Catholic Education in a Secular Society* London and Sydney, Sheed & Ward 1968.

WALLER, W. *The Sociology of Teaching* New York, Wiley 1932.

WEBER, M. *The Sociology of Religion* London, Methuen 1966 (fp 1922).

WESTERGAARD, J. and LITTLE, A. 'Educational Opportunity and Social Selection in England and Wales: Trends and Policy Implications', ch 3 in M. Craft (ed) *Family, Class and Education: A Reader* London, Longman 1970.

WESTERGAARD, J. H. and RESLER, H. *Class in a Capitalist Society: A Study of Contemporary Britain* London and Melbourne, Heinemann 1975.

WINTER, M. M. *Mission or Maintenance: A Study in New Pastoral Structures* London, Darton Longman & Todd 1973.

WISEMAN, S. *Education and Environment*, Manchester, Manchester University Press 1964.

WRIGHT, D. and COX, E. 'Changes in Moral Belief among Sixth-form Boys and Girls over a Seven Year Period in Relation to Religious Belief, Age and Sex Difference', *Brit J Soc Clin Psychol 10* 1971, 332–41.

WRIGHT, D. and COX, E. 'Changes in Religious Belief among Sixth-form Boys and Girls in English Grammar Schools between 1963 and 1970' (unpublished) 1973 (quoted in G. W. Pilkington et al).

YOUNG, M. F. D. (ed) *Knowledge and Control: New Directions for the Sociology of Education* London, Collier-Macmillan 1971.

YUDKIN, S. and HOLME, A. *Working Wives and Their Children* London, Michael Joseph 1963.

Index